Political Thought in the Mamluk Period

Edinburgh Studies in Classical Islamic History and Culture
Series Editor: Carole Hillenbrand

A particular feature of medieval Islamic civilization was its wide horizons. The Muslims fell heir not only to the Graeco-Roman world of the Mediterranean, but also to that of the ancient Near East, to the empires of Assyria, Babylon and the Persians; and beyond that, they were in frequent contact with India and China to the east and with black Africa to the south. This intellectual openness can be sensed in many inter-related fields of Muslim thought, and it impacted powerfully on trade and on the networks that made it possible. Books in this series reflect this openness and cover a wide range of topics, periods and geographical areas.

Titles in the series include:

The Body in Arabic Love Poetry: The 'Udhri Tradition
Jokha Alharthi

Arabian Drugs in Early Medieval Mediterranean Medicine
Zohar Amar and Efraim Lev

Towards a History of Libraries in Yemen
Hassan Ansari and Sabine Schmidtke

The Abbasid Caliphate of Cairo, 1261–1517: Out of the Shadows
Mustafa Banister

The Medieval Western Maghrib: Cities, Patronage and Power
Amira K. Bennison

Christian Monastic Life in Early Islam
Bradley Bowman

Keeping the Peace in Premodern Islam: Diplomacy under the Mamluk Sultanate, 1250–1517
Malika Dekkiche

Queens, Concubines and Eunuchs in Medieval Islam
Taef El-Azhari

Islamic Political Thought in the Mamluk Period
Mohamad El-Merheb

The Kharijites in Early Islamic Historical Tradition: Heroes and Villains
Hannah-Lena Hagemann

Classical Islam: Collected Essays
Carole Hillenbrand

Islam and the Crusades: Collected Essays
Carole Hillenbrand

The Medieval Turks: Collected Essays
Carole Hillenbrand

The Books of Burhān al-Dīn: Literacy and Book Ownership in Mamluk Jerusalem
Said Aljoumani and Konrad Hirschler

Medieval Damascus: Plurality and Diversity in an Arabic Library – The Ashrafiya Library Catalogue
Konrad Hirschler

A Monument to Medieval Syrian Book Culture: The Library of Ibn ʿAbd al-Hādī
Konrad Hirschler

The Popularisation of Sufism in Ayyubid and Mamluk Egypt: State and Society, 1173–1325
Nathan Hofer

Defining Anthropomorphism: The Challenge of Islamic Traditionalism
Livnat Holtzman

Making Mongol History: Rashid al-Din and the Jamiʿ al-Tawarikh
Stefan Kamola

Lyrics of Life: Saʿdi on Love, Cosmopolitanism and Care of the Self
Fatemeh Keshavarz

Art, Allegory and the Rise of Shiism in Iran, 1487–1565
Chad Kia

The Administration of Justice in Medieval Egypt: From the 7th to the 12th Century
Yaacov Lev

Zoroastrians in Early Islamic History: Accommodation and Memory
Andrew D. Magnusson

A History of Herat: From Chingiz Khan to Tamerlane
Shivan Mahendrarajah

The Queen of Sheba's Gift: A History of the True Balsam of Matarea
Marcus Milwright

Ruling from a Red Canopy: Political Authority in the Medieval Islamic World, From Anatolia to South Asia
Colin P. Mitchell

Islam, Christianity and the Realms of the Miraculous: A Comparative Exploration
Ian Richard Netton

The Poetics of Spiritual Instruction: Farid al-Din 'Attar and Persian Sufi Didacticism
Austin O'Malley

Sacred Place and Sacred Time in the Medieval Islamic Middle East: An Historical Perspective
Daniella Talmon-Heller

Conquered Populations in Early Islam: Non-Arabs, Slaves and the Sons of Slave Mothers
Elizabeth Urban

edinburghuniversitypress.com/series/escihc

Political Thought in the Mamluk Period

The Unnecessary Caliphate

Mohamad El-Merheb

EDINBURGH
University Press

This book is dedicated to Mona and Rasheed
اتييد نور حيرشد و يرقة عميى صدنم إلى

Edinburgh University Press is one of the leading university presses in the UK. We publish academic books and journals in our selected subject areas across the humanities and social sciences, combining cutting-edge scholarship with high editorial and production values to produce academic works of lasting importance. For more information visit our website: edinburghuniversitypress.com

Edinburgh University Press Ltd
The Tun – Holyrood Road
12 (2f) Jackson's Entry
Edinburgh EH8 8PJ

Typeset in 11/15 Adobe Garamond by
Cheshire Typesetting, Cuddington, Cheshire

A CIP record for this book is available from the British Library

ISBN 978 1 4744 7964 6 (hardback)
ISBN 978 1 4744 7966 0 (webready PDF)
ISBN 978 1 4744 7967 7 (epub)

Contents

Acknowledgements vi

Introduction 1

1 Reading Islamic Political Thought 11

2 Ibn Jamaʿa's Synthesis and Praxis of Shafiʿi Political Thought 47

3 Sufi Political Thought 85

4 The Late Ayyubid and Early Mamluk Context: Ibn Talha and al-Qarafi 122

5 Mamluk Historiography as a Form of Political Thought 156

Bibliography 193

Index 207

Acknowledgements

This book developed out of my PhD thesis at the School of Oriental and African Studies (SOAS), under the supervision of Konrad Hirschler. It could not have been completed without his support and guidance. I owe Konrad an ever-increasing debt of gratitude for his constant encouragement, guidance in developing my argument, and patience in discussing, challenging and refining my ideas. I thank him for helping me to identify and access relevant primary sources, participate in research forums in the UK and internationally, and complete my first publications.

I am deeply grateful to Roy Fischel for all his support and for making the submittal stage of my PhD an enjoyable experience.

The indispensable and unwavering assistance of Hilary and Hugh Kennedy throughout the past years was a real privilege. I would particularly like to thank Hugh for giving me great and vital opportunities to advance my research.

Thanks are due to Suzanne Ruggi whose meticulous corrections and valuable suggestions helped see this work to completion.

I am indebted to Tayeb El-Hibri for initiating me into the history of Islamic political thought, the important part he played in the shaping of my thesis, and for the boundless supply of pertinent sources and studies. I would also like to thank both John Meloy, who directed my first ventures into Mamluk history, and Nadia Maria El Cheikh for many years of kindness, support, advice and hospitality. Thanks are due to Bilal Orfali and Bashar Haydar for continuously encouraging me to complete and publish my research.

I was fortunate to receive support from the Institute of Historical Research (IHR) in London. This book greatly benefited from feedback and conversations with my cohort of IHR fellows and the institute's director, Jo Fox, who gave me the opportunity to present, discuss and develop my research in its unique and stimulating environment.

I am very grateful to Nathan Hofer for his valuable and encouraging feedback; to Quentin Skinner for the opportunity to sit in on his class at Queen Mary University of London; and to Radwan al-Sayyid for familiarising me with a treasure of medieval political treatises. I hope the influence of these three scholars on this book will be discernible to the reader.

I am grateful to the following individuals who read parts of my PhD thesis or this book and helped with obtaining sources: Caterina Bori, Tayeb El-Hibri, Nathan Hofer, Yossef Rapoport, Debora Spini and Jo Van Steenbergen.

This work owes a great deal to the wonderful staff of the SOAS library, the British Library and the Topkapi Palace directorate in Istanbul, especially Esra Müyesseroglu. Thanks are due to the staff of the Jaffet Library at the American University of Beirut, the Austrian National Library and the Bodleian at Oxford.

Other individuals were too of great help, patiently listening to my ideas, providing valuable advice or offering crucial assistance in different ways: Christopher Bahl, Mehdi Berriah, Ghena Hariri, Patrick Lantschner and Gowaart Van Den Bossche. Thanks are due to my awesome SOAS doctoral cohort: Nattanee Amornpradubkul, Mattin Biglari, Tyolumun Kinga-Upaa, Peter Law, Brandi Simpson Miller, Susannah Savage and Yingzi Wang. Special thanks to Mattin and Susannah for being always available during difficult and stressful periods of the writing-up process.

The time I spent at New York University (NYU) Shanghai was important for developing and enriching some of the book's ideas and I am grateful to Joanna Wiley-Cohen and Maria Montoya for this opportunity. Of great help were the long enriching and stimulating conversations with other members of the 'Shanghai Saturday Club': Emily Bauman, Hye Eun Choi, Jennifer Egloff, Ruth de Llobet, Tom Mazzone and Debora Spini.

The arguments in this book benefited from feedback, questions, comments and discussions at conferences and workshops where I presented parts of it. I am grateful to the organisers and participants of the Third Annual Conference of the British Association for Islamic Studies; the Fourth and

Fifth Conferences of the School of Mamluk Studies in Beirut and Ghent; the workshop *Ǧihād et fitna* at the Sorbonne made possible by Mehdi Berriah, Sylvie Denoix and Clément Onimus; the *Criticizing the Ruler* conference in Bonn organised by Karina Kellermann, Alheydis Plassmann and Christian Schwermann; the *Arabic Pasts* conference organised by Sarah Bowen Savant and Hugh Kennedy; and the IHR Fellows Seminar in London.

Lastly, I am thankful to Nicola Ramsey and Edinburgh University Press for accepting the book for publication. It is a great privilege for any medievalist to see their book published in the Edinburgh Studies in Classical Islamic History and Culture series, currently edited by Carole Hillenbrand.

I only wish my mother, Amal, an avid reader of history, was still with us to see this book completed.

Introduction

This book is about the history of political thought produced in the late Ayyubid and early Mamluk period. It highlights various concerns raised and solutions devised by Muslim legal theoreticians, jurists, judges and administrators of the Syro-Egyptian lands in their attempts to tackle a central question: how best to govern their communities. In the words of Ibn Jamaʿa (639/1241–733/1333), a renowned jurist and chief judge and one of the key thinkers treated in this work, this was a challenge of achieving optimal governance for the purpose of 'running the affairs of the people of Islam' (*tadbir ahl al-Islam*).[1]

There are two main aims of this venture. First, the book proposes a taxonomy of the themes of the political thought produced in this period under the three ideals of the rule of law, limited government and legitimate delegation of power. Secondly, it recommends contextualism, as employed in the history of political thought of late medieval and early modern Europe, as a suitable approach for interpreting Islamic political texts based on their narrow social, intellectual and political contexts. These two aims are achieved through the examination of treatises by five selected authors who flourished in the period between *c.* 1250 and *c.* 1350. In so doing, the book deals with other important questions of authorship, readership and dedicatees, authorial motives and intentions, genres and literary styles, sources and influences, and applicability.

[1] Refer to the full discussion in Chapter 2, below.

The history of Islamic political thought is approached from the fundamental tenet that Muslim thinkers believed that fallible humans can be entrusted with governing their societies. They theorised and proposed solutions in order to moderate and limit the exercise of power by other fallible humans and to improve all aspects of governance based on knowledge derived from legal and ethical traditions, personal administrative experiences, and historical precedents. There is no evidence in any of the texts examined in this book to suggest that Muslim thinkers considered themselves constrained by a perceived divine role that would limit the agency of humans in matters of governance. Nor is there any suggestion that they conceived of the *shariʿa* either as a doctrine of duties whose enforcement was the sole purpose of government or intended to uphold the institution of the caliphate as the perennial and highest form of political authority in Islam. Accordingly, they could freely advise rulers and ruling elites on various aspects of governance and address concerns that they considered relevant for their own time. It follows that the aspirations of Muslim political thinkers may not have been so different from some of their counterparts in Europe: securing stability, locating legitimate authority, and ensuring a just and durable system of governance – to the extent that this was possible in the thirteenth and early fourteenth centuries.

What is Islamic Political Thought?

Presently, scholarly interest in the study of the history of political thought does not match that in other vigorous disciplines in Islamic studies such as the legal, social and cultural histories of the Mamluk period. The field is still dominated by the twentieth-century works of H. A. R. Gibb, Ann K. S. Lambton, Erwin E. J. Rosenthal, Patricia Crone and others, in addition to a few more recent ones including those by Antony Black.[2] As formative and valuable as they are, these authoritative works circumscribed the scope of inquiry in the field to a very limited set of themes that concerned medieval Muslim thinkers: the preservation of the historical institution of the caliphate; the duty of the state to implement divine law; and the legitimation of usurpation of power by the sultans. Furthermore, these studies unintention-

[2] Refer to Chapter 1, below, for a detailed discussion.

ally obscured important contributions by various medieval Islamic thinkers and led to a distorted reading of political texts, as I shall discuss in detail subsequently in Chapter 1. Fortunately, recent contributions by historians of Islamic law and new perspectives on the work of the Hanbali theologian Ibn Taymiyya (661/1263–728/1328) have led to some incidental yet significant advances in the study of the political thought of the Mamluk period.[3] Further progress was achieved by scholars who studied representations of power and the remembrance of the shadow ʿAbbasid caliphate in Cairo.[4]

Defining political thought in a field as vast as the history of the pre-modern Islamic world is an ambitious endeavour, but a necessary one. With the political, religious, ethical, philosophical, theological and spiritual all encroaching on my attempts to identify a suitable definition in existing secondary literature, I eventually opted to construct an all-inclusive one befitting of the high political culture of medieval Islamic urban centres. Hereafter, political thought in the late Ayyubid and early Mamluk period refers to any discourse dealing with the origins of a state or polity, the legitimacy of the ruler and ruling elites, the limits of their power and authority, the moderation of their exercise of power, their relations with the people they ruled, the necessary qualifications for governing, institutions of government and order, institutions and modes of dispensing justice, individual and group rights, taxation and the distribution of wealth, and the justification and rules of war. This definition applies to any channel or form of expression, be it common among the intellectual and ruling elites or lay individuals, and whether expressed in high literary or material culture, or even spontaneously on the streets of Cairo or Damascus. This definition notwithstanding, the foci of this book are literary works by political thinkers of the Ayyubid and Mamluk period.

To a certain extent, the present book's definition of Islamic political thought overlaps with what Ibn Khaldun (732/1332–808/1406) accused Muslim philosophers of failing to discuss. He observed in his *Muqaddima*:

---

3 I will discuss in Chapter 1 such works by Ovamir Anjum, Caterina Bori, Yossef Rapoport, Baber Johansen, Mohamed Fadel and Sherman Jackson.

4 This includes works of Mona Hassan which will be treated in Chapter 1, and Anne F. Broadbridge's *Kingship and Ideology in the Islamic and Mongol Worlds*, Cambridge Studies in Islamic Civilization (Cambridge: Cambridge University Press, 2008) and Mustafa Banister's *The Abbasid Caliphate of Cairo, 1261–1517: Out of the Shadows*, Edinburgh Studies in Classical Islamic History and Culture (Edinburgh: Edinburgh University Press, 2021).

> By 'government of the city' (*al-siyāsa al-madaniyya*), the philosophers mean simply *the disposition of soul and character* which each member of a social organisation must have if, eventually, people are completely to have no need of rulers. They call the social organisation that fulfils these requirements the 'virtuous city' (*al-madīna al-fāḍila*). The norms observed in this connection are called 'government of the city'. *They do not mean the kind of government that the members of a social organisation are led to adopt through laws for the common interest. That is something different.* The 'virtuous city' of the philosophers is something whose realisation (*wuqū'*) is rare and remote. They discuss it only as a hypothesis.[5]

For Ibn Khaldun, philosophers did not treat *siyasa* or 'political government'.[6] We have to look elsewhere for thinkers who theorised on practical and attainable *siyasa*.

Sources

There exists a rich and extensive pre-Khaldunian tradition of authoring works of political thought by legal theoreticians, jurists, judges and administrators. This book examines the political conceptions expressed in the treatises of the following five carefully selected late Ayyubid and early Mamluk period authors from among what is available to us of this vast corpus: (1) Ibn Jamaʿa's (639/1241–733/1333) *Tahrir al-ahkam fi tadbir ahl al-Islam* (*Drafting Ordinances towards Running the Affairs of the People of Islam*), which I will argue was the synthesis of the Shafiʿi–Ashʿari strain of political thought of the period; (2) *Misbah al-hidaya fi tariq al-imama* (*The Guiding Lamp to the Path of the* imama), a Sufi expression of political thought dedicated by an unknown author probably to al-Zahir Baybars (r. 658/1260–676/1277); (3) parts of the work of the Maliki legal theoretician al-Qarafi (626/1228–

5 This passage is translated by Dimitri Gutas and the emphases are his throughout in 'The Study of Arabic Philosophy in the Twentieth Century: An Essay on the Historiography of Arabic Philosophy', *British Journal of Middle Eastern Studies* 29(1) (2002): 24. For Gutas, before Ibn Khaldun there is 'no independent field of study within Arabic philosophy which investigates political agents, constituencies, and institutions as autonomous elements that operate according to their own dynamic within the structure of the society', in ibid., p. 23.

6 This translation of *siyasa* in the same passage of the *Muqaddima* is from Erwin I. J. Rosenthal, *Political Thought in Medieval Islam: An Introductory Outline* (Cambridge: Cambridge University Press, 1958), 93–4.

682/1283 or 684/1285) titled *al-Ihkam fi tamyiz al-fatawa ʿan al-ahkam wa-tasarrufat al-qadi wa-al-Imam* (*The Book of Perfection in Distinguishing Legal Opinions from Judicial Rulings and the Discretionary Actions of Judges and Rulers*); (4) Ibn Talha's (582/1186/7–652/1254) *al-ʿIqd al-farid li-al-malik al-Saʿid* (*The Unique Necklace for a Content King*), a juristic treatise that resembles what is often termed mirrors for princes; and, lastly (5) parts of the historiographical work by Taj al-Din al-Subki (d. 771/1370), *Tabaqat al-Shafiʿiyya al-kubra* (*The Great Shafiʿi Biographical Dictionary*) and his treatise *Muʿid al-niʿam wa-mubid al-niqam* (*The Restorer of Favours and the Restrainer of Chastisements*), which will both be interpreted as political texts.

The above authors are not randomly selected. In addition to chronological and regional factors, the selection considers their professional backgrounds, their intended audiences and dedicatees, their aims in writing, the literary styles they opted for, their adherence to specific legal schools and intellectual currents, and the main political concerns they treated. All selected treatises were authored in the Syro-Egyptian lands during the late Ayyubid and early Mamluk period. The authors are known to be legal theoreticians and jurists or – as in the case of the Sufi *Misbah* – trained as such. Each of these authors belonged to the Ashʿari intellectual tradition and, with the exception of al-Qarafi, they all adhered to the Shafiʿi legal tradition. While the intended audiences were Ayyubid or Mamluk rulers and ruling elites, these treatises were not presented as mere panegyrics or works of flattery as they did not shy away from passing criticism or calling for accountability; nor were they authored for the sole purposes of critique, satire or to threaten in any way the stability of a realm or the legitimacy of a ruler. Moreover, these were not diplomatic exchanges concerned with reflecting certain images or ideologies of power. The selected works are all treatises that express clear political ideals using well-founded and recognisable repertoires of legal and ethical languages. Most importantly, these treatises fit this book's definition of Islamic political thought since, as professed by their authors, they dealt with themes of legitimacy of rulers, the limits and origins of power, ideal governance, justice and taxation.

Reading Ayyubid and Mamluk Political Thought

Identifying where and how to find Islamic political thought is only one aspect of the methodological challenges facing historians of the field. There is, likewise, the crucial issue of 'reading' – that is, interpreting – political texts, with which this book is equally concerned. This methodological concern must be kept in mind in order that the main themes, intended ideas and concerns treated by Islamic political thinkers of the period are not missed and, also, that ones that are not relevant to their time or simply did not concern them are not imposed. It follows that only a proper 'reading' of premodern Islamic political texts can unravel the rich and innovative tradition of authoring works of political thought that existed in the late Ayyubid and early Mamluk period and offset any artificial impositions on this thought. Such a reading can inform us whether the above-mentioned five authors – as is often believed – strived for the revival of the caliphal institution and the legitimation of usurped power, or conversely – as I shall argue – expressed first and foremost their concern for the moderation and limitation of the exercise of power.

This is a question of reading political thought as much as it is one of locating it. To this end, I shall propose contextualism (or linguistic contextualism) as an expedient methodology to interpret the political thought of the late Ayyubid and early Mamluk period. The well-tested broad guidelines of contextualism have been employed extensively in the history of medieval and early modern European political thought by historians of the 'Cambridge School', including Quentin Skinner and J. G. A. Pocock. The approach of this school proved to be beneficial for this book and, I argue, is indeed necessary at this stage of the development of the field of the history of Islamic political thought since it provides the required framework to counter anachronisms, misrepresentations of political texts, and the imposition of political ideas and concerns that could not have been relevant to the authors of the Ayyubid and Mamluk period.[7] Accordingly, as per the guidelines of contextualism, which are discussed in Chapter 1, the political texts treated throughout this

7 However, it is in no way the aim of this book to suggest it as the only way to interpret medieval Islamic political texts.

book will be interpreted against their narrow political, social and intellectual contexts. Furthermore, the political languages used by the five authors to express their ideas and concerns will be unlocked and the conventions that governed the prevalent ideological and political discourses of their time will be identified, both as prerequisites for 'reading' their treatises.

The late Ayyubid and early Mamluk period is the optimal proving ground for applying the guidelines of contextualism in the history of Islamic political thought. This was a period of a highly 'bookish' culture that thrived in the Syro-Egyptian lands and led to a prolific production and consumption of works of political advice.[8] Additionally, various well-recorded features of the social, cultural and political history of this period allow the reconstruction of the narrow context within which its political thought was produced, including the professionalisation and bureaucratisation of the scholars who authored works of political advice; various social and intellectual networks that flourished around legal schools, theological trends, and ideological debates and boosted intellectual production; the proliferation of educational and charitable institutions under military patronage states, which furthered competition for jobs and shaped the patterns of knowledge transfer in great urban centres such as Damascus and Cairo; and, lastly, the absence of an effective caliphate and the rule of the sultans and military elites.

Themes, Concerns and Ideals

All things considered, what is Islamic political thought of the late Ayyubid and early Mamluk period? Close scrutiny of the treatises authored by the previously mentioned five authors demarcates the following main themes: the moderation of the exercise of power by the ruler and ruling elites; the limits of this power; and the concern for stability and the smooth running of government and the affairs of the populace, irrespective of power struggles at the top and, consequently, locating legitimate political, judicial and administrative powers for every eventuality. As already mentioned, the present monograph argues that these themes can be classified under the three overlapping and interlocked ideals of the rule of law, limited government and legitimate

[8] Konrad Hirschler, *Medieval Damascus: Plurality and Diversity in an Arabic Library: The Ashrafiya Library Catalogue* (Edinburgh: Edinburgh University Press, 2016), 3, 37–8.

delegation of power. This taxonomy is intended to convey what the five authors strived to express and uphold in their treatises.

The rule of law describes the authors' effort to moderate the arbitrary exercise of power based on written systems of checks and balances. Such systems were rooted in Islamic legal reasoning, various ethical concepts from within and outside the religious tradition, and pertinent historical precedents. Each thinker understood these systems of checks and balances differently and opted for his own carefully selected repertoire of sources, authoritative texts, traditions and precedents in order to present his call for the rule of law in a distinctive way. Some resorted to legal and juristic reasoning and conceptions, others used Sufi ethical systems, and others still compiled what resembled tailor-made proto-constitutions to uphold their own conceptions of the rule of law.

Limited government refers in this book to attempts to restrain the discretionary exercise of power by the ruler by implementing a division of political, judiciary and administrative labour. This was possible owing to the sophistication of the late Ayyubid and Mamluk administration. Despite the overlap with the above-mentioned ideal of the rule of law, a more precise portrayal of these authors' detailed discussions of various senior offices dictates the identification of a separate and distinct ideal termed limited government. The examined treatises discussed various high-ranking administrative, military and judicial offices, including viziers, *amir*s, judges, market inspectors, chancery and fiscal secretaries, and other posts in what can be described as detailed administrative manuals. Such treatments aimed at securing the interests of the populace, the smooth running of government, and the just dispensing of justice outside the discretionary power of the ruling elites and independently from their struggles.

The theory of the legitimate delegation of power refers to careful attempts made by the five authors to secure a lawful and durable transfer of the original caliphal functions to different sultanic, judicial and administrative powers. This theory was an advanced political discourse that aimed to locate legitimate power at all levels of government for every eventuality and, accordingly, must not be confused with the legitimation expressed in panegyrics. Each author presented a distinct version of the theory of delegation and opted for his own cautiously selected sources and conceptions to ensure that the exercise of power was legitimate. Some thinkers expressed their concern for this ideal using juristic reasoning, while others relied on Sufi conceptions that fixed the origins of political power within the sultanate as the successor of prophethood.

Chapter Outlines

There are five chapters in this book. Although each one is written to be read and understood independently, the purpose of every chapter is the same: to highlight the aims and concerns of authors and how they expressed them thematically and stylistically. The chapters have deliberately not been placed in chronological order, so as not to give the reader a misleading impression of a causal or teleological relationship between the texts discussed in this book. All chapters treat an understudied source and some bring new ones to light for the first time.

Chapter 1 outlines the book's methodology and gives an overview of the prevalent impediments and impaired approaches in the field of the history of Islamic political thought. It justifies the decision to employ contextualism as a reliable and needed methodology to interpret the political texts of the late Ayyubid and early Mamluk period.

Chapter 2 introduces the reader to Ibn Jamaʿa's career and political thought. It explains the development of his practicable conceptions of the rule of law and his elaboration of a new system of checks and balances to moderate the ruler's discretionary exercise of power, which was rooted in Shafiʿi juristic reasoning and greatly benefited from the author's administrative and judicial experience. The chapter treats Ibn Jamaʿa's tripartite conception of political authority, which ruled out the normative need for the caliphal institution, advanced what resembled a proto-constitution that regulated all aspects of public life and empowered the administration, and proposed an advanced theory of the legitimate delegation of power to high-ranking functions of government.

Chapter 3 examines the anonymous *Misbah* as a model for thirteenth-century Sufi conceptions of highest political authority that identified the sultanate as the legitimate heir of prophethood. It introduces the reader to the intellectual and socio-political milieu within which these ideas emerged and treats the active participation of Sufis in the circles of politics in Mamluk

Cairo and Damascus. The chapter explores how the *Misbah*'s unknown author proposed moderating sultanic power through a Sufi proprietary political language rooted in the *shariʿa* and Islamised ethical systems deriving from Graeco-Arabic philosophy.

Chapter 4 demonstrates how the original contributions of Ibn Talha and al-Qarafi were formative to the political thought produced in this period and challenges the scholarly focus on the study of literary genres of political texts. It highlights the influence of the social, professional and ideological contexts of both authors in shaping their innovative postulations and conceptions of the rule of law. The chapter provides further proof that medieval political thinkers only treated concerns and ideas that were available to them in their empirical and intellectual worlds.

Chapter 5 examines Mamluk historiography, namely, specific anecdotes in al-Subki's biographical dictionaries, as a form of political thought. These selected anecdotes aimed to emphasise the self-proclaimed prerogatives of Shafiʿi scholars to legitimate rulers and moderate their exercise of power, and defend the populace against the perceived excesses of the rising military elites. The final chapter, likewise, highlights the role of competition between legal schools (*madhhab*s) in the production of political thought.

Hopefully, what will emerge from this book is a surprisingly innovative Islamic political thought that centred on the limitation and moderation of power and empowered the professional administration and judiciary in order to secure the smooth running of government. In the process, this thought completely ignored the institution of the caliphate or, at best, deemed it unnecessary.

1

Reading Islamic Political Thought

This chapter outlines the methodology followed in the present book. It aims to identify the impediments in the field of the study of the history of Islamic political thought and to recommend a suitable approach for 'reading' political texts. The chapter will propose contextualism or linguistic-contextualism as a reliable methodology to interpret the writings of the five authors who will be treated in the four subsequent chapters. By making this proposition, I am also contending that the prevailing approaches applied in the field are no longer adequate for reading Islamic political texts since they fail to benefit from the advances made in the history of medieval and early modern European political thought. One only needs to contrast the scholarship produced on political texts from the two sides of the Mediterranean between the mid-thirteenth to the mid-fourteenth century to find examples of this great disparity.

To justify this criticism, I propose a simple comparison of the available historiography written on the two contemporaneous authors Ibn Jamaʿa (639/1241–733/1333) and Marsilius of Padua (*c.*1275/80–1343). The scholarly interpretations of their writings highlight the dire state of the field of the history Islamic political thought when compared with its European counterpart. Both authors flourished around the same time, the first in Damascus, Jerusalem and Cairo, and the second in Padua, Paris and Munich. Each author produced one main political work and two lesser ones. Marsilius completed his main political work, *Defensor pacis* (*Defender of Peace*) in Paris on 24 June 1324, and composed two short ones, *De translatione imperii* (*On the Translation of the Empire*) also in Paris between 1324 and 1326, and the *Defensor minor* (*Lesser Defender*) in Munich between 1339 and 1341.[1] Ibn

[1] Joseph Canning, *Ideas of Power in the Late Middle Ages, 1296–1417* (Cambridge: Cambridge

Jamaʿa authored *Tahrir al-ahkam fi tadbir ahl al-Islam* (*Drafting Ordinances towards Running the Affairs of the People of Islam*) during his final years. The *Tahrir* followed a chain of two lesser political works the *Mustanad* and the *Mukhtasar*; the latter work was completed between 689/1290 and 693/1293.[2] While the writings of Marsilius of Padua have generated a pool of varying, sometimes opposing, and lively interpretations among modern historians, political theorists and philosophers, the historians of Islamic political thought handed down a near unanimous and rather dull verdict on Ibn Jamaʿa.

The contested readings of Marsilius' writings reflect the advanced and vigorous state of the field of the history of European political thought. They can be classified into three main approaches: 'the republican, the imperial and (within the imperial) the providential-historical'.[3] Within the various contributions to the first approach, Quentin Skinner regards Marsilius as a republican and a supporter of popular sovereignty.[4] Skinner argues that Marsilius considered that 'the ruler should be the whole body of people' in order to avoid internal fighting and keep the peace and that, furthermore, Marsilius 'provided the fullest and most systematic defence of Republican liberty against the coming of the despots'.[5] The second and opposite interpretation contends that the *Defensor pacis* was pro-imperial. For instance, Annabel Brett maintains that Marsilius posited that only an emperor could bring peace being 'the supreme civic legislator' who was rightfully entrusted with 'all power over spirituals'.[6] The third approach is similarly pro-imperial. It is advanced by George Garnett who bases his interpretation on Marsilius' providential view of history.[7] Lastly, Joseph Canning considers that Marsilius'

University Press, 2011), 81; Marsilius and Annabel S. Brett, *The Defender of the Peace* (Cambridge: Cambridge University Press, 2005), xi–xiii; Frank Godthardt, 'The Life of Marsilius of Padua', in Gerson Moreno-Riaño and Cary J. Nederman (eds), *A Companion to Marsilius of Padua* (Leiden: Brill, 2012), 13–55.

2 Refer to Chapter 2, 58–77, below.

3 Canning, *Ideas of Power*, 84, 81–106 and *passim*; I am grateful to Debora Spini for suggesting this work to me. For a similarly useful summary, refer to George Garnett, *Marsilius of Padua and 'the Truth of History'* (Oxford: Oxford University Press, 2006), 1–14.

4 Canning, *Ideas of Power*, 84.

5 Quentin Skinner, *The Foundations of Modern Political Thought*, vol. I (Cambridge: Cambridge University Press, 1978), 61, 65.

6 Canning, *Ideas of Power*, 88; Marsilius and Brett, *The Defender of the Peace*, xxxi.

7 Refer to Canning, *Ideas of Power*, 88–9; Garnett, *Marsilius of Padua*, especially ch. 4, 'Christian Providential History: A Dialectic of Perfection and Perversion', 146–59.

political thought centred on questions of power and legitimate authority and, through these questions, Marsilius made a distinction between the political community and the church and exposed the illegitimate papal claims to plenitude of power.[8]

On the other hand, the scholarly readings of Ibn Jamaʿa's thought are homogeneous since they stem from a less vigorous field. They unanimously reduce the essence of the *Tahrir* to the single view that 'might equals right' and that usurped power is unquestionably legitimate.[9] H. A. R. Gibb posits that Ibn Jamaʿa's thought reflected 'the abandonment of the Law in favor of a secular absolutism'.[10] Similarly, Ann K. S. Lambton states that Ibn Jamaʿa justified the 'extinction of the caliphate' and was not even concerned with legitimating the coercive sultan's authority since 'seizure of power itself gave authority'.[11] Likewise, Rosenthal sees in the *Tahrir* a 'principle of acquiescence in bad rule' in order to avoid anarchy and that Ibn Jamaʿa 'compromised to an astonishing degree with political realities and stretched his concept of legality very nearly to breaking-point'.[12] Antony Black, however, is more original, describing Ibn Jamaʿa's views on political authority as 'broadly Hobbesian'; he moreover notes how some modern Islamic thinkers regarded Ibn Jamaʿa's theory as a corruption of Islamic thought.[13] Fundamentally, the above interpretations are different formulations of the same view.

There are two ways to explain this disparity between the rigour of the two bodies of scholarship. One might say that the two authors emerged from two intellectual traditions alien to each other and treated different sets of problems conceived within disparate political contexts and, therefore, their texts are of varying complexity and it is only reasonable that one author would engender more scholarly interpretations. Yet a closer inspection reveals that the intellectual spheres of Marsilius and Ibn Jamaʿa were not so unconnected after

[8] Canning, *Ideas of Power*, 104, 106, 102–6.

[9] H. A. R. Gibb, 'Constitutional Organization', in Majid Khadduri and Herbert J. Liebesny (eds), *Law in the Middle East* (The Middle East Institute, 1955), 19.

[10] Ibid., 23.

[11] Ann K. S. Lambton, *State and Government in Medieval Islam: An Introduction to the Study of Islamic Political Theory; the Jurists* (Oxford: Oxford University Press, 1981), 138, 139.

[12] Rosenthal, *Political Thought*, 43–4, 45.

[13] Antony Black, *The History of Islamic Political Thought: From the Prophet to the Present*, 2nd edn (Edinburgh: Edinburgh University Press, 2011), 148.

all. Antony Black astutely highlights a striking similarity between Marsilius and al-Ghazali and considers that some aspects of the *Defensor pacis*, such as its views on the origins of the state, may have been influenced by Ibn Rushd (Averroes, 520/1126–595/1198) and other Muslim philosophers.[14] Indeed, there are various and ongoing discussions on the nature and extent of Marsilius' Averroeism.[15] Furthermore, the set of problems treated by the two authors was not so different. Both were trying to locate legitimate authority: Marsilius for the purpose of securing peace; and Ibn Jamaʿa to guarantee stability and the continuous functioning of government in all eventualities, as I shall argue in Chapter 2. It follows that a second and more reasonable explanation for this disparity resides in the current shape of the field of the history of Islamic political thought. Its impaired approaches to reading political texts have yielded fewer interpretations of Ibn Jamaʿa's thought. Four of these impediments are treated in the following discussion: the longue durée; imposed paradigms such as the theory of the caliphate and fall of Baghdad; the mythology of genre; and the availability of texts.

The Longue Durée

The longue durée is a genealogical approach that looks at the development of political thought from the early Islamic days down to varying stages of Islamic history, as attempted by Rosenthal, Lambton, Crone, Black and others.[16] These well-known studies remain essential since they situate various political ideas within the broad context of Islamic history and are, as such, the inescapable starting point for new scholars of the field. Nevertheless, they also present an array of challenges for any study of political thought – such as this monograph – that is circumscribed chronologically or geographically. For instance, Patricia Crone's *Medieval Islamic Political Thought* reflects the longue durée's emphasis on the themes of the early Islamic period, including

[14] Antony Black, *The West and Islam: Religion and Political Thought in World History* (New York: Oxford University Press, 2008), 52, 53.

[15] To cite one such discussion, see Michael J. Sweeney, 'The Spirituality of the Church: Scripture, Salvation, and Sacraments', in Gerson Moreno-Riaño and Cary J. Nederman (eds), *A Companion to Marsilius of Padua* (Leiden: Brill, 2012), 181–227.

[16] Rosenthal, *Political Thought*; Lambton, *State and Government*; Black, *History of Islamic Political Thought*; Patricia Crone, *Medieval Islamic Political Thought* (Edinburgh: Edinburgh University Press, 2005).

the formation of sects and the nature of the early caliphal institution. This inevitably impacts the perceived importance of subsequent political thought, such as that of the thirteenth and fourteenth centuries when these themes ceased to capture the imagination of Muslim writers.

Some historians were well aware of the limitations of the longue durée approach while others were not. Ann Lambton warned her readers that her selection of authors was 'guided partly by personal choice, partly by the work of others in the field before me, and partly by the availability of texts'.[17] Accordingly, she presented her seminal book as a mere 'introduction to the study of the political ideas of the jurists'.[18] On the other hand, Antony Black aspired to nothing short of a 'complete' survey and an analysis of the history of Islamic political thought 'from the beginning (*c.* 622) to the present' while relying solely on secondary works.[19] Aspiring to offer the first 'complete' history led to peculiar conclusions, like regretting that the US and UK governments had failed to benefit from Ibn Khaldun's analysis of 'less sophisticated humans' in responding to the terrorist attacks of 11 September 2001.[20]

The shortcomings of a longue durée perspective are evident in some conclusions that were rushed into in order to bridge developments over a wide chronological period. Black, for instance, stated that, 'Nizam's [Nizam al-Mulk (d. 485/1092)] tolerant and statesmanlike approach to religious politics appears to have left its mark on later Sunni regimes, particularly the Ottoman.'[21] Aside from the risk of drawing conclusions based on the highly questionable attribution of *Siyar al-muluk* or *Siyasat-nama* (*Book of Government*) to Nizam al-Mulk, there is clearly a need to revisit this statement.[22] 'Tolerant' and 'statesmanlike' need to be defined in a medieval context. Moreover, I find 'approach to religious politics' difficult to comprehend without further delineation, especially given Nizam al-Mulk's role in the spread of Shafiʿi colleges. Finally, one struggles with what is meant by 'later

17 Lambton, *State and Government*, xviii.

18 Ibid., xviii.

19 Black, *History of Islamic Political Thought*, xvi.

20 Ibid., xvii.

21 Ibid., 96.

22 Ibid., 91; while Black was aware of the dubious attribution to Nizam al-Mulk, he concluded that the *Siyar al-muluk* 'appears, nonetheless, to advocate something like Nizam's strategy for the religious polity'. Refer to the discussion in fn. 68, below.

Sunni regimes': the Ottomans did not view themselves primarily as a mere Sunni regime (and most certainly not a Shafiʿi one), but as a universal empire that inherited the ʿAbbasid caliphate, Byzantium and more besides.[23] The wide chronological gap between the Seljuqs and the Ottomans cannot simply be bridged with a single sentence – unless one considers far-reaching transformations that occurred over a period of two or three centuries irrelevant for studying political thought.

The longue durée is a very ambitious project that attempts to survey as many thinkers as possible, which comes at the high cost of ignoring the narrow historical contexts of most developments in political thought. The demands of this approach impact the granularity of the study of political thought. By granularity I am referring to period-specific conditions that may or may not relate to perceived developments in the broader Islamic history of ideas. As such, the longue durée perspective implies that Muslim political thinkers always dealt with a fixed set of paradigms that concerned various intellectual currents throughout the history of Islam. Moreover, it implicitly assumes that those thinkers formed a decontextualised network where the history of ideas becomes a self-referential circle of discussion among great men. With such assumptions we risk missing more concrete and pertinent factors that concerned Muslim thinkers, such as competition within the ruling classes or dynasties, the rise of new types of political elites (military slaves, for example), the Crusades, lawful and unlawful taxation, the evolution of the schools of law (*madhhab*s) into corporate entities held together by legal conformity, rivalries among the four *madhhab*s, emerging juristic discourses, major developments in the operation of the legal system, the popularisation of Sufism, the professionalisation and *adab*isation of scholars and their competition for offices, and other concerns.

Despite their unquestionably beneficial contribution to the field, existing works of the longue durée resulted in a simplified pantheon of pre-modern authors. Such a pantheon is insufficiently broad to incorporate all major

[23] The Ottoman sultan's titles included *Kayser-i Rum* (Caesar of the Eastern Roman Empire), *padishah* and 'sultan over all the sultans of East and West and [undefeated] conqueror of the territories of the Byzanto-Roman world, Persian, and Arabia'; refer to Rhoads Murphey, *Exploring Ottoman Sovereignty: Tradition, Image and Practice in the Ottoman Imperial Household, 1400–1800* (London: Continuum, 2008), 83, 98, ch. 2, 41–75.

contributions to Islamic political thought and, accordingly, the wide chronological approach obscured important thinkers and ideas. This misleading hierarchy from a list of a limited number of medieval thinkers emanated from prevalent biases among historians, which were caused by accessibility to original manuscripts and texts in translation, trends set by previous studies, present-day political concerns, and other imposed paradigms such as the theory of the caliphate to which this chapter now turns.

Imposed Paradigms

The study of the history of Islamic political thought has similarly been impaired by subjective and constant impositions of political paradigms that, I argue, were hardly relevant to thinkers of the Mamluk period. It is striking that examining such an immense and diverse corpus of Islamic political, ethical and legal texts has resulted in historians identifying a very narrow set of paradigms that supposedly consumed Muslim political thinkers for fourteen centuries, including the 250 years of Mamluk history of concern to the present book. One paradigm is often cited, the theory of the caliphate/*imamate* and its tributary concept of the legitimation of the usurpation of power (*imarat al-istila'*). As summarised by E. I. J. Rosenthal, Muslim jurists were continuously attempting to 'bring constitutional theory into line with political reality' and accommodate the authority of the wielder of power with the *shari'a*.[24]

We are repeatedly told that Ibn Jama'a was the final stage in the development of the theory of the caliphate following al-Mawardi and al-Ghazali. Lambton presented this progression eloquently: al-Mawardi established the difference between vizierate (*wizara*) and amirate (*imara*) and legitimised the 'amirate of usurpation'; al-Juwayni and al-Ghazali established the importance of the sultanate, while al-Razi recognised 'the dissociation of religious and temporal power'; finally, Ibn Jama'a (and Ibn Taymiyya) justified the 'extinction of the caliphate'.[25] Rosenthal suggested a similar evolution.[26] Both Lambton and Rosenthal in point of fact were reiterating, albeit more subtly, H. A. R. Gibb's view that Ibn Jama'a's thought marked 'a complete divorce

[24] Rosenthal, *Political Thought*, 22.
[25] Lambton, *State and Government*, 96, 133, 138–51.
[26] Rosenthal, *Political Thought*, 27–61.

of the imāmate from the Sharīʿa and the abandonment of the Law in favor of a secular absolutism'.[27]

I find this mapping simply too convenient and based on two imposed paradigms. It is reliant upon the artificial ascription of a continuous concern among the jurists for the preservation of the role of the caliphal institution and, consequently, for the tributary 'justification of usurpation'. This problem originated, no doubt, in Gibb's interpretation of *Kitab al-Ahkam al-sultaniyya wa-al-wilayat al-diniyya* (*The Book of Ordinances of Government*). He considered this work – as did other scholars who followed him – as a 'post eventum justification' of the usurpation of the caliph's powers by sultans.[28] Consequently, when studying later political texts from different contexts, like Ibn Jamaʿa's, for instance, scholarship has tended to ask similar questions: who or what was the author justifying? How crude was the justification? Unfortunately, the study of pre-modern Islamic political thought has thus practically been reduced to a study of the justification of usurpation or even, a mere 'justification of the precedents'.[29]

This reduction is, moreover, the product of a deep-rooted misunderstanding of the nature of the *shariʿa* and its relation with government in Islam. In a nutshell, the prevalent scholarly opinion was that the *shariʿa* – being religious law – is utopian, rigid and, as such, was impractical for the governance of a growing empire and changing Islamic society.[30] Accordingly, the *shariʿa*'s role in Islamic society inhibited any urge that medieval Muslim jurists may have entertained to develop an all-encompassing political theory or a workable constitutional law. The long trajectory that led to the formation of this opinion, as was well summarised by Mohammad Fadel, started with Max Weber's typology of law down to the works of Lambton, Malcolm Kerr, Crone and others, via Joseph Schacht and Noel Coulson.[31]

---

[27] Gibb, 'Constitutional Organization', 23. Crone does not even refer to Ibn Jamaʿa in her *Medieval Islamic Political Thought*.

[28] Lambton, *State and Government*, 84; Hamilton A. R. Gibb and Stanford J. Shaw, 'Al-Mawardi's Theory of the Caliphate', in *Studies on the Civilization of Islam* (Princeton, NJ: Princeton University Press, 1982), 162.

[29] Ibid.

[30] This is no longer the prevalent view among historians of Islamic law.

[31] Refer to Mohammad Fadel, 'State and Sharia', in Rudolph Peters and P. J. Bearman (eds), *The Ashgate Research Companion to Islamic Law* (Farnham: Ashgate, 2014), *passim* and especially 93–7.

1. Theory of the Caliphate

The theory of the caliphate was the predictable outcome of such a line of reasoning. Since the *shariʿa* was a mere 'doctrine of duties'[32] towards God and since the function of the state was 'essentially' to execute the *shariʿa*,[33] what kind of constitutional law were the jurists really capable of producing? And what sort of political theory could they pen if – unlike their Greek antecedents – Muslim political thinkers were not even interested in 'the basis of the state's authority and the source if its laws', as Lambton claimed?[34] According to this reasoning, the answer can only be a rudimentary theory centred on a legitimate ruler, the caliph, who was entrusted with enforcing a deficient religious law on his community. It follows that a derivative of this theory would be that any usurper of caliphal authority would rapidly be granted the backing of the jurists. As such, the institution of the caliphate was transformed into the perennial orbit of any Islamic political theory that the jurists may propose. I shall challenge this opinion when I treat below the question of *shariʿa* and government and the meanings and usages of *shariʿa* in the political language of the Mamluk period. Yet at this point in the introduction, I simply wish to show how these prevalent views led to the imposition of artificial paradigms on the political thought of the Mamluk period.

I propose one aspect the theory of the caliphate for further dissection. *Khalifat Allah* (deputy of God) versus *khalifat Rasul Allah* (deputy of the Prophet) has been presented as a critical discourse that concerned jurists and determined legitimation strategies of Muslim rulers and dynasties. The authors of *God's Caliph*, Patricia Crone and Martin Hinds, claimed:

> In short, from ʿUthmān to Numayrī, or in other words from about 644 to about 1984, Muslims of the most diverse political, religious, geographical and ethnic backgrounds had taken the title khalīfa to stand for khalīfat

[32] First from ibid., 94; Christiaan Snouck Hurgronje, *Selected Works of C. Snouck Hurgronje*, ed. Georges-Henri Bousquet and Joseph Schacht (Leiden: E. J. Brill, 1957), 261.

[33] Hamilton A. R. Gibb, 'The Heritage of Islam in the Modern World (I)', *International Journal of Middle East Studies* 1(1) (1970): 11; Lambton, *State and Government*, xiv.

[34] Lambton, *State and Government*, xiv.

> Allāh, 'deputy of God'. It thus seems natural to infer that this is what the title always meant.[35]

But what did political thinkers of the Mamluk period, a good 250 years of Islamic and world history, really make of this supposedly paradigmatic title that troubled Islam from the first year of the reign of ʿUthman (23/644–35/655) until the second Sudanese civil war of 1983? Unsurprisingly, they did not invest much effort in pondering this issue nor did they consider the caliphal title to mean 'deputy of God'. Ibn Jamaʿa, at the end of a section of his *Tahrir* dedicated to the institution of the caliphate, offered only one sentence to this issue, 'the elected one can be named *khalifa*, or *khalifat Rasul Allah*, as he is a caliph among his community; *khalifat Allah* is not to be used because when Abu Bakr was called this way, he replied, "I'm not the Caliph of God but the Caliph of his Prophet."'[36] A similar verdict came from al-Qalqashandi (756/1355–821/1418), a jurist whose interests lay mostly in the secretarial art of writing (*insha*ʾ) and also in geography and mathematics.[37] In his *Maʾathir al-inafa fi maʿalim al-khilafa* (*Foregoing Glories of the Caliphate Landmarks*), which he presented to caliph al-Muʿtadid III (r. 817/1414–845/1441), al-Qalqashandi dedicated a short discussion to 'God's caliph', in which he merely listed three different positions on this issue.[38] One would have expected a longer treatment as the *Maʾathir al-inafa* was focused on the caliphate and was dedicated to a caliph, yet that was not the case. The issue of God's caliph did not seem to be of major relevance to political thinkers, at least not in this period.[39] The discussion on *khalifat Allah*

[35] Patricia Crone and Martin Hinds, *God's Caliph: Religious Authority in the First Centuries of Islam* (Cambridge: Cambridge University Press, 2003), p. 19.

[36] Ibn Jamaʿa, *Tahrir al-ahkam fi tadbir ahl al-Islam*, ed. Fuʾad ʿAbd al-Munʿim Ahmad (Qatar: Riʾasat al-Mahakim al-Sharʿiyya wa-al-Shuʾun al-Diniyya, 1985), 57; at the end of the first section titled 'Regarding the necessity for the imam, the conditions of the imama, and the imam's injunctions', 48–57.

[37] For a more detailed interpretation of al-Qalqashandi, refer to Mona Hassan, *Longing for the Lost Caliphate: A Transregional History* (Princeton, NJ: Princeton University Press, 2017), 126–31. See also C. E. Bosworth, 'al-Ḳalḳashandī', *EI²*.

[38] Al-Qalqashandi, *Maʾathir al-inafa fi maʿalim al-khilafa*, ed. ʿAbd al-Sattar Ahmad Farraj (Beirut: ʿAlam al-Kutub, 2006), 15–16.

[39] The argument in Crone and Hinds' *God's Caliph* is based on a contested translation of a fraction of a letter drafted by an Umayyad caliph and preserved in al-Tabari; refer to Uri Rubin, 'Prophets and Caliphs: The Biblical Foundations of the Umayyad Authority', in Herbert Berg (ed.), *Method and Theory in the Study of Islamic Origins* (Leiden: Brill, 2003), 87–93.

is therefore a perennial paradigm that has been imposed on Islamic political thought of the Mamluk period.

Some scholars insisted on the unanimous commitment of Muslim jurists to the theory of the caliphate even when faced with ample and compelling contradictory evidence. Wilferd Madelung's explanation of the waiving of the necessity of Qurashi descent for the eligibility to the *imamate* by the *Misbah*, a thirteenth-century anonymous Sufi treatise, is an emblematic example.[40] He contended that the unknown author of the *Misbah* 'deviated' from the tradition of the jurists as 'the requirement of the imam being of Qurayš had been a matter of consensus among Sunnite scholars until the recent overthrow of the ʿAbbāsid caliphate in Baghdad . . .'.[41] However, more than two centuries before the *Misbah*, the prominent Sunni jurist and theologian al-Juwayni (d. 478/1085) did not consider Qurashi descent to be a 'reasonable' requirement for eligibility to the caliphate in his treatise, *Ghiyath al-umam fi-iltiyath al-zulam* (*Aid to Nations Shrouded in Darkness*).[42] Although Tilman Nagel brought the possible influence of the *Ghiyath* on the *Misbah* to his attention, Madelung insisted on his interpretation and argued that the author of the *Misbah* was not even 'acquainted' with al-Juwayni's work![43] Additionally, he dismissed Wael Hallaq's findings on the *Ghiyath*, judging that it went 'far beyond what may be reasonably inferred from al-Ǧuwaynī's discussions'.[44] Madelung maintained that al-Juwayni 'insists' on the necessity of Qurashi descent, despite the fact that the latter considered this stipulation to be 'unreasonable' and cast serious doubt on a prophetic saying that 'imams are from Quraysh'.[45]

---

40 For a more detailed discussion, refer to Chapter 3, 103–7, below.

41 Wilferd Madelung, 'A Treatise on the Imamate Dedicated to Sultan Baybars I', in *Proceedings of the 14th Congress of the Union Européenne Des Arabisants et Islamisants, Pt. 1* (Budapest, 1995), 95.

42 In Al-Juwayni, *Al-Ghiyathi: Ghiyath al-umam fi iltiyath al-zulam*, ed. ʿAbd al-ʿAzim al-Dib (Cairo: Matbaʿat Nahdat Misr, 1981 or 1982), 79–81; I use the translated title based on Ovamir Anjum, 'Political Metaphors and Concepts in the Writings of an Eleventh-Century Sunni Scholar, Abū al-Maʿālī al-Juwaynī (419–478/1028–1085)', *Journal of the Royal Asiatic Society* 26(1/2) (2016): 7.

43 Madelung, 'A Treatise on the Imamate', 91, fn. 1.

44 Ibid., 95, fn. 7. Refer to Wael B. Hallaq, 'Caliphs, Jurists and the Saljūqs in the Political Thought of Juwaynī', *The Muslim World* 74(1) (1984): 26–41.

45 Madelung, 'A Treatise on the Imamate', 95, fn. 7; al-Juwayni, *Ghiyath al-umam*, 79–81.

The scholarly interest in the theory of the caliphate persists. Recently, Mona Hassan's *Longing for the Lost Caliphate* examined Muslim conceptions of the caliphate following the destruction of Baghdad in 656/1258 by the Mongols and the abolition of the Ottoman caliphate in 1924. She argues that the caliphate was continuously 'a pivotal cultural symbol' for Muslims, who were constantly attempting to 'redefine the caliphate for their times'.[46] While there is no denying the significance of the institution of the caliphate in the historical memory of many Muslims, this rarely translated into a yearning for the caliphate in the Islamic political thought produced during the Mamluk period, as will be shown in the subsequent four chapters. Hassan's well-researched work is one of only a few to acknowledge the relevance of Mamluk political thinkers such as Ibn Jamaʿa and al-Subki, yet her book still considers them as 'Post-656/1258 Theorists of the Caliphate'.[47] I shall present differing interpretations of the political theories of both thinkers in Chapters 2 and 5 and, furthermore, frequently stress throughout this monograph that the caliphate was a long gone ideal well before and after the fall of Baghdad.

2. *The Fall of Baghdad*

In the history of pre-modern Islamic political thought, the fall of the ʿAbbasid caliphate in Baghdad in 656/1258 is still regarded as a '*terminus ad quem*'.[48] While this paradigm has been retired in other fields of Islamic history and although Lambton argued, in 1962, that the Mongol invasion did not cause a fundamental break in Islamic political theory, this paradigm still resonates in the history of political thought.[49] The attempts of modern scholars to periodise centuries of intellectual history, include a large number of authors, and treat a

46 Hassan, *Longing for the Caliphate*, 2, 19.

47 Ibid., on Jamaʿa, 108–11 and al-Subki, 118–20.

48 Sherman A. Jackson, *Islamic Law and the State: The Constitutional Jurisprudence of Shihāb al-Dīn al-Qarāfī* (New York: Brill, 1996), xxxix; Jackson notes a 'conceptualization of history' that considers this period as 'an epoch that was not expected to produce much in the way of constitutional thought'. Such works consider the death of al-Ghazali in 1111 as the end of serious intellectual activity; the political thought of authors like Ibn Jamaʿa is viewed as 'irrelevant', in Marshall G. S. Hodgson and Edmund Burke, *Rethinking World History: Essays on Europe, Islam, and World History*, Studies in Comparative World History (Cambridge: Cambridge University Press, 1993), 182–3.

49 A. K. S. Lambton, 'Justice in the Medieval Persian Theory of Kingship', *Studia Islamica* 17 (1962): 108.

massive corpus of political thought writings biases them towards the thinkers of the golden age and exceptional later thinkers. In the process the actual history of political thought has been lost. For instance, in the introduction to *The Princeton Encyclopedia of Islamic Political Thought*, Gerhard Böwering segregated Islamic political thought of the High Middle Ages (1055–1258) from that of the Late Middle Ages (1258–1500), from which, he stated, only two writers 'stand out': Ibn Taymiyya and Ibn Khaldun.[50] Crone's *Medieval Islamic Political Thought* covers Islamic political thought from the rise of Islam and stops at the Mongol destruction of the caliphate in Baghdad in 656/1258. Even Ibn Taymiyya and Ibn Khaldun are outside the scope of this book, never mind thinkers like al-Qarafi and Ibn Jamaʿa.

This idea of 656/1258 being a watershed in Middle Eastern history of political thought does not tie in well with this book for several reasons. For one, the Mongols never invaded Egypt and their presence in Syria was short-lived. Seljuq and Ayyubid polities and potentates existed before and continued to exist well after 656/1258. Furthermore, the scholarly networks and the social and educational institutions of the Syro-Egyptian urban centres that produced political thinkers survived and flourished. This diminishes any resultant influence of the event on political writings in Egypt and Syria. Secondly, the caliphate, as a primary ideal for political thinkers living in thirteenth-century Syria and Egypt, was outweighed by other considerations; this book will argue that many developments in political thought ascribed to the fall of Baghdad were already in place by the end of the Ayyubid period. Such important developments are lost in this pre- and post-Mongol invasion perspective and can be redeemed only by a precise study of the late Ayyubid and early Mamluk period.

The Mythology of Genre

In addition to the emphasis on the longue durée approach and imposed paradigms, the field was – and still is – impaired by a fixation on the study of literary genres. Some scholars contend that the genre of a political text is fixed in both content and style and, therefore, dictates the postulated political

---

50 Gerhard Böwering, Patricia Crone and Mahan Mirza (eds), *The Princeton Encyclopedia of Islamic Political Thought*, Princeton Reference (Princeton, NJ: Princeton University Press, 2013), xi–xii.

ideas within the text. Furthermore, the genre is occasionally reconstructed along fictional dichotomies and an elusive and highly problematic pursuit of cultural continuity. The scheme such scholars propose is simple: the writings of jurists only treated religion and the above-mentioned theory of the caliphate, while the literati – broadly defined as non-jurists – were interested in the themes of kingship and sultanate, the arts of statecraft and administration, and ancient conceptions of justice. Chapters 2, 4 and 5 will challenge the mythology of genre by highlighting the importance that the jurists of the Ayyubid and Mamluk period accorded to the arts of administration, the blending of different literary genres in their political treatises, their focus on the sultanate as opposed to the caliphate, and their reliance on non-religious ethical systems to moderate the exercise of power.

Relentless attempts by scholarship aimed to uphold fixed and continuing genres, especially mirrors for princes. This fixation somehow transformed the discourse on medieval Islamic political thought to one of genre as opposed to one of conceptions of political authority and governance. Lambton delimited three main 'formulations' of political thought: 'theory of the jurists', 'theory of the philosophers' and 'literary theory'.[51] In this once widely accepted – and still resonant – scheme, literary theory is understood to include the genres of mirrors for princes and administrative manuals.[52] Lambton's categorisation assumed that the first formulation was 'the most truly Islamic of the three'.[53] The third formulation, on the other hand, 'is concerned with the practice rather than the theory of government and seeks in some measure to assimilate Islamic norms to Sassanian traditions of kingship. Its basis is justice rather

[51] Lambton, *State and Government*, xvi.

[52] This argument was a refined version of one proposed by Lambton in 1962 when she made a distinction between 'medieval' and 'classical' theory; refer to 'Justice in the Medieval Persian Theory of Kingship'. According to Lambton's classification, the 'classical theory' was a 'purely Islamic' one put forward by jurists like Abu Yusuf (d.182/798), al-Mawardi, al-Ghazali and Ibn Jamaʿa (93–5). These jurists, Lambton argued, were concerned only with religion and the caliphate, not with 'offices and functions' or administration (99). However, all these authors dedicated writings to taxation, administration, the sultanate and the art of governance; as an illustration, refer to Louise Marlow, *Counsel for Kings: Wisdom and Politics in Tenth-Century Iran: The Naṣīḥat Al-Mulūk of pseudo-Māwardī: Contexts and Themes*, vol. 1 (Edinburgh: Edinburgh University Press, 2016), 11–12, for a list of titles authored by al-Mawardi on statecraft, political authority and administration.

[53] Lambton, *State and Government*, xvi.

than right religion or knowledge.'[54] The issue was, however, that ultimately the boundaries between formulation, theory and genre were lost and the focus became exclusively on the genre. Moreover, so unchanging and blurred was this categorisation that, with time, it almost became sufficient for some scholars to recognise the genre of a political text in order to presume its postulated theory.

Post-classical texts do not fit well into this categorisation, which proved to require continuous scaffolding to be sustained. Lambton, for instance, conceded that the three formulations had much in common and that the same authors wrote in their different capacities as jurists, philosophers and advisers of rulers.[55] Although Islamic advice literature employed pre-Islamic Arab, Greek, Indian and Sassanian inspirations that aimed to instruct rulers through an appealing and reachable style, political texts were often more complex than mere repetitive etiquette formulas, verses or poetry, aphorisms and homily. Rather, these texts often reflected clear and confident conceptions of government relevant to their own age. I will present two cases where complications arose from assuming that the genre determines the content of a political text.

The first case is the mirror titled *Bahr al-fawa'id* (*Sea of Precious Virtues*).[56] Composed in mid-twelfth-century Syria, this anonymous Persian work counters any suggestion that the mirrors for princes genre was any less an Islamic formulation of political thought than that of treatises written by jurists.[57] Despite the indisputable administrative background of its author, there is nothing in this mirror that supports the stigma of being less Islamic, which Lambton associated with this genre.[58] On the contrary, there is in *Bahr*

[54] Ibid., xvii.

[55] Ibid.

[56] Julie Scott Meisami (ed.), *The Sea of Precious Virtues: A Medieval Islamic Mirror for Princes (Baḥr Al-Favā'id)* (Salt Lake City: University of Utah Press, 1991). Refer to Geert Jan van Gelder, 'Mirror for Princes or Vizor for Viziers: The Twelfth-Century Arabic Popular Encyclopedia "Mufīd al-ʿulūm" and Its Relationship with the Anonymous Persian "Baḥr al-Fawāʾid"', *BSOAS* 64(3) (2001): 313–38; van Gelder noted the influence on the *Bahr al-fawa'id* of an Arabic work titled *Mufid al-ʿulum wa-mubid al-humum*, authored in 551/1156.

[57] Ann K. S. Lambton, 'Islamic Mirrors for Princes', in *La Persia Nel Medioevo* (Rome: Accademia Nazionale dei Lincei, 1971), 426–36; refer to the introduction of Scott Meisami in *The Sea of Precious Virtues*, especially vii.

[58] Even Lambton noted that this treatise was '*sharʿī* based'; 'Islamic Mirrors for Princes', 426.

al-fawa'id great emphasis on the religious scholars (*'ulama'*), the duty of *jihad*, the companions of the Prophet, jurisprudence and prophetic tradition, and juristic discussions such as the law of rebellion. Furthermore, this treatise reflects an unembellished Shafi'i–Ash'ari and Sufi tone, an Islamic conception of justice and a clear influence of al-Ghazali.[59] *Bahr al-fawa'id* contradicts the idea that the genre itself dictates the political content of mirrors for princes.[60]

The second case is *Kitab nasihat al-muluk* (*Book of Counsel for Kings*), a mirror attributed wrongly to al-Ghazali, as Crone established in 1987.[61] This work was in two parts: the anonymous mirror *Nasihat al-muluk* and the *Risala* (epistle), which may have been by al-Ghazali or based on his writings.[62] The catalogue of the Damascene Ashrafiyya Library listed this work in two entries: *Nasihat al-muluk* (Counsel for kings) and *Risalat al-Ghazali* (al-Ghazali's epistle), and the thirteenth-century cataloguer noted suspiciously *fihi nazar* (requires further consideration), thus casting doubts on its attribution to al-Ghazali.[63] Similar doubts were voiced in Cairo in 1924 by Zaki Mubarak, who noted that 'the book was weak in the treatment of several topics', and consequently unlike al-Ghazali.[64] However, in his 1938 first Persian edition of *Nasihat al-muluk*, J. Huma'i fiercely defended the authenticity of the work; later in the second edition of 1972, Huma'i accepted that there was a part of this work that was 'uncharacteristic' of al-Ghazali.[65] The consensus of leading scholars was until recently to accept the attribution to al-Ghazali.[66] It

---

59 Scott Meisami, *The Sea of Precious Virtues*, xii–xiv.

60 I do not suggest this confusion was a universal trend, as several scholars including Julie Scott Meisami did not consider the mirror genre to be less Islamic. Likewise, refer to the introduction of the English translation of *Naṣīḥat al-mulūk*; *Counsel for Kings*, trans. F. R. C. Bagley (London: Oxford University Press, 1964), ix–x.

61 Patricia Crone, 'Did Al-Ghazālī Write a Mirror for Princes? On the Authorship of Naṣīḥat al-Mulūk', *Jerusalem Studies in Arabic and Islam* 10 (1987): 167–91.

62 Ibid., 169–70.

63 The catalogue dates from the early Mamluk period; refer to Hirschler, *The Ashrafiya Library Catalogue*, 40–2.

64 Zaki Mubarak, *Al-Akhlaq 'ind-al-Ghazali* (Cairo: Dar al-Sha'b, 1924), 115.

65 Crone, 'Did Al-Ghazālī Write a Mirror for Princes?', 167–8.

66 Lambton, 'Justice in the Medieval Persian Theory of Kingship'; for a relevant study, refer to Carole Hillenbrand, 'A Little-Known Mirror for Princes of al-Ghazālī', in Rüdiger Arnzen, Jörn Thielmann and Gerhard Endreß (eds), *Words, Texts and Concepts Cruising the Mediterranean Sea: Studies on the Sources, Contents and Influences of Islamic Civilization and Arabic Philosophy and Science* (Leuven: Peeters, 2004), 593–601.

took over sixty years to recognise the concern that had been voiced in Cairo in 1924 and seemed rather obvious to an average medieval scholar like the Damascene cataloguer.[67]

There is a simple explanation for this confusion. Scholars considered *Nasihat al-muluk* to be a 'fixed' mirror for princes rather than a work that comprised political conceptions that could not have been expressed by al-Ghazali. Examining this mirror as a work of Islamic political thought would have led the same scholars to different conclusions. The attribution to al-Ghazali, an Ashʿari–Shafiʿi–Sufi thinker, ought to have immediately alarmed a historian of Islamic political thought. They should have concluded, *fihi nazar*.[68]

Availability of Texts

The fourth major impediment follows from the first three. Simply put, it is the staggering lack of availability of properly edited, let alone translated, pre-modern Islamic political texts. Even the full range of writings by al-Mawardi, arguably the most renowned of all Muslim political thinkers, are insufficiently accessible to new scholars of the history of Islamic political thought. Only his *Ahkam al-sultaniyya* (*Ordinances of Government*) is translated into English, possibly owing to the interest in the theory of the caliphate and the presumed genre of the theory of the jurists. His other – equally essential in my opinion – writings on the themes of political authority, the virtues that

[67] Muzaffar Alam, likewise, attributed *Nasihat al-muluk* to al-Ghazali and made rather important conclusions based on this, in *The Languages of Political Islam: India 1200–1800* (London: Hurst, 2004), 27–8.

[68] In 2008 and again in 2015, Alexey Khismatulin confirmed beyond any doubt the forgery of Nizam al-Mulk's *Siyar al-Muluk* (the *Siyasat-Nama*) and parts of al-Ghazali's *Nasihat al-muluk*. He even succeeded in unmasking the identity of the potential counterfeiter; refer to Alexey Khismatulin, 'The Art of Medieval Counterfeiting: The Siyar al-Mulūk (The Siyāsat-Nāma) by Niẓām al-Mulk and the "Full" Version of the Naṣīḥat al-Mulūk by al-Ghazālī', *Manuscripta Orientalia* 14(1) (2008): 3–31; Alexey Khismatulin, 'Two Mirrors for Princes Fabricated at the Seljuq Court: Nizām al-Mulk's Siyar al-Mulūk and al-Ghazālī's Nasīhat al-Mulūk', in Edmund Herzig and Sarah Stewart (eds), *The Age of the Seljuqs* (London: I. B. Tauris, 2015), 94–130. Yet subsequent studies still insist on ascribing the *Nasihat al-muluk* to al-Ghazali and *Siyar al-Muluk* to Nizam al-Mulk, basing major arguments and conclusions on this false attribution; for instance, see Neguin Yavari, *Advice for the Sultan: Prophetic Voices and Secular Politics in Medieval Islam* (Oxford, 2014) and Seyed Sadegh Haghighat, "Persian Mirrors for Princes: Pre-Islamic and Islamic Mirrors Compared," in *Global Medieval: Mirrors for Princes Reconsidered*, ed. Regula Forster and Neguin Yavari, (Harvard, 2015), 83–93.

the ruler should cultivate, and the art of governance have not been translated and, moreover, are in dire need of new utilisable editions. These writings include *Qawanin al-wizara (wa-siyasat al-mulk)* (*Principles of the Vizierate [and the Governance of Sovereignty]*); *Tashil al-nazar wa-ta'jil al-zafar* (*The Facilitation of Reflection and the Hastening of Victory*); and *Adab al-dunya wa-al-din* (*The Ethics of the Realms of the World and Religion*).[69] There may be more works, but this will not be ascertained until a comprehensive study on al-Mawardi is undertaken.

Fortunately, in recent years, there have been arduous individual efforts to preserve, edit and publish works of Islamic political thought. Radwan al-Sayyid's efforts made a rich corpus of edited 'Abbasid, Seljuq, Ayyubid and Mamluk political texts available to researchers.[70] Additionally, his introductions to these editions highlighted the richness and originality of the medieval period's production of political thought and helped to place its authors within their relevant intellectual and socio-political contexts. Similarly, Louise Marlow helped to rescue the field from stagnation through her continuous rethinking of the genres, and the origins and influences of the sources beyond the prevalent biases.[71] Her works included a notable attempt to understand the motivation of authors of mirrors and a seminal article on Islamic advice literature.[72]

Marlow's recent *Naṣīḥat al-mulūk of pseudo-Māwardī* provides an exemplary approach to editing texts and the study of the history of political thought.[73] It is a detailed research on a tenth-century anonymous work attributed to al-Mawardi. Marlow did not limit herself to the genre to draw

[69] Refer to Marlow, *Counsel for Kings: Naṣīḥat al-mulūk of pseudo-Māwardī*, 1:11–12. The translations of the first two titles are taken from Marlow.

[70] I have come across over twenty published sources in which Radwan al-Sayyid was involved, some of which are used in this book. His recent involvement in the Ibn al-Azraq Center for Political Studies resulted in seventeen titles, in addition to previous editions with different publishers.

[71] Louise Marlow, *Hierarchy and Egalitarianism in Islamic Thought* (Cambridge: Cambridge University Press, 1997); Louise Marlow, 'Kings, Prophets and the 'Ulamā' in Mediaeval Islamic Advice Literature', *Studia Islamica* 81 (1995): 101–20.

[72] Louise Marlow, 'The Way of Viziers and Lamp of Commanders (Minhāj al-Wuzarā' Wa Sirāj al-Umarā') of Aḥmad al-Iṣfahbādhī and the Literary and Political Culture of Early Fourteen-Century Iran', in Beatrice Gruendler and Louise Marlow (eds), *Writers and Rulers: Perspectives on Their Relationship from Abbasid to Safavid Times* (Wiesbaden: Reichart, 2004), 169–93; Louise Marlow, 'Advice and Advice Literature', *EI*^{3}.

[73] Marlow, *Counsel for Kings: The Naṣīḥat al-mulūk of pseudo-Māwardī*.

hasty conclusions, but strived to consider various crucial factors: the author's language of choice, his repertoire of political and ethical ideas, the relevant intellectual discourses of his time, the importance of knowing his legal school – Hanafi in this case – and the theological background of his work, the social, intellectual and political networks within which he operated, and the different literary genres with which the work flirted. She noted how the author uses 'ancient wisdom to bear on recent developments' thus responding to and reflecting on the particular circumstances of his time and location.[74] Marlow thus showed that the genre was not static and – most importantly – did not dictate the content of the treatise. Her model work shows how the above impediments can be countered by making more texts available to researchers.

Despite such efforts, the combined effect of the longue durée approach, imposed paradigms, the mythology of genre and the lack of edited texts has been severe on the study of the history of Islamic political thought of the post-Seljuq period. Political thinkers between the time of al-Ghazali and Ibn Khaldun were simply denied originality, the capacity to engage with the political conditions of their time, and the production of any meaningful set of reflections. Their agency to quote judiciously from earlier traditions and accessible repertoires of aphorisms and maxims in order to express their own arguments and political ideas was dismissed. Their work was, accordingly, ignored for being devoid of reason and serving to stamp authority on the oriental despot. Furthermore, the professionalised and *adab*ised nature of these authors was overlooked, and, as such, they were denied any contribution to the art of statecraft and administration. Likewise, the intellectual and ideological milieux and scholarly networks within which they flourished were disregarded. These four impediments eventually led to a distorted understanding of the languages of political thought of the Ayyubid and Mamluk period.

Contextualising Political Thought

The stage is now set to propose a contextualist interpretation of political texts from the Mamluk period. Indeed, this book aims to pull a well-established debate in the history of medieval and early modern European political thought

[74] Ibid., 20.

– one that some may even deem slightly outdated – into the field of Islamic history. From what is loosely labelled 'The Cambridge School', I especially intend to benefit from the writings of Quentin Skinner and J. G. A. Pocock when approaching the political texts treated in this book. Although not the first to refer to these two scholars in Islamic political historiography, this work aims to apply the methodologies and broad guidelines they provided in order to avoid any anachronism, distortion of the meaning of political texts or imposition of irrelevant paradigms on the period's authors. My rough blueprint for a contextualist interpretation of the political thinkers treated in this book is, in addition to considering their social, cultural and political contexts, to understand their intellectual and empirical worlds, retrieve the political languages within which they conducted their debates and expressed their ideas, and reconstruct the prevalent discourses of their time.[75] Before pushing further the agenda of the school of contextualism and my slightly modified version of its broad methodology, a quick word is warranted on the two opposing theoretical camps to contextualism, ahistoricism and the paradigmatic approach, and how they intersect with three of the four above-mentioned impediments.

Ahistoricism – also referred to as textualism or literalism – treats timeless political ideas and problems by focusing solely on the texts and completely disengaging them from their narrow historical contexts. Ahistoricism can lead to serious distortions as it approaches Islamic political thought based on a limited set of perennial problems that concerned 'great' classical thinkers and were transmitted to later political thinkers and actors. As mentioned above, one such anachronism is Black's suggestion that Ibn Khaldun's theory could have served Western governments in devising policies towards the post-2001 Middle East and that his observations are still directly applicable to our age. Likewise, another case of distortion, albeit unintended, can be observed in Malcolm Kerr's study of modern theories of Islamic reform.[76] Kerr offers a teleological interpretation of pre-modern political texts, including al-Mawardi's, not within the context in which they were written, but in

[75] These steps stem from trademark guidelines by Skinner and Pocock as will be explained subsequently.

[76] Malcolm Kerr, *Islamic Reform: The Political and Legal Theories of Muḥammad 'Abduh and Rashīd Riḍā* (Berkeley: University of California Press, 1966).

terms of the greater purpose they serve in elucidating the road to the perceived unavoidable failure of political and intellectual reform in the modern Islamic world. By considering 'ambiguities in the classical constitutional theory' as a factor behind the failure of the theories of modern reformers like Rashid Rida (1865–1935), Kerr fell into the same anachronistic interpretation of classical political texts that the object of his study committed before him.[77] Answers to the question why modern reform theories failed cannot be found in the incoherence of medieval texts, but are better pursued in the intellectual, social and political landscapes of the modern Middle East.

The paradigmatic school, likewise, presents a plethora of complicated challenges to the study of Islamic political texts.[78] Any attempt to apply it to the history of political thought is faced with the following questions: what constitutes a paradigm, and who defines it? As discussed above, some scholars imposed a specific date or event such as the fall of Baghdad in 656/1258, or a perceived model of political authority such as 'God's caliph' as paradigms of Islamic political thought. Others identified paradigm shifts in intellectual history engendered by the doctrines of outstanding thinkers, which begs the questions: who qualifies to be classified as such, and why? As a case study that addresses these challenges in the context of the Mamluk period and exposes the limits of the paradigmatic method, I propose Ovamir Anjum's *Politics, Law and Community in Islamic Thought: the Taymiyyan Moment.* He presents the intellectual contributions of the theologian Ibn Taymiyya (661/1263–728/1328) as a Kuhnian paradigm shift in the history of Islamic political thought.[79] Ibn Taymiyya, Anjum argues, transformed the community of believers (*umma*) into the ultimate epistemic authority in interpreting

[77] Ibid., 24–32

[78] Quentin Skinner considered that the application of paradigms leads to the development of a 'mythology of doctrine' which 'contaminate' the 'historical study of ethical, political, religious, and other such ideas'; refer to Quentin Skinner, 'Meaning and Understanding in the History of Ideas', *History and Theory* 8(1) (1969): 7. Likewise, J. G. A. Pocock found the paradigmatic approach inapplicable to the history of political thought; refer to, J. G. A. Pocock, 'Languages and Their Implications: The Transformation of the Study of Political Thought', in *Politics, Language, and Time: Essays on Political Thought and History* (Chicago, IL: University of Chicago Press, 1989), 13–19.

[79] Ovamir Anjum, *Politics, Law and Community in Islamic Thought: The Taymiyyan Moment* (Cambridge: Cambridge University Press, 2012). 'Kuhnian paradigm shift' refers to the concept identified by Thomas S. Kuhn in his ground-breaking work *The Structure of Scientific Revolutions* (Chicago, IL: University of Chicago Press, 1962).

revelation and consequently into 'the site of political authority', against the backdrop of a prevalent legalistic 'elitism'.[80] Additionally, he posited that Ibn Taymiyya attempted to bring back political and religious life to the purview of the *shari'a* by limiting legal formalism; this explained – according to Anjum – Ibn Taymiyya's unremitting challenge to the authority of the jurists over the *shari'a*, the Sufis over 'mystical reality' (*haqiqa*) and the political elite over the *siyasa*.[81] The 'Taymiyyan moment' was a 'radically political one' that revived the political life of the Muslim community, and Anjum went as far as comparing it with the way in which the emergence of Christianity rejuvenated the sense of community in the Roman Empire.[82] There is, however, a stark precedent to this supposed paradigm shift. Two and half centuries before Ibn Taymiyya, al-Juwayni had forged a direct connection between epistemology and political thought. As established in Sohaira Siddiqui's recent study, al-Juwayni's epistemological views prioritised continuity, political stability and the preservation of religion.[83] Consequently, his political thought as articulated in the *Ghiyath* was not centred on the ruler and, well before Ibn Taymiyya, he conceived the *shari'a* as a dialectical nomos that guaranteed the community's continuity and its place as the locus of political authority. This example illustrates the limitations of the paradigmatic approach.

In contra-distinction to these two methods, contextualism – also referred to as historicism or linguistic contextualism – rejects the existence of answers that possess a 'perennial' relevance and the application of paradigms that are irrelevant to the past.[84] A truly contextualist approach is essentially an

---

80 Anjum, *Politics, Law and Community*, *passim* and 267, 269.

81 Ibid., 236–7, 244. For a radically different interpretation of Ibn Taymiyya's thought refer to Baber Johansen, 'A Perfect Law in an Imperfect Society. Ibn Taymiyya's Concept of "Governance in the Name of the Sacred Law"', in Peri J. Bearman et al. (eds), *The Law Applied: Contextualizing the Islamic Shari'a* (London: I. B. Tauris, 2008), 259–94. Johansen saw no prominent role for the community in the Taymiyyan theory as its conceptions of governance in the name of the sacred law (*siyasa shar'iyya*) was restricted to 'narrow groups of stakeholders' whereby the '*ulama*' legitimised and directed the exercise of power by political and administrative elites to the exclusion of all other social groups (285). For another useful study on Ibn Taymiyya's thought, refer to Yossef Rapoport, 'Ibn Taymiyya's Radical Legal Thought', in Yossef Rapoport and Shahab Ahmed (eds), *Ibn Taymiyya and His Times*, Studies in Islamic Philosophy 4 (Karachi: Oxford University Press, 2010), 191–226.

82 Anjum, *Politics, Law and Community*, 271.

83 Refer to part 4 (chs 9 and 10) of Sohaira Siddiqui, *Law and Politics under the Abbasids: An Intellectual Portrait of al-Juwayni* (Cambridge: Cambridge University Press, 2019).

84 Refer to Skinner, 'Meaning and Understanding', *passim*.

empirical endeavour, one that aims to situate a political text within its narrow historical context, decode the author's intentions in writing the text, and identify 'the "language" or "vocabulary" with and within which the author operated'.[85] While there is no denying that 'perennial questions' do exist, for instance, who can be considered a legitimate ruler or how best to govern a society, the answers to such questions are only meaningful in their own narrow historical context;[86] they are neither useful for the past nor the future. As far as Skinner is concerned, there are no timeless answers and, accordingly, a contextualist understanding or 'reading' of a political text hinges on grasping the author's intentions. Identifying the political languages is a prerequisite to a historian's attempt to decode 'the actual intention' of a writer in pronouncing an utterance and, therefore, one must first trace 'the relations between the given utterance' and its 'wider *linguistic* context'.[87] It follows that, as historians of political thought, we must only concern ourselves with interpreting political ideas and discourses within the political, social and intellectual context in which the text or author under study emerged and, furthermore, focus on demarcating the political languages used to express these ideas and the conventions that governed these discourses.

Contextualism left very broad guidelines, yet they are field-proven. Skinner and Pocock produced a series of ground-breaking works on medieval and early modern European intellectual history; they did not, however, impart a detailed methodology or rulebook to follow. For instance, Skinner suggests two simple yet effective rules for historians of political thought – both of which are followed closely in this present book – the first is to 'focus not just on the text to be interpreted, but on the prevailing conventions governing the treatment of the issues or themes with which that text is concerned'; and the second is to focus on 'the writer's mental world, the world of his empirical beliefs'.[88] Likewise and as already mentioned, Pocock recommends

---

85 Ibid.; Pocock, 'Languages and Their Implications', 25 and *passim*. For another beneficial and related article by Pocock, refer to J. G. A. Pocock, 'The Reconstruction of Discourse: Towards the Historiography of Political Thought', *MLN* 96(5) (1981): 959–80.

86 Skinner, 'Meaning and Understanding', 52.

87 Ibid., 49.

88 Quentin Skinner, 'Motives, Intentions and the Interpretation of Texts', *New Literary History* 3(2) (1972): 406, 407. The same discussion can be found in Quentin Skinner, *Visions of Politics, vol. 1: Regarding Method* (Cambridge: Cambridge University Press, 2002), 101–2.

the detection of 'the "language" or "vocabulary" with and within which the author operated'.[89] Such broad guidelines can be invaluable, especially if we familiarise ourselves with Skinner and Pocock's works on authors like Marsilius of Padua, Niccolò Machiavelli, Thomas Hobbes, John Locke and others. If applied carefully, such basic recommendations can yield the desired results in the case of pre-modern Islamic political thought, as I will show throughout the length of this monograph.

A caveat is warranted here. It is not the intention of this work to advocate contextualism as the only way to read Islamic political texts, rather, that it is a desideratum at this stage in the development of the field of the history of Islamic political thought. It provides the necessary framework to counter prevailing impediments and casts the net wide in order to understand the political thinkers treated in this book beyond the usual fixation on specific themes which are irrelevant to the late Ayyubid and early Mamluk period.

Intellectual, Social and Cultural Context

I shall start with Skinner's second rule, which is to focus on 'the writer's mental world, the world of his empirical beliefs'.[90] This recommendation is useful to avoid ascribing to a text or an author an idea that they could not possibly have held. This could be simply because such ideas were not known or available to them. Consequently, any interpretation of a political treatise drafted by thinkers from the Mamluk period, for example, should take into consideration what ideas were available to them every day in the souk, mosque, *madrasa*, street, citadel, tavern and chancery, or even better in the library that they frequented.

We can catch a better glimpse of the 'mental world' of a thirteenth- and early fourteenth-century Damascene or Cairene author by examining the catalogue of the Ashrafiyya Library of Damascus. This library's eponym is the Ayyubid sultan al-Malik al-Ashraf (d. 635/1237) and it became accessible to the public some years after his death.[91] This catalogue itself, however, dates from the early Mamluk period and boasts over seventy titles linked to political

89 Pocock, 'Languages and Their Implications', 25.
90 Skinner, 'Motives, Intentions and the Interpretation of Texts', 407.
91 Hirschler, *The Ashrafiya Library Catalogue*, 40–2.

thought which is, as Konrad Hirschler noted, a strikingly high number compared with other fields of knowledge in the collection.[92] The books available on the shelves of the library include works attributed to Aristotle (including the Aristotelian–Alexandrine apocryphal correspondence); Plato, Socrates; Ibn al-Muqaffaʿ (d. *c.* 139/756–7) and other Indic-influenced sources; al-Jahiz (d. 255/868–9); Ibn Qutayba (d. 276/889); al-Farabi (d. 339/950); Miskawayh (d. ?421/1030); al-Thaʿalibi (d.429/1038); al-Mawardi (d. 450/1058); Abu Yaʿla (d. 458/1066); al-Ghazali (d. 505/1111); al-Turtushi (d. 520/1126); and Sibt Ibn al-Jawzi (d. 654/1256). The catalogue also includes epistles and testaments ascribed to caliphs and rulers including Abu Bakr, ʿUmar, ʿAli, ʿUmar II b. ʿAbd al-ʿAziz, Aḥmad b. Tulun, al-Maʾmun, Hadrian, Ardashir, Khusraw and to Indian kings. Furthermore, the catalogue boasts a collection of statecraft and administrative manuals and mirrors for princes by a variety of known and unknown authors.[93]

---

[92] Ibid., 37–8.

[93] As highlighted by Hirschler, the following entries figure in the catalogue: the *Siyasa* or *Sirr al-asrar: al-siyasa wa-al-farasa fi tadbir al-riʾasa* (Politics), which is the famous pseudo-Aristotelian *Secretum secretorum* that was transmitted later from Arabic to Latin, Hebrew and other languages, *Risalat Aristatalis ila al-Iskandar* (*Aristotle's Epistle to Alexander the Great*); *ʿAhd Adriyanus al-Malik ila ibnihi* (*The Testament of King Hadrian to His Son*) and *Risala fi al-ʿuhud al-yunaniya* (*A Treatise on the Greek Testaments*); *Risalat Suqratis fi siyasat al-malik* (*Socrates' Epistle on the Ruler's Governance*); *ʿAhd Ardashir* (*The Testament of Ardashir*), *Risalat Ibn al-Muqaffaʿ fi adab al-wuzaraʾ* (*A Treatise on the Rules for Viziers*), *Adab Ibn al-Muqaffaʿ al-kabir*, *al-Yatima fi siyasat al-mulk* (*The Unique [pearl] on the Conduct of Kingship*) by Ibn al-Muqaffaʿ (d. *c.* 139/756–7); various works of al-Jahiz (d. 255/868–9); *ʿUyun al-akhbar* (*Choicest Reports*) of Ibn Qutayba (d. 276/889); *Khidmat al-muluk* (*Service of Rulers*) of al-Sarakhsi (d. 286/899); *Majmuʿ Akhlaq al-muluk* (multiple-text manuscript with the *Morals of the Kings*) of Muhammad b. al-Harith al-Thaʿlabi (fl. third/ninth century) (attr. to al-Jahiz); *al-Siyasa* (*[Communal] Governance*) of al-Farabi (d. 339/950); *Muntakhab Jawidhan* (*Choices from the Eternal Wisdom*) Miskawayh (d. ?421/1030); *Adab al-muluk* (*Rules for Kings*) of al-Thaʿalibi (d.429/1038); *Min al-Sahil wa-al-shahij* (*[Parts] of The Neigher and the Brayer*) of Abu al-ʿAlaʾ al-Maʿarri (d. 449/1058); *Adab al-din wa-al-dunya* (*On Conduct in Religious and Worldly Matters*), *Qanun al-wizara* (*Ordinance of the Vizier's Office*) and *Tashil al-nazar wa-taʿjil al-zafar* by al-Mawardi (d. 450/1058); *Rusul al-muluk* (*The Kings' Envoys*) and *Min al-Ahkam al-sultaniya* (*[Parts] of the Ordinances of Government*) of Abu Yaʿla Ibn al-Farraʾ (d. 458/1066); *Ihyaʾ ʿulum al-din* (*The Revival of the Religious Sciences*), *Maqasid al-falasifa* (*The Philosophers' Intentions*), the *Mustazhiri* in different titles by al-Ghazali (d. 505/1111); *Siraj al-muluk* (*The Light for Kings*) of al-Turtushi (d. 520/1126); the sermons of Ibn al-Jawzi (d. 597/1200); *al-Jalis al-salih* of Sibt Ibn al-Jawzi (d. 654/1256); various epistles and testaments attributed to Greek kings, Ardashir, ʿAli b. Abi Talib, al- Maʾmun and Khusraw; *Hadith malik min muluk al-hind*, a book of wisdom attributed to an Indian king; and various other collection of titles like *Sirat Ahmad b. Tulun* (*The life of Ahmad b. Tulun*).

The catalogue reflected the priorities of the cultured ruling, administrative and religious elites.[94] The library was consulted by rulers, *adab*ised scholars and administrators, other cultivated civilians, and some prominent military individuals.[95] The catalogue suggests that attention to the administrative arts was considered essential to good governance, as reflected by the multitude of administrative handbooks covering taxation (*kharaj*), the art of chancery writing and composing letters, the selection and proper conduct of viziers and secretaries, and the dispensation of justice.[96] The abstract themes of distribution of wealth, selection of companions and senior officials, justice and court etiquette are, likewise, present. Furthermore, the catalogue shows that those concerned with political thought were able to consult a variety of genres and sources attributed to various traditions and periods. Greek political wisdom seems to have been particularly prized. One can visualise an author like Ibn Jamaʿa browsing the shelves of this or a similar library in Damascus and Cairo.

There are clues in the Ashrafiyya catalogue to captivate any historian of political thought. They point to a highly proficient readership that faced similar academic challenges to ours. Remarkably, one such clue is the mirror for princes wrongly attributed to al-Ghazali, the authorship of which has since been resolved, as discussed above.[97] It is captivating that scholars then and now struggle to identify authors of political texts. The comprehensiveness of the catalogue is also remarkable: my attempts to trace the sources and influences of the political treatises covered in the present book in the catalogue were always successful, yielding material from one or more of its titles.

---

[94] The library was mostly based on the two private collections of al-Ashraf and the son of al-Qadi al-Fadil (529/1135–596/1200), the prominent Ayyubid administrator; Hirschler, *The Ashrafiya Library Catalogue*, 27–32.

[95] Most of the books had previously been in the private court library of al-Ashraf, though we do not know exactly which.

[96] This is reflected in the multitude of administrative handbooks such as, for example, *Adab al-wuzaraʾ wa-al-kuttab* (*Rules for Viziers and Secretaries*), titles on the selection of viziers, military manuals, and titles on dispensing justice like *Adab al-mazalim* (*The Manual for Dispensing the Ruler's Justice*) and other more intriguing titles on this topic such as *Irshad ila ma laysa li-l-salatin tafwiduhu ila al-qudat* (*Guidance on What Rulers Cannot Delegate to Judges* by unknown authors). There are likewise several titles of mirrors for princes by unknown authors.

[97] Refer to the discussion at 26–7, above.

Yet library catalogues are only one of several tools available to us to investigate the intellectual and empirical worlds of the five thinkers treated in this work. We can, additionally, benefit from the growth in scholarship on the middle period of Islam in order to grasp the interrelatedness between the production of political thought during that period and various developments in legal theory and tradition, theology, epistemology and speculative Sufism. Furthermore, advances in social and cultural history allow for detailed scrutiny of the milieux within which these political thinkers emerged. Fortunately, this investigative task is made easier by the fact that all five thinkers were jurists and legal theoreticians (*usulis*) who thrived in the late Ayyubid and early Mamluk Syro-Egyptian lands, all five were Ashʿaris, four of them were Shafiʿis and Sufis, and the Maliki one was trained by Shafiʿi–Ashʿari legal theoreticians.

Understanding historical developments in the legal sphere is central to this investigation. Well before the Mamluk sultanate, the Sunni *madhhab*s had 'settled down' from groups loosely gathered around broad legal and theological concepts into well-defined 'corporate' units tied by normative legal conformity (*taqlid*).[98] The 'integrity' and 'corporate' status of the *madhhab* was established on a shared approach to interpreting the law, a collective commitment to prevalent legal opinions or trends within the school on specific issues, and the adoption of a carefully selected set of authoritative legal texts.[99] However, this did not result – as per the prevalent misconception – in the doors of independent legal reasoning (*ijtihad*) being closed nor in Islamic law becoming incapable of evolving and adjusting to social changes and political requirements.[100] Rather than prohibiting jurists from adopting novel views that contradicted prevailing doctrines and trends within their own *madhhab*s, the *taqlid* system merely provided a stable framework that regulated the ability of these jurists to provide new legal opinions on all aspects of personal and societal life.[101]

[98] For a more detailed discussion on this process refer to Jackson, *Islamic Law and the State*, xx, xxix, 225–7.

[99] Ibid., xx, 226; according to Jackson the *madhhab* emerged as the 'sole repository of legal authority'. Refer also to Mohammad H. Fadel's introduction in al-Qarafi, and Mohammad H. Fadel, *The Criterion for Distinguishing Legal Opinions from Judicial Rulings and the Administrative Acts of Judges and Rulers* (New Haven, CT: Yale University Press, 2017), 7.

[100] For a list of several studies that refute this conception refer to Fadel, 'State and Sharia', 94–100.

[101] Fadel, in *Criterion*, 7–8.

As a matter of fact, it is under the *taqlid* tradition and out of concern for it that the Maliki jurist al-Qarafi (d. 684/1285) conceived one of the most radical and innovative contributions to Islamic political thought. So how did this Cairene jurist – trained by Shafiʿi–Ashʿari legal theoreticians – express his concern for the independence of his own *madhhab* and the inviolability of its corporate status? Al-Qarafi developed a constitutional theory based on the granularisation of the Prophet's authorities by splitting them into three: executive, legislative and judicial.[102] In a discussion supposedly centred on speculative jurisprudence and law, he articulated far-reaching political views on the limitation of the exercise of power, the delegation of power and the origins of legitimate authority. As eloquently explained by Jackson and later Fadel, and as will be discussed in Chapter 4, al-Qarafi's theory was the product of his effort to normalise the relationship between speculative jurisprudence, human application of divine law, and the political institutions and judicial system of the late Ayyubid and early Mamluk period. In line with Skinner and Pocock's guidelines, the constitutional relevance of al-Qarafi's discussions can be grasped only by first comprehending his concerns as a Maliki–Ashʿari jurist operating in Cairo under the judicial dominance of an obstinate Shafiʿi chief judge, and reading his work as a political text written in the context of a juristic polemic that was expressed in a constitutional language.

In addition to law and jurisprudence, theology and epistemology played key roles in shaping the political thought of our authors. Benefitting from recent studies, this work considers prior familiarity with theological discourses on topics such as anthropomorphism and, likewise, the epistemic concern for attaining certain knowledge in theology and law to be prerequisites for reading political texts authored by Shafiʿi–Ashʿari legal theoreticians. The recent work of Siddiqui on the renowned Ashʿari theologian and Shafiʿi jurist al-Juwayni is very useful to this end as it brings the fields of theology, epistemology, law and political thought into one coherent discussion.[103] Al-Juwayni's concern with certainty and continuity marked his approach to the questions of reason and revelation, the firmness of the sources of law,

102 For a detailed discussion, refer to Chapter 4, 145–55, below.

103 Siddiqui, *An Intellectual Portrait of al-Juwayni*; see Mohamad El-Merheb's review in *BSOAS* 82(3) (2019): 533–5.

the imam's political role in society, and the consequences of his absence. Siddiqui connected al-Juwayni's preoccupation with attaining epistemically certain knowledge in theology and law to his concern for preserving the community's social and religious continuity and, accordingly, to his political thought. Subsequent chapters of this monograph identify al-Juwayni's epistemology as a major influence on the Shafiʿi–Ashʿari political thinkers treated in this research.

Likewise, theological debates penetrated the domain of constitutional thought. Although the Shafiʿi judge and devoted Ashʿari author Taj al-Din al-Subki (d. 771/1370) was of the opinion that Ashʿari and Maturidi theologies had become essentially identical, thus ending the rivalry between Shafiʿis and Hanafis,[104] theology never vanished and continued to play a role in the religious, intellectual and political life of the period. Other theological disputes continued in Damascus and Cairo, especially during the thirteenth and fourteenth centuries between, on the one hand, Ashʿari and Shafiʿi–Ashʿari rationalists, and, on the other, Shafiʿi and Hanbali traditionalists; these debates later intensified between Ibn Taymiyya and his opponents.[105] The vast corpus of research on Ibn Taymiyya, which dominates the study of Mamluk political thought, has proven rather beneficial here owing to the depth of some of its studies and has led to a better understanding of the relevance of theology to the politics of the Mamluk period. Most notably in this category, Caterina Bori raised the need to study the 'missing link between theological production and its potential social and political significance'.[106] Similarly, the above-mentioned works of Anjum and Baber Johansen are useful to link theology to politics in the Mamluk period.[107] Within this

104 Wilferd F. Madelung, 'The Spread of Māturīdism and the Turks', in *Religious Schools and Sects in Medieval Islam* (Aldershot: Ashgate/Variorum, 1999), 166–7.

105 Useful here is Caterina Bori's challenge to 'the commonly accepted identification of Ibn Taymiyya with 14th century Syrian Hanbalism'; she described the polemics among jurists, judges, prominent *shaykhs* and other members of the Hanbali community who did not share Ibn Taymiyya's views on Sufism, or his theological and legal doctrines. Refer to Caterina Bori, 'Ibn Taymiyya Wa-Jamāʿatuhu: Authority, Conflict and Consensus in Ibn Taymiyya's Circle', in Yossef Rapoport and Shahab Ahmed (eds), *Ibn Taymiyya and His Times* (Karachi: Oxford University Press, 2010), 24, 33–6.

106 Caterina Bori, 'Theology, Politics, Society: The Missing Link. Studying Religion in the Mamluk Period', in Stephan Conermann (ed.), *Ubi Sumus? Quo Vademus?: Mamluk Studies – State of the Art* (Goettingen and Bonn: V & R Unipress and Bonn University Press, 2013), 58.

107 Refer to 32, above.

context, Chapters 3 and 5 will discuss cases where the debate on anthropomorphism extended from the theological domain into dynastic politics and constitutional thought.

Four of the five authors treated in this study were Sufis and Sufi political conceptions are a key feature in three of their treatises. As will be discussed in Chapters 3 and 4, speculative Sufism helped to shape the ethical systems some of these authors relied upon to moderate the exercise of power and, furthermore, Sufi conceptions influenced their views on the origins of legitimate power. Consequently, it is necessary to understand Sufism in the Ayyubid and Mamluk period and clarify its interrelatedness with the social and intellectual milieu within which political thought was produced. Nathan Hofer's monograph is very beneficial for this purpose since it examines when and how the popularisation of Sufism occurred and provides proof of the mixing of Sufism with politics in the context of Ayyubid and Mamluk Egypt. Hofer rejects the notion that Sufism was a response to the 'dry legalism' of jurists and the 'two-tiered model' of elite and popular culture.[108] On the contrary, his research promotes understanding of how some jurists engaged Sufism to disseminate their political ideas among the political elites.[109] Furthermore, Hofer's work is useful for delineating the heterogeneous composition of any socio-religious group including Sufis. For instance, the state-sponsored Sufis of Cairo were very different from the insubordinate Sufis of Upper Egypt. Hofer cautions, 'The [Sufi] epithet only makes sense within very specific historical, social and political contexts.'[110] Similarly, Richard McGregor noted the spread of Sufism among the elites of Cairo during the fourteenth century in the case of the Wafaʾiyya order.[111] He highlighted further flaws in the prevalent understanding of Sufism during the Mamluk period, such as using 'orthodoxy' to designate the opposition of some scholars and jurists to Sufis and Sufism and to their alleged lower culture.[112] Chapter 3, below, will show that this opposition was often politically motivated.

---

[108] Nathan Hofer, *The Popularisation of Sufism in Ayyubid and Mamluk Egypt, 1173–1325* (Edinburgh: Edinburgh University Press, 2015), 8–9.

[109] Ibid., 8–9.

[110] Ibid., 25.

[111] Richard McGregor, *Sanctity and Mysticism in Medieval Egypt: The Wafāʾ Sufi Order and the Legacy of Ibn ʿArabī* (Albany, NY: State University of New York Press, 2004), 56–61.

[112] Richard McGregor, 'The Problem of Sufism', *Mamlūk Studies Review* 13(2) (2009): 79–81.

Significant advances in the field of social and cultural history help to seal the study of the contexts within which our five thinkers emerged. They reflect how various processes that contributed to the formation of the jurists impacted their modes of thinking and writing about politics. Over the past four decades, a series of comprehensive studies have examined the formation of scholars in Egypt and Syria, their training, and the ensuing two processes of professionalisation and *adab*isation of the *ʿulamaʾ*. These studies include Joan E. Gilbert's article on the professionalisation and bureaucratisation of the scholars in Damascus; Carl Petry's *Civilian Elite of Cairo*; the works of Jonathan P. Berkey and Michael Chamberlain on knowledge transfer in Cairo and Damascus; Thomas Bauer's research on the process of *adab*isation of the scholars as they increasingly employed and produced literary modes of communication like poetry; and more recently Konrad Hirschler's work on the processes of textualisation and popularisation of knowledge transmission in Islamic societies.[113] Moreover, various aspects of the professional mobility of scholars have started to attract scholarly attention, especially the impact of mobility on the production of political thought.[114] These studies show that by the early Mamluk period, bureaucratised and *adab*ised Muslim scholars dominated judicial and teaching posts, high-ranking supervisory roles, including market inspection and the superintendence of charitable endowments, various positions in the chancery and treasury, and in some cases acted as diplomatic emissaries. I will argue throughout the subsequent chapters that political thinkers incorporated these precious experiences into their political thought by conceiving a central role for the administration in

113 Refer to Joan E. Gilbert, 'Institutionalization of Muslim Scholarship and Professionalization of the ʿUlamāʾ in Medieval Damascus', *Studia Islamica* 52 (1980): 105–34; Carl Petry, *Civilian Elite of Cairo in the Later Middle Ages* (Princeton, NJ: Princeton University Press, 1981); Jonathan P. Berkey, *The Transmission of Knowledge in Medieval Cairo: A Social History of Islamic Education* (Princeton, NJ: Princeton University Press, 1992); Michael Chamberlain, *Knowledge and Social Practice in Medieval Damascus: 1190–1350* (Cambridge: Cambridge University Press, 1995); Thomas Bauer, 'Mamluk Literature: Misunderstandings and New Approaches', *Mamlūk Studies Review* 9(2) (2005): 105–32; Konrad Hirschler, *The Written Word in the Medieval Arabic Lands: A Social and Cultural History of Reading Practices* (Edinburgh: Edinburgh University Press, 2012).

114 Mohamad El-Merheb, 'Islamic Political Thought and Professional Mobility: The Intellectual and Empirical Worlds of Ibn Ṭalḥa and Ibn Jamāʿa', in Mohamad El-Merheb and Mehdi Berriah (eds), *Professional Mobility in Islamic Societies (800–1700): New Concepts and Approaches* (Leiden: Brill, 2021), 207–30.

the preservation of the stability and continuity of government, and in the limitation of the ruler's exercise of power.

Political Languages, Conventions and Discourses

The previous section highlighted the social, cultural and intellectual contexts, and the empirical worlds of the five thinkers and, additionally, identified some of their influences and authorities. The term 'influence' as employed subsequently in this book, refers to the repertoire of ideas, ideologies, taxonomies, vocabulary, literary styles, anthologies and authoritative texts that were available to the authors to use and benefit from. This denotes, for instance, the texts and views of authors such al-Mawardi, al-Juwayni, al-Ghazali, Ibn ʿArabi, Ibn ʿAbd al-Salam and many others whose works helped to shape the thought of the five thinkers. Likewise, 'influence' refers to excerpts from classical legal, theological, philosophical and political sources with which these authors were familiar and had access to, both from within or external to the Islamic tradition.

However, as I shall stress and demonstrate recurrently, all five thinkers treated in this book displayed astonishing agency in benefiting from their influences to suit their own aims in writing political texts. They had mastered the delicate art of including and excluding, re-arranging, and altering the passages from earlier writings that they borrowed from and – most importantly – adding to them in order to express their own novel political ideas that dealt with their own concerns. These authors communicated their thought using specific political languages that were intended to be understood as languages by their audiences, dedicatees and interlocutors based on prevailing conventions at the time.[115] Understanding this authorial agency will be key to retrieving the political languages of these five thinkers and reconstructing the discourses with which they were engaging. Such is the present monograph's approach to Skinner's above-mentioned first rule: the need to focus 'on the prevailing conventions governing the treatment of the issues or themes with which that text is concerned', and Pocock's recommendation to detect 'the "language" or "vocabulary" with and within which the author operated'.

---

[115] For more on the use of 'languages' in the plural, refer to Pocock, 'The Reconstruction of Discourse', 963–4.

Predictably with all the existing impediments in the field, the study of the political languages in the middle period of Islam has attracted little scholarly attention. Two contributions stand out: Bernard Lewis' pioneering *The Political Language of Islam* and Ovamir Anjum's more recent article on 'Political Metaphors and Concepts'.[116] Lewis' concise book aimed to explain Islamic political concepts and interactions based on a broad selection of vocabulary. Lewis examined the etymologies of some of this vocabulary and occasionally highlighted their altered meanings, but he often overlooked the continually changing nature of the political concepts they represented. On the other hand, Anjum's insightful article investigated political terms and metaphors and their compatibility with the modern nation-state, and the usefulness of modern readings of older Islamic texts. Anjum focused on terms with perceived relevance to modern politics, including *dawla*, *umma*, *siyasa*, *imam*, *shariʿa* and *shura*. Perceptively he highlighted their varying meanings, different problems associated with their conceptual and linguistic translation, and the challenges of applying them in the modern context.[117] Anjum's article classified some terms such as *umma*, *imam* and *shariʿa* as being of 'fixed conceptual range', while others including *wali*, *amir*, *sultan* were classified as 'variable and substitutable';[118] I contend that all terms – and the political concepts they represented – were continuously variable.

This work does not limit its scope to tracing the ever-shifting meanings of political vocabulary, albeit an important task. It additionally focuses on retrieving the political languages through which the authors conveyed their ideas and treated their concerns by employing modes of speech and conventions that were recognised and even anticipated by their audiences. Pocock explained how political languages varied from vocabulary and metaphors:

[116] Bernard Lewis, *The Political Language of Islam* (Chicago, IL: University of Chicago Press, 1988); Anjum, 'Political Metaphors'. In the context of India, there is, of course, Muzaffar Alam's work, *The Languages of Political Islam: India 1200–1800*. It should be noted that there are other studies that refer interchangeably to language – that is, Arabic, Persian, or Turkish – and political language of pre-modern Islamic texts. These views are utter distortions of the social, religious and cultural mesh of the medieval Middle East and are best left for study under the purview of modernists specialised in the history of nationalism. For a relevant and useful discussion on language in the abstract sense and political language, refer to Pocock, 'The Reconstruction of Discourse', 964.

[117] Anjum, 'Political Metaphors', passim.

[118] Ibid., 12.

'such a mode of speech is not a way of naming things, but of conveying and enjoining a selective view of political activity in general – a way of acting and of determining the actions of others'.[119] He furthermore referred to political languages as 'idioms' and 'rhetorics', which he noted 'may co-exist, converge, diverge or conflict'.[120] I found 'idioms' particularly useful to explicate one important feature of political languages: as opposed to terms or metaphors, political idioms are properly understood only by a specific group of people who are often the intended audiences; idioms do not translate well literally into other languages used in other frameworks and recognised by different audiences.[121]

The intricacies of these conventions and how idioms 'co-exist, converge, diverge or conflict' are best highlighted by examining the use of '*shariʿa*' in the late Ayyubid political treatise *al-ʿIqd al-farid* (*The Unique Necklace for a Content King*). The author Ibn Talha (d. 652/1254), himself a Shafiʿi–Ashʿari legal theoretician and chief judge, advanced seemingly contradictory conceptions of the *shariʿa* in his treatment of the ten duties required of the sultan.[122] In his discussion of the third duty, he urged the sultan to ensure the swift enforcement of penalties outside the *shariʿa* courts (*al-siyasat*) in order to repel corruption, maintain people's safety and secure travel on the roads.[123] In the fifth duty, however, Ibn Talha advised the sultan to abide by the *shariʿa* and cultivate scholars, jurists and judges who upheld it. Yet again in the ninth duty, the author encouraged the sultan to dedicate time to sit in on the sultanic and non-*shariʿa* courts (*mazalim*) in order to expose injustice

119 Pocock, 'The Reconstruction of Discourse', 964.

120 Ibid.

121 Pocock provides a useful illustration by noting that Edmund Burke (1729–97) observed 'that the English [in the sixteenth and seventeenth centuries] had been in the habit of affirming their liberties in a language framed to articulate the inheritance of property'; refer to Pocock, 'The Reconstruction of Discourse', 967, and for the full discussion refer to, J. G. A. Pocock, 'Burke and the Ancient Constitution – A Problem in the History of Ideas', *The Historical Journal* 3(3) (1960): 127, 128, 130–1

122 Ibn Talha, *al-ʿIqd al-farid li-al-malik al-saʿid*, ed. Yūsuf bin ʿUthmān al-Ḥazīm (Riyadh: Ibn al-Azraq Center for Political Studies, 2013), 246–8; for the full discussion, refer to Chapter 4, 136–9, below.

123 *Siyasa* here can also mean the 'legal authority of the sultan'; refer to Yossef Rapoport, 'Royal Justice and Religious Law: Siyāsah and Shariʿah under the Mamluks', *Mamlūk Studies Review* 16 (2012): 75.

and uphold the 'duties of reason and justice'.[124] The coexistence of *mazalim* and *shari'a* courts in the same discussion is hardly shocking. Yossef Rapoport explained that the Mamluk period witnessed the integration of sultanic authority into one symbiotic legal structure wherein the *siyasa* and *mazalim* courts allowed the government to actively participate in and even compete with the jurists in interpreting and adapting the law to social practice.[125] Yet Rapoport's valuable contribution still does not explain why a Syrian Shafi'i chief judge like Ibn Talha would enthusiastically incite the sultan to implement a competing conception of Islamic justice that challenged, first and foremost, the standing of his own *shari'a* court. The explanation is that, in this treatise, the *shari'a* is conceived more creatively by Ibn Talha to hold a constitutional association. The *shari'a* of this political text is certainly not the Schachtian model of Islamic law, nor is it a doctrine of obligations, nor mere substantive law.

Two recent scholarly conceptions of the *shari'a* are useful here. The first is Anver Emon's notion of the *shari'a* as the 'rule of law'.[126] Emon argued that the *shari'a* is neither a mere legal doctrine nor God's law, but a 'conceptual framework' within which 'different claims of justice' are made by different stakeholders of the Islamic community.[127] A second beneficial view is argued by Siddiqui and conceives of the *shari'a* as a nomos or 'a dialectical mechanism of governance influencing society through the production of legal norms and responding to sociopolitical conditions', which allows the organisation and preservation of society.[128] These two notions are more effective to gain an understanding of the constitutional relevance of the use of *shari'a* by medieval political thinkers and tie in well with the argument of this monograph.

As I will discuss in Chapter 2, Ibn Jama'a's treatment of *tafwid* (delegation), *'ahd* (oath), *taqlid* (appointment) and *wilayat* (senior functions)

124 Ibn Talha, *al-'Iqd al-farid*, 247.

125 Refer to Rapoport, 'Royal Justice and Religious Law', 74–5, 86–92, 100.

126 Anver M. Emon, *Religious Pluralism and Islamic Law: 'Dhimmīs' and Others in the Empire of Law*, 1st edn, Oxford Islamic Legal Studies (Oxford: Oxford University Press, 2012), 16. See also Anver M Emon, 'Shari'a and the Rule of Law', in Robin Griffith-Jones and Mark Hill (eds), *Magna Carta, Religion and the Rule of Law* (Cambridge: Cambridge University Press, 2015), 196–214.

127 Emon, *Religious Pluralism and Islamic Law*, 16.

128 Siddiqui, *An Intellectual Portrait of al-Juwayni*, 283; refer to full discussion, 279–83.

similarly held a constitutional relevance. Although Ibn Jamaʿa's discussions resembled those of his main influences, especially al-Mawardi, they were also in fact a reflection of his interest in the moderation of and limitations on the exercise of power by the sultan, and the proper functioning of government in every political eventuality. I referred to these interests in the Introduction as the concern for the rule of law, delegation of power and limited government.

Shariʿa, *tafwid*, *ʿahd*, *taqlid* and *wilayat* should not be interpreted merely as terms or metaphors representing political concepts, but rather as essential and carefully selected constituents of the political languages of Islamic thinkers. They were deployed to convey complex constitutional views and were understood precisely by those target audiences and dedicatees that were acquainted with the specific conventions prevalent among the political thinkers of the late Ayyubid and early Mamluk period. For instance, idioms in political treatises authored by Shafiʿi–Ashʿari legal theoreticians could be opaque to other Shafiʿi jurists or traditionists who were not versed in constitutional discourses or simply not interested in questions of governance. Moreover, the same idioms may hold or be taken to hold drastically different meanings if employed by the same Shafiʿi–Ashʿari legal theoreticians in different fields such as, for instance, works of substantive law; the above-mentioned use of *shariʿa* comes to mind here. Likewise, there is a need to not be deceived by the reuse of excerpts from classical influences, which may appear to relate to the same historical political concepts or interactions but in fact serve purposes in completely different discourses that are pertinent only to the late Ayyubid and early Mamluk context. Only with these nuanced understandings in mind can we begin to retrieve the languages and understand the political discourses of the period, and accordingly 'read' political texts.

2

Ibn Jamaʿa's Synthesis and Praxis of Shafiʿi Political Thought

This chapter examines the synthesis of the Shafiʿi strain of political thought during the Mamluk period and its praxis. It describes its development, precursors, influences and the distinctive literary styles that were used to convey it. This synthesis is embodied in the treatise *Tahrir al-ahkam fi tadbir ahl al-Islam* (*Drafting Ordinances Towards Running the Affairs of the People of Islam*) and the praxis in the life and career of its author, Ibn Jamaʿa. This synthesis and praxis make the *Tahrir* the ultimate manifestation of Shafiʿi political thought.

Several features of the *Tahrir* make it a synthesis of Shafiʿi political thought. For one, the *Tahrir* was the last of the Shafiʿi political treatises of the period, and arguably the last important one ever written by a renowned Shafiʿi thinker. After this period, there was only a yearning for the Shafiʿi lost golden past, as illustrated in the last chapter of this book. Furthermore, layers of Shafiʿi thinkers, including al-Mawardi, al-Juwayni, al-Ghazali and Ibn Talha profoundly influenced the *Tahrir*, both thematically and stylistically. The influence of these and other earlier Shafiʿi writings was, likewise, evident in the style and the distinctive arrangement of sections that Ibn Jamaʿa opted for in his treatise. The *Tahrir*'s arrangement reflected three main clusters of topics: the *imamate* and the conception of political authority; the main offices and the administration; and the rules of war – in this organisation, the *Tahrir* benefited from earlier Shafiʿi treatises.

The praxis of this political thought is attested to by the life and career of Ibn Jamaʿa. It refers to the way the *Tahrir* was moulded by Ibn Jamaʿa's experience in the posts he held and, at the same time, to the way his political thought was applied during a major political change of the Mamluk period. Ibn Jamaʿa's various appointments in high-ranking offices under al-Ashraf Khalil Ibn Qalawun (r. 689/1290–693/1293) and subsequent Mamluk sultans shaped the evolution of his political thought across his three successive political treatises. His political ideas, including his conceptions of political authority, delegation of power and the role of the administration, were put into practice in order to secure a durable and legitimate transfer of power at the start of the third reign of al-Nasir Muhammad. This was a very rare example of documented praxis of political thought. As such, Ibn Jamaʿa offers a unique case in the study of the history of Islamic political thought: specific political ideas posited by an Islamic thinker being put into practice during his own lifetime.

Inspecting the development of Ibn Jamaʿa's political thought in parallel with the progress of his career is a prerequisite to discussing this case of praxis. This entails a detailed study of Ibn Jamaʿa's biography not just as a jurist and judge, but also as a leading administrator and a statesman who was at the centre of major political events. This will show how the ideas of the *Tahrir* were shaped by its author's service in various religious, judicial and administrative posts, his patronage by influential individuals, and his other intellectual interests and affiliations. Furthermore, this will help to explain the roots of the various concerns that the author developed throughout his various writings.

Ibn Jamaʿa's political thought has been misread to a large extent. As discussed in Chapter 1, earlier scholars such as Lambton have argued that following the fall of the ʿAbbasid caliphate, 'the problem for the jurists now was to define' the authority of the sultans who seized power and that this dictated Ibn Jamaʿa's 'restatement of the theory of the caliphate'.[1] However, Ibn Jamaʿa was certainly not concerned with restating the so-called 'theory of the caliphate' to accommodate sultanic rule. By his time, and in fact well before the fall of Baghdad to the Mongols, the caliphate was a long gone ideal. Furthermore, the accommodation of coercive power had already been incorporated into Islamic political thought since the time of al-Mawardi. Ibn Jamaʿa never aimed at reaffirming or rehabilitating the theory of the caliphate.

---

[1] Lambton, *State and Government*, 138. Refer to Chapter 1, 17–23, above.

Ibn Jamaʿa was predominantly interested in the three abstract and interlocked notions of the rule of law, limited government and delegation of power. The first comprised the moderation of the arbitrary exercise of power based on written systems of checks and balances; the second intended to empower the professionalised administration and judiciary, and hence curtail the absolute power of rulers and military elites; and the third was meant to secure a legitimate and durable transfer of political power in the context of frequent changes at the top. In order to uphold these three constitutional notions, Ibn Jamaʿa aimed at guaranteeing the proper functioning of government, irrespective of the Mamluk households and factional competition for power. To achieve this he intended, both in his writings and throughout his career, to secure a constitutional framework that guaranteed a continually functional government via its administrative and judiciary branches. In achieving this aim, Ibn Jamaʿa could advocate these three notions: the rule of law, limited government and delegation of power. This is this essence of the *Tahrir* that has been missed so far in the few studies that have covered Ibn Jamaʿa.[2]

There are three parts to this chapter. The first is a biography of Ibn Jamaʿa, which will identify the important milestones of his career and how they impacted his political thought. This included his service for al-Ashraf Khalil; the roles that he played later, willingly or otherwise, in the deposition and confirmation of three different Mamluk sultans; and the experience that he mustered within the administration and the influence that he came to exert on it. The second and longest part is dedicated to Ibn Jamaʿa's political thought as articulated in his three political treatises. It will trace the evolution of his ideas and the development of new constitutional concerns. This part will show that Ibn Jamaʿa's concern for the three constitutional themes of the rule of law, limited government and delegation of power was expressed in the *Tahrir* under three main topics: the *imamate* or the author's conception of political authority; the main offices and the administration; and the rules of war. Furthermore, this second part will identify at which points in time Ibn Jamaʿa's major political ideas crystallised and the various influences upon

[2] The two main works that included Ibn Jamaʿa are: Lambton, *State and Government* and Rosenthal, *Political Thought*.

him. Finally, the third part of this chapter will present a documented case of the praxis of Ibn Jamaʿa's political thought. It will highlight the use of his political ideas, by Ibn Jamaʿa himself as well as other judges, jurists and chancery secretaries, to complete the political transition at the start of the third reign of sultan al-Nasir Muhammad.

Ibn Jamaʿa: A Biography[3]

Born in 639/1241 in Hama to a prominent Syrian family, Badr al-Din Ibn Jamaʿa was a 'latecomer to celebrity', and there was nothing distinguished about his career until his forties when, in 687/1288, he was appointed as preacher (*khatib*) of the Aqsa Mosque of Jerusalem.[4] His career benefited from his friendships with influential *amir* ʿAlam al-Din Sanjar al-Dawadari (d. 699/1300) and Shams al-Din Ibn al-Salʿus (d. 693/1294), who later became the vizier of al-Ashraf Khalil.[5] Ibn Jamaʿa relied on the support of his two powerful friends, especially Ibn al-Salʿus, whom he met in 687/1288 during the latter's appointment as market inspector (*wali al-hisba*) of Damascus.

Ibn Jamaʿa's belated fame was in large part a result of the 'questionable circumstances' of his first appointment as chief judge in Cairo.[6] Ibn al-Salʿus,

[3] This biography focuses on Ibn Jamaʿa's role in the public sphere, especially events that impacted his political thought. It does not cover other aspects of his career and intellectual life, such as his works on teaching or theology.

[4] This section benefits from Mohamad El-Merheb, 'Ibn Jamāʿa and Family', *EI*[3] 46; El-Merheb, 'Islamic Political Thought and Professional Mobility', 218–20. Refer to ʿAbd al-Jawad Khalaf, *al-Qadi Badr al-Din Ibn Jamaʿa: Hayatuh wa-atharuh* (Karachi: Jamiʿat al-Dirasat al-Islamiyya, 1988), 32, 132; al-Birzali, *Mashyakhat qadi al-qudat shaykh al-Islam Badr al-Din Ibn Jamaʿa*, ed. Muwaffaq Bin ʿAbd a-Qadir, 2 vols (Beirut: Dar al-Gharb al-Islami, 1988), 1:11–12, 95–8; Ibn Hajar al-ʿAsqalani, *al-Durar al-kamina fi aʿyan al-miʾah al-thamina*, 4 vols (Beirut: Dar al-Jil, 1993), 3:281; Ibn Kathir, *al-Bidaya wa-al-nihaya*, ed. Muhyi al-Din Dib Mistu, 20 vols in 11 vols (Damascus-Beirut: Dar Ibn Kathir li-al-Tibaʿa wa-al-Nashr wa-al-Tawziʿ, 2010), 15:529.

[5] Refer to Ibn Kathir, *Bidaya*, 15:529; Ibn Kathir believed that Ibn al-Salʿus was Ibn Jamaʿa's patron. Al-Yusufi claimed that ʿAlam al-Din al-Dawadari al-Salihi was behind the rise of Ibn Jamaʿa; refer to *Nuzhat al-nazir fi sirat al-Malik al-Nasir*, ed. Ahmad Hutayt (Beirut: ʿAlam al-Kutub, 1986), 133–5. So does al-Maqrizi, *al-Suluk li-maʿrifat duwal al-muluk*, ed. Muhammad ʿAbd al-Qadir ʿAta, 8 vols (Beirut: Dar al-Kutub al-ʿIlmiyya, 1997), 2:208. Refer to Robert Irwin, *The Middle East in the Middle Ages: The Early Mamluk Sultanate 1250–1382* (London: Croom Helm, 1986), 76–82; Joseph H. Escovitz, 'Patterns of Appointment to the Chief Judgeships of Cairo during the Baḥrī Mamlūk Period', *Arabica* 30(2) (1983): 162–3. For more on Ibn al-Salʿus, refer to Mathieu Eychenne, *Liens Personnels, Clietélisme et Réseaux de Pouvoir dans le Sultanat Mamelouk Milieu XIIIe–Fin XIVe Siècle)* (Beirut-Damascus: Presses de l'Ifpo, 2013), ch. 7, 341–89.

[6] El-Merheb, 'Islamic Political Thought and Professional Mobility', 219. Refer to Ibn Kathir, *Bidaya*, 15:548; al-Maqrizi, *Suluk*, 2:228; al-Safadi, *al-Wafi bi-al-wafayat*, 29 vols (Beirut: Dar

who had recently been appointed vizier by al-Ashraf Khalil, removed the prominent judge Taqi al-Din Ibn Bint al-Aʿazz (d. 695/1296) after making scandalous accusations against him and, in 690/1291, appointed Ibn Jamaʿa. Therefore, this first major appointment was the consequence of 'a case concocted against Ibn Jamaʿa's predecessor'.[7] This was probably the result of a power struggle involving Ibn Jamaʿa's patron, Ibn al-Salʿus, and other influential Mamluk *amirs* who supported Ibn Bint al-Aʿazz. This political appointment baptised latecomer Ibn Jamaʿa into the intrigues of power, a craft that he quickly mastered, as his career will show. Ibn Jamaʿa, furthermore, obtained other prominent posts in Cairo, including delivering the Friday sermon (the *khutba*) in al-Azhar, the Salihiyya teaching post, the office of chief Sufi (*shaykh al-shuyukh*) and the *khutba* in the Citadel Mosque.

After the assassination of al-Ashraf Khalil in 693/1293 the ascent of Ibn Jamaʿa came to a temporary halt, only to resume again soon after.[8] Despite his close connection to Ibn al-Salʿus, Ibn Jamaʿa managed to successfully disentangle himself from the struggle for power amongst the Mamluks and preserve his life and career. Al-Nasir Muhammad, who was a child at the time, was invested as sultan as per an agreement between the powerful Mamluk *amirs*. Consequently, and following the death of Ibn al-Salʿus under torture, Ibn Bint al-Aʿazz was reinstated as chief judge in 693/1294, but Ibn Jamaʿa kept his teaching post. That same year, he was appointed to the judgeship of Damascus and, in 694/1295, to the *khutba* of the city's Great Umayyad Mosque. This experience decisively marked Ibn Jamaʿa's political thought.

The ascension and deposition of al-Malik al-ʿAdil Kitbugha (r. 694/1294–696/1296) brought Ibn Jamaʿa closer to the power struggles among Mamluk households.[9] In 694/1294, Kitbugha removed al-Nasir Muhammad and

Ihyaʾ al-Turath al-ʿArabi, 2000), 2:16; al-Suyuti, *Husn al-muhadara fi akhbar Misr wa-al-Qahira*, ed. Muhammad Abu Fadl Ibrahim, 2 vols (Cairo: Dar Ihyaʾ al-Kutub al-ʿArabiyya, 1968), 2:168; al-ʿAyni, *ʿIqd al-juman fi taʾrikh ahl-al-zaman*, ed. Muhammad Muhammad Amin, 5 vols (Cairo: Dar al-Kutub wa-al-Wathaʾiq al-Qawmiyya, 2009), 3:85–8. Refer to the two excellent studies by Eychenne, *Liens Personnels*, ch. 7, 341–89 and Nathan Hofer, 'The Origins and Development of the Office of the "Chief Sufi" in Egypt, 1173–1325', *Journal of Sufi Studies* 3(1) (2014): 28.

7 'Ibn Jamāʿa and Family', *EI*[3].

8 Ibid. Al-Maqrizi, *Suluk*, 2:246–52; Ibn Kathir, *Bidaya*, 15:573–6; Ibn Hajar, *Durar*, 3:281.

9 'Ibn Jamāʿa and Family', *EI*[3]. Ibn Kathir, *Bidaya*, 15:581–602; Ibn Taghribirdi, *al-Nujum al-zahira fi muluk Misr wa-al-Qahira*, ed. Muhammad Husayn Shams al-Din, 17 vols (Beirut: Dar al-Kutub al-ʿIlmiyya, 1992), 8:54–8.

seized the sultanate. However, within two years he found his grip on power was weakening and, in Muharram 696/November 1296, he summoned Ibn Jamaʿa to the citadel of Damascus along with the Hanafi judge, where the Mamluk *amirs* renewed their oath of allegiance to Kitbugha in the presence of the two judges. Nevertheless, this did not end Kitbugha's woes; his main competitor, al-Mansur Lajin (r. 696/1296–698/1299), declared himself sultan in Safar 696/December 1296.[10] Shortly afterwards, several Mamluk *amirs* visited the citadel of Damascus along with Ibn Jamaʿa and successfully persuaded Kitbugha to abdicate in favour of Lajin. Later that year, Ibn Jamaʿa was 'honourably discharged from the judgeship' and replaced by Imam al-Din al-Qazwini, but he still held the *khutba* of the Grand Mosque and a professorship in the Qaymariyya *madrasa* in Damascus.[11] For the following three years, Ibn Jamaʿa held the *khutba* of the Grand Mosque. In 698/1299 Lajin was killed and al-Nasir Muhammad was brought back from Karak.

The Mamluk–Ilkhanid war brought Ibn Jamaʿa to the centre of political events in Damascus.[12] Following the Mamluk defeat at Wadi al-Khaznadar in 699/1299 by the armies of the Ilkhanid ruler Ghazan (r. 694/1295–703/1304), chief judge al-Qazwini escaped Damascus, leaving Ibn Jamaʿa as the leading Shafiʿi scholar in the city. Damascus was now abandoned except for its citadel, which kept up resistance under its commander Arjuwash. In this period of great insecurity, Ibn Jamaʿa joined a delegation of notables that attempted to secure an amnesty from Ghazan.[13] Furthermore, Ibn Jamaʿa and Ibn Taymiyya went to the citadel and attempted to broker a peace between Arjuwash and the Ilkhanids.[14] As soon as the Ilkhanid armies retreated, Ibn

---

[10] Ibn Kathir, *Bidaya*, 15:598–602; Ibn Taghribirdi, *Nujum*, 8:56–7; al-Maqrizi, *Suluk*, 2:277–80; al-ʿAyni, *ʿIqd al-juman*, 3:350–3.

[11] 'Ibn Jamāʿa and Family', *EI*[3].

[12] Ibn Kathir, *Bidaya*, 15:619–27; Ibn al-Dawadari, *Kanz al-durar wa-jamiʿ al-ghurar*, 9 vols (Deutsches Archäologisches Institut, 1960), 9:19–35; al-Yunini, *Dhayl mirʾat al-zaman*, ed. Hamza Ahmad ʿAbbas, 3 vols (Abu Dhabi: Hayʾat Abu Dhabi li-al-Thaqafa wa-al-Turath, al-Majmaʿ al-Thaqafi, 2007), 1:253–54, 299; al-ʿAyni, *ʿIqd al-juman*, 4:30–1, 80–1; al-Maqrizi, *Suluk*, 2:321, 331.

[13] 'Ibn Jamāʿa and Family', *EI*[3]. Ibn Kathir, *Bidaya*, 15:620; possibly concerned with presenting a leading role for Ibn Taymiyya, Ibn Kathir skipped Ibn Jamaʿa's name from the delegation. This is contradicted by the accounts of Ibn al-Dawadari, *Kanz*, 9:19; al-Yunini, *Dhayl mirʾat al-zaman*, 1:253–4; al-ʿAyni, *ʿIqd al-juman*, 4:30–1; al-Maqrizi, *Suluk*, 2:321.

[14] Ibn al-Dawadari, *Kanz*, 9:35; al-Yunini, *Dhayl mirʾat al-zaman*, 1:299.

Jamaʿa was reassigned to the chief judgeship of Damascus and its *khutba* in 699/1300. His distinguished career in Damascus continued as, in 701/1301, the Sufis of the Sumaysati *khanqah* selected him as their *shaykh al-shuyukh*.[15] According to Syrian historian Ibn Kathir (d. 774/1373), no one had ever managed to hold the positions of chief judge, *khatib* and *shaykh al-shuyukh* in Damascus simultaneously before Ibn Jamaʿa.[16]

In 702/1302, the sultan appointed Ibn Jamaʿa as chief judge of Egypt. In this capacity, he was later dragged into some of the controversies surrounding Ibn Taymiyya.[17] Ibn Jamaʿa succeeded in distancing himself from these affairs until 707/1308, when the Sufis of Cairo brought charges against Ibn Taymiyya for his comments on Ibn ʿArabi.[18] The case boiled down to Ibn Taymiyya's refusal to invoke the Prophet for help (*la yustaghath bi-al-nabi*), which Ibn Jamaʿa saw as 'mere insolence' and refused to take further action against Ibn Taymiyya.[19] However, the pressure mounted and many jurists and Sufis insisted on Ibn Jamaʿa sentencing Ibn Taymiyya to jail, which he finally did.[20] Throughout this controversy, Ibn Jamaʿa attempted to distance himself from doctrinal debates, factionalism and the dangerous political split between Baybars II, on the one hand, who was under the influence of the influential Sufi Nasr al-Manbiji, and Salar and some of Ibn Taymiyya's Hanbalis, on the other.[21]

The period between the second and third reigns of al-Nasir Muhammad brought Ibn Jamaʿa dangerously close to power struggles between Mamluk households. Nonetheless, this period was crucial in shaping his political thought and, congruently, his thought contributed to the unfolding political events.[22] For example, when al-Nasir Muhammad left Cairo for Karak, he

15 Ibn Kathir, *Bidaya*, 16:13; al-Yunini, *Dhayl mirʾat al-zaman*, 1:662.

16 As enviously noted by Ibn Kathir; Ibn Kathir, *Bidaya*, 16:13–14. The editor's helpful footnote (2) mentions others who later held these three posts together based on Ibn Jamaʿa's precedent. Refer to El-Merheb, 'Islamic Political Thought and Professional Mobility', 219–20.

17 Ibn Kathir, *Bidaya*, 16:19; al-Yunini, *Dhayl mirʾat al-zaman*, 1:682–3; al-Suyuti, *Husn al-muhadara*, 2:171.

18 For a fuller explanation of the case, see Chapter 3, below.

19 'Ibn Jamāʿa and Family', *EI*[3].

20 Ibn Kathir, *Bidaya*, 16:62–3; a similar account is related in al-Yunini, *Dhayl mirʾat al-zaman*, 2:1174.

21 For a more detailed discussion on this split, refer to Chapter 3, 96–8.

22 Refer to 77–83 below.

asked secretary ʿAlaʾ al-Din Ibn al-Athir to draft his resignation letter.[23] On Friday, 22 Shawwal 708/ 4 April 1309, this letter was read aloud in the citadel of Cairo and upon the request of some prominent Mansuri *amirs*, the judges and the caliph corroborated the authenticity of the resignation letter.[24] As chief judge, Ibn Jamaʿa could not possibly have avoided taking part in this process, at the end of which Baybars al-Jashankir became sultan. Shortly afterwards, in 709/1309, Ibn Jamaʿa assumed the directorate (*mashyakha*) of the *khanqah* of Saʿid al-Suʿada in Cairo upon the request of the Sufis.[25]

The above-mentioned resignation letter kept on dragging Ibn Jamaʿa into the centre of Mamluk politics. This letter was important for Baybars al-Jashankir and his loyal *amirs* as it rendered any possible return of al-Nasir Muhammad to power as illegitimate. To underline this, the sultan summoned the four judges, including Ibn Jamaʿa, and read them al-Nasir's resignation letter to secure another legal ratification of his own reign.[26] Mindful of the risks involved, Ibn Jamaʿa subsequently endeavoured to distance himself from this matter as much as possible. Although this carefulness eventually earned him the clemency of the returning and triumphant sultan al-Nasir Muhammad, a price had to be paid and in 710/1310 Ibn Jamaʿa was removed from the judgeship of Egypt.[27]

Al-Nasir Muhammad quickly reversed his decision and reinstated Ibn Jamaʿa with greater influence. In 711/1311, he was appointed to the chief judgeship of Egypt, the superintendence of Dar al-Hadith in Ibn Tulun's mosque, and the professorships at al-Salihiyya and al-Nasiriyya colleges.[28] In 712/1312, the sultan appointed Ibn Jamaʿa *khatib* of a newly built mosque and he, in turn, assigned his son Jamal al-Din ʿAbdallah (d. 716/1316) as his deputy for this commission.[29]

---

23 Al-Maqrizi, *Suluk*, 2:422–3.

24 Ibn Taghribirdi, *Nujum*, 8:184; Ibn Kathir, *Bidaya*, 16:66.

25 Al-Yunini, *Dhayl mirʾat al-zaman*, 2:1264. Refer also to al-ʿAyni, *ʿIqd al-juman*, 5:81. The arrangement was that Ibn Jamaʿa would visit the *khanqah* every Tuesday afternoon to read *hadith* and attend to the needs of the Sufis. 'Ibn Jamāʿa and Family', *EI*[3].

26 Ibn al-Dawadari, *Kanz*, 9:179–85.

27 Al-Yunini, *Dhayl mirʾat al-zaman*, 2:1318–19; al-Suyuti, *Husn al-muhadara*, 2:171; al-ʿAyni, *ʿIqd al-juman*, 5:190.

28 "Ibn Jamāʿa and Family", *EI*[3]. Al-Yunini, *Dhayl mirʾat al-zaman*, 2:1434; al-Suyuti, *Husn al-muhadara*, 2:171; al-ʿAyni, *ʿIqd al-juman*, 5:249.

29 Al-Maqrizi, *Suluk*, 2:479; 'Ibn Jamāʿa and Family', *EI*[3].

Meanwhile, Ibn Jamaʿa continued to wield great power over the administration and among the ruling elite. For instance, in 713/1313 he acted against a certain Ibn al-Waziri, who had been appointed to supervise the Sultanic Hall of Justice (*dar al-ʿadl*) and the charitable endowments (*waqfs*).[30] When Ibn al-Waziri accused some judges of malpractice, Ibn Jamaʿa decided to fight back and defend his peers and, according to Maqrizi, he 'knew [the right] manoeuvres' to achieve his aim.[31] Ibn Jamaʿa contacted several influential individuals in the bureaucracy, powerful judges, the inspector of the army, the head of the chancery and several of the elite Mamluks (*khassakiyya*) of the sultan, and succeeded in removing al-Waziri. Understandably, such wide-ranging influence earned Ibn Jamaʿa a place in some defamatory poems from his enemies.[32] Generally, the sources referred to Ibn Jamaʿa throughout those years as commanding great influence, which he employed to moderate the relation between the populace and the ruling elite.[33] Ibn Jamaʿa resigned in 727/1327 and probably dedicated his time to writing until his death in 733/1333 at the age of 94.[34] Even after his resignation he continued to exert considerable authority, as his son ʿIzz al-Din ʿAbd al-ʿAziz (694/1294–767/1366) was appointed to a teaching post at the Mosque of ʿAmr b. al-ʿAs in 730/1330.[35]

Ibn Jamaʿa's writings spanned a wide array of subjects.[36] Although he authored three doctrinal works, Ibn Jamaʿa was a firm but moderate

30 Al-Maqrizi, *Suluk*, 2:487–8. For more on *dar al-ʿadl*, refer to Rapoport, 'Royal Justice and Religious Law', 71–102.

31 Al-Maqrizi, *Suluk*, 2:487–8.

32 Al-Sharmasahi was encouraged by Ibn Sayyid al-Nas to compose a defamatory poem about Ibn Jamaʿa; in al-Maqrizi, *Suluk*, 2:487–8. Refer also to al-Yusufi, who mentions that some poets praised him while others like al-Sharmasahi attacked him, see *Nuzhat al-nazir*, 134–5.

33 Al-Maqrizi related one such incident that took place in 714/1314; in *Suluk*, 2:495–6.

34 'Ibn Jamāʿa and Family', *EI*[3].

35 Berkey noted that ʿIzz al-Din Ibn Jamaʿa 'owed his appointment to his father Badr al-Din', in *Transmission of Knowledge*, 108. The letter is preserved by al-Qalqashandi (d. 821/1418) in *Subh al-aʿsha fi sinaʿat al-insha*, 4 vols (Cairo: al-Matbaʿa al-Amiriyya, 1913), 11:227–9.

36 For a list of his books refer to Khalaf, *Ibn Jamaʿa: Hayatuh*, 243–73. For a recent study that mentions Ibn Jamaʿa's theological production, refer to Jon Hoover, 'Early Mamluk Ashʿarism against Ibn Taymiyya on the Nonliteral Reinterpretation (Taʾwīl) of God's Attributes', in Ayman Shihadeh and Jan Thiele (eds), *Philosophical Theology in Islam: Later Ashʿarism East and West*, Islamicate Intellectual History, vol. 5 (Leiden: Brill, 2020), 195–230. Hoover notes that 'it is possible' that Ibn Jamaʿa wrote a theological work, *Idah al-Dalil*, 'to counter Ibn Taymiyya', although he did not mention him explicitly (217).

Ash'ari and nothing in his career suggested that he was at any time primarily concerned with polemics and doctrinal debates.[37] Furthermore, Ibn Jama'a almost continuously held a teaching post in either Cairo or Damascus and hence was closely involved in the teaching profession.[38] His treatise, *The Guide for the Listener and the Speaker on the Etiquette of the Teacher and the Pupil* reflected this vast experience.[39] Moreover, he may have composed a treatise on the astrolabe (*Risala fi-al-asturlab*).[40] Most importantly for our purposes, Ibn Jama'a authored three treatises of political thought, the *Mustanad*, *Mukhtasar* and the well-known *Tahrir*.[41]

The Political Thought of Ibn Jama'a

The title *Tahrir al-ahkam fi tadbir ahl al-Islam* (*Drafting Ordinances towards Running the Affairs of the People of Islam*) captured the essence of Ibn Jama'a's synthesis of Shafi'i political thought.[42] My translation of the title encompasses two principal processes that are central to this thought: *tahrir* and *tadbir*. The first is the process of arriving at and issuing the ordinances needed to run a government, and the second is the process of running the affairs of both populace and government. Neither sultan nor caliph was referred to in this title. This treatise proposed a comprehensive system wherein the pristine functioning of government was assured for all eventualities: a weak or powerful sultan, a nominal or effective caliph and whether the leader was present or absent. This was secured through the *Tahrir*'s two processes, *tahrir* and *tadbir*.

[37] The three treatises are listed in Khalaf, *Ibn Jama'a: Hayatuh*, 326.

[38] Refer to Berkey, *Transmission of Knowledge*, 54.

[39] 'Ibn Jamā'a and Family', *EI*³. Ibn Jama'a, *Tadhkirat al-sami' wa-al-mutakallim fi adab al-'alim wa-al-muta'allim*, ed. Muhammad Ibn Mahdi al-'Ajami (Beirut: Dar al-Basha'ir al-Islamiyya li-al-Tiba'a wa-al-Nashr wa-al-Tawzi', 2008). This treatise covered the merits of learning and the learned, and the etiquette of teaching and learning, including the relation between teacher and students, and among students; the classification of knowledge; various pedagogical techniques and methods; how to handle books; hygiene; protocols of conversing; and the etiquette of residing in a *madrasa*.

[40] Al-Safadi, *al-Wafi bi-al-wafayat*, 2:15–16.

[41] The full titles of the first two treatises are: *Mustanad al-ajnad fi alat al-jihad* and *Mukhtasar fi fadl al-jihad*.

[42] Ibn Jama'a, *Tahrir al-ahkam fi tadbir ahl al-Islam*. Other older and more recent editions exist, including *Tahrir* (ed. and German trans. H. Kofler in *Islamica* 6 (1934), 7i (1935), *Schlussheft* (1938)). Furthermore, the *Tahrir* was sometimes mentioned wrongly as *Tadbir jaysh al-Islam*, see al-'Ulaymi, *Kitab al-uns al-jalil bi-tarikh al-Quds wa-al-Khalil*, ed. 'Adnan Yunus 'Abd al-Majid Abu Tabbana, 2 vols ('Amman: al-Khalil, 1999), 2:228.

Accordingly, the *Tahrir* should be examined first and foremost as a political and constitutional text. Whilst relying on jurisprudence, law and ethics, this treatise was intended to devise a coherent constitutional framework to ensure the smooth running of government. Labelling it as a 'theory of the jurists' that was only concerned with the 'religious ideal in opposition to practice' leads to grave misunderstandings that are disputed in this chapter.[43] The essence of the *Tahrir* was its strong constitutional flavour. Its process of *tahrir* used Islamic legal reasoning and ethical precedents to set checks and balances on the ruler's discretionary exercise of power and as such can be associated with the ideal of the rule of law. Likewise, the process of *tadbir* outlined by Ibn Jamaʿa did not, as scholars have argued, espouse the so-called 'theory of the caliphate', which centred on the authorities of the caliph. The executive arm of government as conceptualised by Ibn Jamaʿa was not supposed to depend solely on the ruler, but rested on the professionalised and powerful administrative and judicial bureaucracy. By distributing the executive functions of the ruler, Ibn Jamaʿa was effectively invoking the ideal of limited government.

This coherent constitutional framework differentiated the *Tahrir* from earlier treatises and confirmed its role as a synthesis of Shafiʿi political thought. In both processes, *tahrir* and *tadbir*, Ibn Jamaʿa proposed legal provisions for exercising power that were not necessarily linked to 'sultanic ordinances' or to caliphal authority, as was normally the case in earlier treatises such as al-Mawardi's *Ahkam*. On the contrary, in Ibn Jamaʿa's conception of government, the administration, legal offices, jurists, and the military and civilian elites contributed vigorously and independently to the processes of *tahrir* and *tadbir* and upheld the rule of law and limited government. The subsequent discussion of the praxis of Ibn Jamaʿa's thought will show how the *Tahrir*'s ideas on delegation of power were put into practice by jurists and chancery secretaries to legitimate the third reign of al-Nasir Muhammad.

There are other crucial originalities in the *Tahrir*, such as the concern for the rules of war. These were equally at the heart of Ibn Jamaʿa's constitutional themes and warrant a treatment of their own. Probably motivated by his concern for the rule of law, Ibn Jamaʿa displayed an exceptional concern for the

43 Lambton, *State and Government*, xvi–xvii.

rules of war unmatched in Islamic legal and intellectual history. He expressed this by consolidating and rearranging earlier legal discussions of topics like the law of rebellion, the treatment of non-Muslims, taxation and the spoils of war. While those topics had been covered in depth in earlier political and legal treatises, the novelty of the *Tahrir* was reflected in the way Ibn Jamaʿa organised these topics as part of a unique and coherent single discussion on the topic of the rules of war.

The development of Ibn Jamaʿa's constitutional ideas in his political works also reflected the progress of his career.[44] The *Tahrir* was the cumulative product of a chain of 'lesser' political works that were influenced by this progress. This development can be traced across two earlier treatises that have been left out of modern scholarship: *Mustanad al-ajnad fi alat al-jihad* (*The Soldiers' Guide to War Engines*) and *Mukhtasar fi fadl al-jihad* (*A Compendium of the Virtues of* jihad).[45] Since the life of Ibn Jamaʿa is well-documented, it is possible to link his writings to the progress of his career in the judiciary and the administration and argue for the cumulative development of his political thought. His first political work, the *Mustanad*, contained some seeds of his political thought expressed in the genre of a military arts manual (*furusiyya*). Later, Ibn Jamaʿa developed further his ideas on the duties and rights of the sultan, and on the resulting effects of war, in the *Mukhtasar*. Generally, one can claim that his basic political views on the duties and rights of the ruler had crystallised by the time he authored the *Mukhtasar*. Lastly, Ibn Jamaʿa conveyed in the *Tahrir* his profound attentiveness to the three constitutional themes of the rule of law, limited government and delegation of power in order to ensure the smooth running of the government in any eventuality.

Before engaging in the analysis of each of the three treatises, it is important to consider the various influences upon Ibn Jamaʿa as an author. He was a teacher, and this was continuously reflected in his concise and clear style, as professed in his aim for the *Tahrir* to be 'easy to refer to'.[46] Ibn Jamaʿa was, likewise, a Shafiʿi jurist and an Ashʿari, which impacted his mode of reason-

---

44 Refer to El-Merheb, 'Islamic Political Thought and Professional Mobility', 221–4.

45 It is possible that one of Ibn Jamaʿa's political writings is missing. Refer to the introduction of the editor, which mentions *Hujjat al-Suluk fi maharat* (or *muhadat*) *al-muluk*, *Tahrir*, 20.

46 Ibn Jamaʿa, *Tahrir*, 46.

ing and influenced the themes that he opted to cover. Finally, he was a judge, a statesman and a bureaucrat, which was reflected in the value he accorded to administrative discussion. At some points, all of these backgrounds combined in Ibn Jamaʿa's writing.

Beginnings: the Mustanad

The study of the development of Ibn Jamaʿa's political thought begins with the *Mustanad*, which contained some seeds of his later writings.[47] The examination of this treatise reveals much about his nascent political ideas, style and influences. Three traits of Ibn Jamaʿa's political writings can already be identified in the *Mustanad*: his use of some non-Islamic sources in conjunction with his heavy reliance on the Qurʾan and *hadith*; the immaculate organisation of the work's sections; and the concurrent use of legal opinions of all four *madhhab*s, often with a surprisingly neutral approach.[48] These traits continued in his later works and became a trademark of his writing style. Most importantly, Ibn Jamaʿa's concern for just rule, his call for obedience in return for justice and his interest in the rules of war were also evident in the *Mustanad*. Despite the impressive and detailed section titles, there was practically no military value to the *Mustanad*.

At first glance a military manual seemed an uncharacteristic work for Ibn Jamaʿa. Yet the *Mustanad* represented a continuation of the idea that the religious scholars (*ʿulamaʾ*) and Sufis had inherited some of the roles of the ʿAbbasid caliph, including, in this case, the education of new military elites by instructing them in the conduct and ethics of war. The *Mustanad* was a military manual (*furusiyya*) largely based on ʿAbbasid works of *adab* and *hadith*, and was one of the few Mamluk treatises that dealt with arms and armour.[49] The roots of this literary genre were in the ʿAbbasid court concept

47 Refer to El-Merheb, 'Islamic Political Thought and Professional Mobility', 221–3.

48 Ibn Jamaʿa, *Mustanad al-ajnad fi alat al-jihad wa-Mukhtasar fi fadl al-jihad wa-fadaʾil al-rami fi sabil Allah*, ed. Usama Nasir al-Naqshabandi (Damascus: Dar al-Wathaʾiq li-al-Dirasat wa-al-Tabʿ wa-al-Nashr wa-al-Tawziʿ, 2008), 5–8; the editor notes that Ibn Jamaʿa's sources in the *Mustanad* include some lost works of the third/ninth century, *Siraj al-muluk* of al-Turtushi, both *Ahkams* of al-Mawardi and Abu Yaʿla, and the book of *Kharaj* of Abu Yusuf. I have identified below al-Juwayni's *Ghiyath al-umam* as an additional and major influence on Ibn Jamaʿa.

49 Refer to El-Merheb, 'Islamic Political Thought and Professional Mobility', 221–2; Shihab al-Sarraf, 'Mamluk Furūsīyah Literature and Its Antecedents', *Mamlūk Studies Review* 8(1) (2004): 142.

of noble *furusiyya* (*al-furusiyya al-nabila*), which was closely associated with the ʿAbbasid Sufi chivalry (*futuwwa*).[50]

In the first section of this supposedly military handbook, Ibn Jamaʿa treated the duties and rights of the ruler.[51] As Ibn Jamaʿa's main concern was justice (*ʿadl*), there was one basic proposition in his discussion: justice in return for obedience.[52] This proposition was confirmed by his choice of various well-known maxims and sayings from within and without the religious tradition, including 'A single day of just rule by a just *imam* is superior to sixty years of [ritual] worship', and 'No rank is higher than that of a just sultan except that of a Prophet or a favoured angel'.[53] In this section Ibn Jamaʿa listed some of the duties and rights of the sultan in what was a mere bridgehead for his detailed discussions in the later two treatises, the *Mukhtasar* and the *Tahrir*.[54] He argued that the sultan was in charge of attending to his subjects, protecting the lands of Islam, preserving religion, dispensing justice and upholding prescribed legal punishments (*hudud*). In return, obedience was required from his subjects, except in sinful decisions where the duty of obedience was waived, thus reflecting al-Juwayni's (419/1028–478/1085) influence on his thought.[55]

The above-mentioned nascent political ideas additionally treated the rules of combat (*ahkam al-qital*). Despite resembling a piece of *adab* more than anything else, the *Mustanad* heralded Ibn Jamaʿa's interest in the rules of war that would later become central to his call for the rule of law. His discussion of swords, bows, the participation of women in warfare, the Prophet's horses, arms and armour were all subjects of an *adab* work based on anecdotes of early Islamic conquests (*futuh*) rather than a source of practical military knowledge. Nevertheless, the *Mustanad* heralded an early appearance of Ibn Jamaʿa's interest in the rules of war, for instance, section twenty-nine titled,

50 Al-Sarraf, 'Mamluk Furūsīyah', 144–6.

51 Ibn Jamaʿa, *Mustanad*, 32.

52 As Lambton observed in the case of the *Tahrir* in *State and Government*, 140.

53 Ibn Jamaʿa, *Mustanad*, 33 (my translation). According to the editor they are quoted from *Siraj al-muluk*. Ibn Jamaʿa will repeat such sayings and maxims verbatim in the *Tahrir*.

54 Ibn Jamaʿa, *Mustanad*, 33–5.

55 Al-Juwayni is very unforgiving to the *imamate* of the sinful; refer to al-Juwayni, *Ghiyath al-umam*, 92–3 of the editor's introduction, and 88, 311, 327 of the main text where al-Juwayni clearly states, 'the *imamate* is impermissible to a sinful person'.

In Seeing Off the Raiders and Receiving Them, the Imam's Directive to Them, and the Rules of Combat.[56] The rules of combat in this section of the *Mustanad* is a stepping stone for later treatises, as Ibn Jamaʿa develops a fascination for the rules of war and this became a central theme of the *Tahrir*, where he dedicated several consecutive sections to the subject.

Crystallisation: the Mukhtasar

The *Mukhtasar fi fadl al-jihad* (*A Compendium of the Virtues of jihad*) was pivotal in the elaboration of Ibn Jamaʿa's political thought for several reasons. While it reiterated some of the ideas of the *Mustanad*, the *Mukhtasar* also reflected major new developments, including his conceptualisation of political authority. For one, Ibn Jamaʿa treated in depth the theme of the sultan's duties and rights towards his subjects. Moreover, he dealt with new themes such as legal provisions (*ahkam sharʿiyya*) related to the effects of war hitherto mentioned only briefly in the *Mustanad*. Most importantly, the *Mukhtasar* marked the crystallisation of Ibn Jamaʿa's principal political idea of equating the sultanate with the *imamate*.

Ibn Jamaʿa's identification of the *imam* with the sultan was a critical development in political thought, which emerged in the *Mukhtasar* and coincided with the start of his high-profile career.[57] In this treatise, dedicated to sultan al-Ashraf Khalil on the occasion of his decisive victories against the Frankish lordships, Ibn Jamaʿa consistently equated the just *imam* (*al-ʿadil*) with the sultan.[58] In the first section of the *Mukhtasar* titled, *Regarding the Sultan, His Benevolence, and the Esteem He Acquires through Justice*, he argued that in the presence of a powerful and just sultan, the *imamate* was held by the sultan.[59] He was to expound this idea in more detail in the later *Tahrir*; nonetheless, the *Mukhtasar* shows that this notion crystallised during the author's service under al-Ashraf Khalil.

56 Ibn Jamaʿa, *Mustanad*, 91–2 (my translation).

57 Refer to El-Merheb, 'Islamic Political Thought and Professional Mobility', 223–4.

58 Ibn Jamaʿa, *Mukhtasar*, 99–100. Most likely vizier Ibn al-Salʿus was the 'great benefactor' who commissioned (*ashara*) Ibn Jamaʿa to author the treatise. Yet Ibn Jamaʿa expected his work to be consulted by both, sultan and vizier (*bi rasmi nazarihi al-ʿali wa nazarihi al-sharif*), otherwise he would have worded it *nazarihi al-ʿali wa-al-sharif*.

59 Refer to Ibn Jamaʿa, *Mukhtasar*, 101–3; when Ibn Jamaʿa quotes a *hadith* related to the justice of the *imam*, he quickly points out that he is referring to the sultan.

In this same section of the *Mukhtasar*, Ibn Jamaʿa treated and adapted the familiar theme of the requirement for the sultan. The author resorted to a collection of Qurʾanic verses, *hadith*, and known maxims that were often used in classical treatises, yet he now equated the requirement for the *imamate* with the requirement for the sultanate.[60] Ibn Jamaʿa noted that God secured victory for rulers when four conditions were met: the preservation of ritual prayer; observing the alms tax (*zakat*) and being charitable; enjoining what is good; and forbidding what is reprehensible.[61] As order and stability were paramount to Ibn Jamaʿa, he justified the requirement for a sultan by stating, 'If God hadn't established a sultan to shelter the weak from the powerful and the oppressed from the oppressor, the unjust would have annihilated the weak, and people would have been at each other's [throats].'[62] Moreover, he explained that the sultan was bestowed by God on people to 'manage their affairs (*siyasatuhum*), protect them, uphold justice for the oppressed, deter the unjust among them, and this is why it was said, "Forty years of tyrannical rule is preferable to [the affairs of] people being neglected for a single hour".'[63] Ibn Jamaʿa was later to echo those well-known maxims in his *Tahrir*.[64]

Ibn Jamaʿa displayed in the *Mukhtasar* a paramount concern for justice (*ʿadl*) similar to that in the *Mustanad* and almost every work of Islamic political thought.[65] He reiterated the notion of justice in return for obedience that he had discussed in the *Mustanad*. Ibn Jamaʿa even used the same maxims, including 'No rank was higher than that of a just sultan, except that of a Prophet or a favoured angel.'[66]

In the *Mukhtasar*, one can clearly discern the synthesis of Shafiʿi political thought. Ibn Jamaʿa's discussion on the rights and duties of the sultan was proof that the fundamentals of his synthesis had crystallised by the time he

60 The editor's very helpful notes identified the sources of the maxims with *Siraj al-muluk* being a main influence.

61 Ibn Jamaʿa, *Mukhtasar*, 101; based on verse 22:41 of the Qurʾan.

62 Ibid., 101.

63 My translation. The editor again identifies the source as *Siraj al-muluk*.

64 Refer to Lambton, *State and Government*, 139–40. Although this discussion treats the *Tahrir*, it discusses the same maxims.

65 Ibn Jamaʿa, *Mukhtasar*, 103–4.

66 Ibn Jamaʿa reiterates those ideas and maxims in his *Tahrir*. Refer to Lambton, *State and Government*, 140. The maxim is found in al-Turtushi, *Siraj al-Muluk*, ed. Muhammad Abu Bakr (Cairo: al-Dar al-Misriyyah al-Lubnaniyya, 1994), 186.

authored the *Mukhtasar*. This was evident in the subsection titled, *Regarding the Duties and Rights of the Sultan*.[67] While this discussion resembled earlier similar ones by other Shafiʿi thinkers, most notably al-Mawardi and al-Juwayni, it was distinctive and reflected Ibn Jamaʿa's own ideas, changes and rearrangements.[68]

Prior to an examination of the *Tahrir*, the development of Ibn Jamaʿa's political thought between the two 'lesser' treatises must be traced. The transformation from the *Mustanad*, a pseudo-*furusiyya* manual that contained seeds of his political thought, into the *Mukhtasar* should be understood as a move towards an enhanced articulation of his political ideas and the crystallisation of his conceptualisation of political authority. Ibn Jamaʿa's concise and well-organised style is notable in both treatises. Moreover, the consistent presentation of the opinions of other *madhhab*s in a remarkably impartial way was another feature of Ibn Jamaʿa's works, and so was his use and synthesis of sources like al-Mawardi, Abu Yaʿla, Abu Yusuf and al-Turtushi.[69] Most importantly, Ibn Jamaʿa systematically and unequivocally referred in the *Mukhtasar* to the powerful and just sultan as the *imam*. As such, he adapted earlier discussions on the requirement for the *imamate* to argue for the requirement for the sultanate. Lastly, other notable developments were Ibn Jamaʿa's ideas on the duties and rights of the sultan and his concern for the rules of war, which had similarly crystallised by the time he authored his *Mukhtasar*.

Synthesis: the Tahrir

The *Tahrir* was the ultimate synthesis of Shafiʿi political thought. It highlights Ibn Jamaʿa's novel conception of political authority, the role he envisioned for the professionalised judiciary and administrative branches of government in the political sphere, and an unprecedented concern for the rules of war.

67 Ibn Jamaʿa, *Mukhtasar*, 104.

68 This subsection is repeated in the *Tahrir* with minor rearrangements in the lists of duties and rights. Ibn Jamaʿa uniquely referred to the sultan in the *Mukhtasar*, while in the *Tahrir* he referred to both caliph and sultan. For a similar discussion, refer to al-Mawardi, *Kitab al-ahkam al-sultaniyya wa-al-wilayat al-diniyya*, ed. Ahmad Mubarak al-Baghdadi, 2 vols (Kuwait: Dar Ibn Qutayba, 1989), 2:22–3.

69 The footnotes by the editor of the *Mustanad* /*Mukhtasar* greatly facilitated my search for Ibn Jamaʿa's sources and influences.

These conceptions and ideas are rooted in the author's wider concern for the rule of law and limited government, and to his theory of delegation.

In the *Tahrir*'s prologue, Ibn Jamaʿa presented his main arguments, methodology, sources, dedicatee and the various sections of his work. He explained that his treatise was divided into seventeen sections that covered: the *imamate*; the requirement for the sultanate; the appointment of viziers; the amirs and their duties; a variety of discussions on the branches of administration, the preservation of the *shariʿa*, and its related judicial and administrative offices; the revenues and spending of the treasury; the distribution of grants and stipends; the recruitment of and payments to soldiers; war machines and the art of war; booty and spoils of war; the rules of truce-making; the law of rebellion; the treatment of *dhimmis*; and the rules of granting safe conduct.[70] Although the *Tahrir* was – almost certainly – completed during the third reign of al-Nasir Muhammad and during Ibn Jamaʿa's final years, he opted for a universal dedication to any ruler who wished to benefit from his treatise.[71]

Political authority: the unnecessary caliphate

The few scholars who studied the *Tahrir*, including Lambton and Rosenthal, misinterpreted its principal contributions to Islamic political thought. Primarily, this treatise upheld a tripartite conception of *imam*, caliph and sultan in order to secure the proper functioning of government; any other interpretation of the *Tahrir*, whether as a legitimation of sultanic usurpation or an attempt to preserve the caliphate, is in my view an imposed paradigm. Lambton believed that Ibn Jamaʿa accepted 'the absorption of the caliphate itself into the sultanate'.[72] However, the *Tahrir* did not view the caliphate in the same way as, for instance, al-Mawardi's *Ahkam*. The *imam* in Ibn Jamaʿa's *Tahrir* could be either the caliph or the sultan, but the sultan could not be caliph. By contrast, Rosenthal saw in the *Tahrir* a 'principle of acquiescence in bad rule' in order to avoid anarchy, which accordingly saw jurists compromise with the usurped power – the sultan – but insist on swearing

70 Ibn Jamaʿa, *Tahrir*, 45.

71 Ibid., 45. Ibn Jamaʿa mentions the *Mustanad* at 162.

72 Lambton, *State and Government*, 141, 140–2.

allegiance to the *imam* – the caliph.[73] That was also neither the intention nor the concern of the *Tahrir*. What really mattered in Ibn Jamaʿa's definition of the *imam*, whether caliph or sultan, were the processes of *tahrir* and *tadbir* and the proper functioning of government. This treatise was concerned with the delegation of power amongst the three offices for the purpose of upholding these two processes.

Ibn Jamaʿa first discussed his conception of political authority. Section one of the *Tahrir*, titled *Regarding the Necessity for the Imamate and its Requirements*, did exactly what its title suggests.[74] In this section, Ibn Jamaʿa reiterated some of the arguments on the necessity for the *imam* that he had used in the *Mukhtasar* solely for the sultan.[75] Furthermore, Ibn Jamaʿa treated the investiture to the *imamate*, and mentioned that it could be acquired electively or coercively (*ikhtiyariyya* or *qahriyya*).[76] Eligibility for the elective *imamate* stipulated ten conditions: the candidate should be male, free, mature in age, judicious, Muslim, just, brave, of Qurashi descent, learned and competent in running the affairs of the state.[77] Once he was elected, his *imamate* became effective and obedience obligatory upon all. Nevertheless, obedience was not expected in sin; this again reflected al-Juwayni's influence on Ibn Jamaʿa.[78] It should be noted that these ten requirements applied only to an elective *imam* and not to a coercive one.[79]

Ibn Jamaʿa then explained that the elective *imamate* could be conferred in two ways. The first was through the oath of allegiance (*bayʿa*) of the 'people who loosen and bind' (*ahl al-hall wa-al-ʿaqd*), who were made up of commanders, leading scholars, and community leaders and prominent individuals.[80] The second method was through designation by the predecessor. In this

---

73 Rosenthal, *Political Thought*, 44.

74 *Fi wujub al-imama, wa shurut al-imam wa ahkamuhu*; in *Tahrir*, 48–57.

75 Compare Ibn Jamaʿa, *Mukhtasar*, 101–2, and *Tahrir*, 48–51. Refer to Lambton, *State and Government*, 139–40; Rosenthal, *Political Thought*, 43–4.

76 Ibn Jamaʿa, *Tahrir*, 51–5. Refer to Lambton, *State and Government*, 140–1.

77 Refer to al-Juwayni's discussion on the required qualities of the *imam* in *Ghiyath al-umam*, 76–97 of the main text. Although al-Juwayni divided his discussion into 'required qualities' and 'acquired qualities', the influence of the *Ghiyath* on the *Tahrir* is difficult to miss.

78 Refer to discussion above in fn. 55 on al-Juwayni's influence.

79 Ibn Jamaʿa, *Tahrir*, 51; '*al-imama darban, ikhtiyariyya wa qahriyya. Amma al-ikhtiyariyya fa li-ahliyyatiha ʿashr shurut*'.

80 Ibid., 52–3.

case, however, both successor and predecessor should meet the ten conditions listed above. Up to this point, there was nothing novel in this discussion.

Subsequently, Ibn Jamaʿa discussed a 'third method' of conferring the *imamate*, which was self-investiture by coercive force (*al-bayʿa al-qahriyya*).[81] Here, Ibn Jamaʿa had only to discuss the way through which a coercive *imamate* was realised, as he had already waived the ten requirements for eligibility to such investiture. Ibn Jamaʿa explained that in the absence of an *imam*, the holder of military power (*sahib al-shawka*) could usurp power rendering his *imamate* effective without the need for an oath of allegiance or a designation from a predecessor. He maintained that this was in the interest of the unity of the Muslims. Ibn Jamaʿa explained that even if the usurper was not learned or happened to be impious (*fasiq*), his *imamate* was considered valid and obedience to him was mandatory. Moreover, if another holder of military power rose up and took over then his *imamate* became valid and obedience was due from all Muslims. As discussed above in the biography, Ibn Jamaʿa was personally involved in a similar situation on three occasions.[82]

Although the discussion of the coercive *imamate* was short, it had far-reaching repercussions. Very early on in his *Tahrir*, Ibn Jamaʿa had practically ended the necessity for the caliphate altogether by making a clear division between *imam* and caliph and by allowing the sultan to be the *imam*.[83] One can argue that, up to this point, there was nothing explicit in the *Tahrir* that suggested waiving the necessity for the caliphate and that the legitimation of the wielder of military force was not new to Islamic political thought. While this is true, there are two important distinctions to consider here. First, the legitimation of military power (i.e., the sultan) had been a long-settled question in Islamic political thought since the time of al-Mawardi and, most importantly, it was not the main paradigm for Ibn Jamaʿa's thought. Despite any apparent linguistic similarity with earlier texts like the *Ahkam*, it is anachronistic to consider the legitimation of coercive power as one of the concerns of the *Tahrir*. Secondly, the chief aim of the *Tahrir* was to secure

81 Ibid., 55–6. Refer to Lambton, *State and Government*, 141–2; Rosenthal, *Political Thought*, 45.

82 In his capacity as a judge, Ibn Jamaʿa was involved in attesting to the resignation of al-Nasir Muhammad and the confirmation of Baybars al-Jashankir, Kitbugha's forced abdication, and finally the confirmation of al-Nasir's third reign.

83 Refer to El-Merheb, 'Islamic Political Thought and Professional Mobility', 224–6.

the proper functioning of government under any political circumstances by upholding the processes of *tahrir* and *tadbir*. In pursuing this aim, Ibn Jamaʿa believed that the wielder of force, that is, the usurper, could be the *imam*. Far from simply stating that the wielder of coercive power – under a nominal caliph – held all the authorities of the office of the *imam*, Ibn Jamaʿa unequivocally stated that the wielder of coercive power *might be* the *imam*. Equally, he did not claim that the wielder of power might be the caliph, which contradicts Lambton's assertion that Ibn Jamaʿa believed 'the sultan might be the caliph'.[84] By waiving the ten requirements for eligibility for the coercive *imam*, including Qurashi descent, Ibn Jamaʿa made this intention very clear. Although this will be mentioned explicitly in a subsequent part of the *Tahrir*, one can already conclude that Ibn Jamaʿa's contribution to the so-called theory of the caliphate was to negate the necessity for the caliphate.

For Ibn Jamaʿa, *imamate*, caliphate and sultanate were three distinct offices, very well demarcated, each entailing different requirements. In this conception, the sultanate and *imamate* were necessary offices, while the caliphate was not. The powers needed to run the state were concentrated in the *imamate*, that is, the 'office' of the *imam*. The elective *imamate* (*ikhtiyariyya*) should be held by a caliph who must either be invested by an oath of allegiance or by designation from a predecessor. On the other hand, any wielder of power – with no requirement of knowledge or pedigree – could hold the coercive *imamate* (*qahriyya*) and his *imamate* becomes legitimate. In this scheme, the eligibility bar for the *imamate* was very high for caliphal candidates who held the elective *imamate*, while it was almost non-existent for sultans who held the coercive *imamate*. Furthermore, the sultan could become *imam* even if there was a caliph in place; in such an eventuality – and it did happen during Ibn Jamaʿa's tenure as chief judge – the caliph would still remain caliph, but he would delegate the authorities of both his caliphate and his *imamate* to the sultan. However, in the absence of a caliph or an *imam*, the sultan would become the legitimate *imam* without the need for delegation. Consequently, sultanate and *imamate* were necessary offices, while the caliphate was not.

---

[84] Lambton, *State and Government*, 142; refer to the discussion below on the duties of the sultan and the *imam*.

With this tripartite scheme, Ibn Jamaʿa skilfully achieved three remarkable objectives simultaneously. The first was that he waived the necessity for the caliphate while preserving it as a cherished and untainted Islamic ideal.[85] Differentiating the *imam* from the caliph solved several long-standing problems that previous prominent Shafiʿi thinkers, like al-Ghazali and al-Juwayni, had struggled with.[86] For one, Ibn Jamaʿa's tripartite scheme succeeded in conserving the symbolic and untainted nature of the caliphate by keeping the bar of eligibility very high. Likewise, he avoided challenging the necessity for Qurashi descent, as opposed to al-Juwayni who put this requirement into question.[87] Moreover, he devised a practical way to circumvent any discussion on the need for a caliph to justify the existence of the state, an issue that al-Ghazali had struggled to keep a consistent opinion about.[88] For Ibn Jamaʿa, no longer was the presence of a caliph as the head of state compulsory to justify its very existence. Secondly, Ibn Jamaʿa created a practical constitutional framework within which a sultan could rule legally even in the complete absence of a caliph. The earlier model of al-Mawardi still required an existing nominal caliph to legitimise a sultan's rule; likewise, al-Ghazali accepted the designation of a caliph by the sultan, but still required the existence of a caliph as head of state. On the other hand, al-Juwayni's lengthy discussion on the absence of the caliph was very theoretical and impracticable.[89] Ibn Jamaʿa's solution was ingenious, the *imamate* was still

[85] 'Effectively, the *Tahrīr* negated the need for the caliphate without calling for an end to it', in El-Merheb, 'Islamic Political Thought and Professional Mobility', 225.

[86] Refer to Rosenthal, *Political Thought*, 44. Rosenthal attempted the same comparison with al-Mawardi and al-Ghazali, and came very close when he said, 'Ibn Jamāʿa obviously has in mind a powerful military leader usurping the supreme authority by appointing himself to the office of *imām*'. Yet Rosenthal missed the *Tahrir*'s distinction between caliph and *imam* and limited Ibn Jamaʿa's aims to justifying the coercive power. Rosenthal was by far the most developed attempt to understand the *Tahrir* in earlier scholarship.

[87] Refer to al-Juwayni's discussion on Qurashi lineage in *Ghiyath al-umam*, 79–82, of the main text. For more on this, refer to Hallaq, 'Political Thought of Juwaynī'; Anjum, 'Political Metaphors'.

[88] Refer to Rosenthal, *Political Thought*, 38–43 and especially 42–43, for a very helpful discussion on *al-Mustazhiri* and the *Ihyaʾ*; al-Ghazali recognised that 'the *imāma* in his day was really a sham', but still stressed that recognising the caliph's authority is a condition for legitimate government (42).

[89] The *Ghiyath* is divided into three parts: the first deals with the ideal *imamate*, the second covers the absence of an *imam* or the existence of non-ideal one, and the third deals with the absence of experts on the *shariʿa*; see Hallaq, 'Political Thought of Juwaynī', 31. Refer to Siddiqui, *An Intellectual Portrait of Al-Juwayni*, especially to pt 4 (chs 9 and 10), which discuss al-Juwayni's concern for continuity and political stability, and to Chapter 1, 32, above.

a must but the sultan could become the *imam* in the absence of a caliph or in the absence of another *imam*. Ibn Jamaʿa thus created a maintainable constitutional framework within which the practical did not conflict with the ideal, the exercise of power was not subject to unattainable requirements, and the legitimacy of the head of the state was upheld without confronting nostalgia for ideal and earlier times. In so doing, Ibn Jamaʿa secured a framework for the smooth running of government in every constitutional eventuality. Thirdly, Ibn Jamaʿa succeeded in decoupling the impact of the struggles for power at the top from the judiciary and the administration by devising a simple solution to the Mamluks' frequent changes at the seat of the sultanate: whenever a holder of military power rose up and took power then his *imamate* became valid and obedience was due to him. As already mentioned, the author was personally involved in confirming or removing three different Mamluk sultans.

Ibn Jamaʿa then buttressed his conception of political authority by further outlining the scope of both sultanate and *imamate*. The second section of the *Tahrir* dealt primarily with the delegations of power (*tafwid*), and the rights and duties of the ruler.[90] In his discussion of the delegation of the *imam*'s powers, the author confirmed his tripartite conception of caliph, sultan and *imam* by describing both caliph and sultan as delegatees of the *imam*'s office. This attention to delegation of power was motivated by the primacy of upholding the executive process of *tadbir*. Ibn Jamaʿa discussed, like al-Mawardi and Abu Yaʿla, the special and general delegations of power (*khass* and *ʿam*).[91] When treating the general delegation (*tafwid ʿam*), he said 'it was as per the custom of kings and sultans in our own time'.[92] This reflected how, during his time, the sultan enjoyed the full powers of the *imam*, including appointing judges and governors, tax collection and spending, and fighting external and internal enemies.

The process of *tadbir* and continuity of government was thus practically secured by two equally legitimate and effective methods that confirmed the sultan's powers: a general delegation from the caliph and/or a coercive

---

[90] Section two of the *Tahrir*, 58–74, titled *Regarding the Rights and Duties of the Caliph and the Sultan*.

[91] Ibid., 60–1.

[92] *ka-ʿurf al-muluk wa-al-salatin fi zamanina*.

acquisition of the *imamate*. Ibn Jamaʿa adapted earlier discussions on the delegation of power by a caliph to the sultan, like al-Mawardi and Abu Yaʿla, in order to buttress his earlier argument on the validity of the sultan as *imam*. To this end, Ibn Jamaʿa stated that the investiture of a sultan by a caliph entailed the delegation of the full caliphal authorities and even his standing except in pedigree.[93] Following that, he reiterated that when a wielder of military power took over a province by force, the caliph should recognise him and the delegation of power became immediately effective. The fact that this usurper may not be qualified did not impact the legitimacy of his delegation, as the latter should simply appoint qualified regents so that both religious and worldly greater interests (*masalih*) were in order and properly administered.[94]

This discussion on delegation provides further proof of how existing scholarship has consistently misinterpreted the *Tahrir*. Ibn Jamaʿa aimed at guaranteeing the sultan full delegation of powers not in the interest of legitimating coercive power, but to uphold the process of *tadbir* within a constitutional framework that suited the early Mamluk period. Rosenthal saw that Ibn Jamaʿa 'unashamedly and openly' made further concessions to legalise the general delegation of authority to the usurper, 'by associating it with the vizierate of delegation or the general emirate'.[95] While Rosenthal astutely noted the adaptation of earlier forms of delegation by Ibn Jamaʿa, his explanation did not account for various aspects of the early Mamluk context. The legitimation of the coercive power paradigm failed to consider such factors as the growing role of the professionalised administration, the role of legal *madhhab*s in the political and administrative spheres, the nature of Mamluk household competition, and the uses and misuses of the presence of a nominal ʿAbbasid caliph in Cairo in such struggles. In fact, the reason behind this adaptation of existing forms of delegation was not to legalise the usurper: this legitimation was achieved mostly through military power and, besides, that was a long-settled issue in Islamic political thought. The

---

93 Ibn Jamaʿa, *Tahrir*, 60. Rosenthal explained *yuʿtabar* differently: 'he must possess the same qualifications as the *imām* in whose place he rules, no doubt a purely theoretical demand in the interests of the supreme authority of the *Sharīʿa*'; in *Political Thought*, 46.

94 Ibn Jamaʿa, *Tahrir*, 61: 'He [the usurper] should delegate authorities to a qualified individual, in order to administer matters as he [the delegatee] possesses the qualities that are lacked by the usurper.'

95 Rosenthal, *Political Thought*, 46.

main purpose was rather to ensure the process of *tadbir* and the continuity of government in every possible eventuality, including, for instance, the full delegation of the *imam*'s powers to the sultan, even in the presence of a legitimate caliph. This very scenario will be discussed later in this chapter.

Equally vital in section two was Ibn Jamaʿa's discussion of the duties and rights of the *imam* towards his subjects (*raʿiyya*) and community (*umma*).[96] Although this was similar in his previous treatise, the *Mukhtasar* was only concerned with the sultan's rights while the *Tahrir* mentioned both caliph and sultan. Both treatises covered the mutual obligations of both community and *imam* and the study of the two in conjunction explains the development of Ibn Jamaʿa's thought and his use of *imam*, sultan and caliph. In short, they both listed the same rights and duties, but they were differently ordered in the *Tahrir*. Furthermore, Ibn Jamaʿa referred solely to the sultan in the *Mukhtasar*, whereas in the *Tahrir* he referred to both caliph and sultan. The reason was that Ibn Jamaʿa dedicated the *Mukhtasar* to al-Ashraf Khalil, who was *imam* and sultan at that time. The *Tahrir*, on the other hand, was a more universal discussion in which the *imam* might have been, in theory at least, a caliph or sultan as per the tripartite scheme of this treatise.

The Tahrir *on leading offices and administration*

Having laid out his conception of political authority, Ibn Jamaʿa shifted his attention to the main offices and administration. In sections three to ten, the author covered various senior offices essential to the process of *tadbir* and the continuity of government, including the vizier, *amirs*, judges, market inspectors and others. In this part, the *Tahrir* resembles more an administrative manual than a typical juridical treatise; as mentioned in the Introduction and as will be discussed in other chapters, such an amalgamation of genres was characteristic of Shafiʿi and other political treatises of this period.

Ibn Jamaʿa started by discussing the vizierate, but his real interest therein was the full delegation of powers to the sultan. More particularly, his attention was focused on the vizier's full delegation (*wizarat al-tafwid/ tafwid muwazara*), which became relevant at the start of the third reign of al-Nasir

[96] *The sultan and the caliph have ten rights over the umma, and they have ten rights over him* in Ibn Jamaʿa, *Tahrir*, 61–74 and *Mukhtasar*, 104–7. For other discussions on this topic refer to Rosenthal, *Political Thought*, 49–50; Lambton, *State and Government*, 142–3.

Muhammad. At first glance, the *Tahrir*'s discussion of the vizierate resembled that in the *Ahkam*.[97] Like al-Mawardi, Ibn Jamaʿa identified two types of vizierate: the one of full delegation (*tafwid*) and that of special delegation (*tanfidh*). The former was a general delegation that granted the vizier the full authorities of the caliph short of his Qurashi lineage. One wonders about the relevance of such a discussion in the *Tahrir*, since under the Mamluks, with some exceptions, the vizier often held a short-term and trivial post and the other senior offices of the administration were more influential and long-lasting.[98] However, in the *Tahrir* there was another more relevant practical purpose for this form of delegation (*tafwid muwazara*), which was to secure and legitimate the delegation of the *imam*'s full authorities to the sultan even in the presence of a legitimate caliph. This was a very particular legal case that was shaped by Ibn Jamaʿa's personal experience; he proposed this specific type of delegation as the constitutional framework to complete the transition to the third reign of al-Nasir Muhammad. This is discussed in detail in the final part of this chapter, which deals with the praxis of Ibn Jamaʿa's thought. It suffices, at this point, to note how a discussion focused seemingly on the vizierate was intended in fact to secure the sultan a full delegation of authorities.

Subsequently, the *Tahrir* focused on the senior military commanders (*umara*ʾ).[99] Ibn Jamaʿa treated this group as another layer of professionals attached to government. He defined their role in the Mamluk period as follows:

> when one is accorded the supervision of a group of soldiers, he must be dedicated to their affairs and should not supervise other soldiers, as is the case of the prominent *umara*ʾ of these days in the Egyptian and Syrian lands – may God safeguard them along with the other lands of Islam – [that is] the holders of grants dedicated to the war in the path of God where each

[97] Section three is titled *Regarding the Appointment of Wazirs and Their Duties* in Ibn Jamaʿa, *Tahrir*, 75–8; refer to al-Mawardi, *Ahkam*, 30–9.

[98] For more on the vizierate under the Mamluks refer to D. Ayalon, 'Studies on the Structure of the Mamluk army [III]', in Gerald R Hawting (ed.), *Muslims, Mongols and Crusaders: An Anthology of Articles Published in 'The Bulletin of the School of Oriental an African Studies'* (London: Routledge, 2007), 61.

[99] Section four titled, *Regarding the Appointment of* umaraʾ *for the Duty of* jihad, in *Tahrir*, 79–86; refer to *Mukhtasar*, 113.

> one of them is assigned a limited group of soldiers whose affairs he should tend to and whose subsistence he should secure.[100]

Ibn Jamaʿa's description of the Mamluk *umaraʾ* as another professionalised group reflected his own administrative outlook. The *amir*, Ibn Jamaʿa explained, should be allocated a durable source of income (*rizq* and *iqtaʿ*) in order to secure a comfortable life for him and his household and, more importantly, to ensure that his soldiers were ready for combat irrespective of the political situation.

Following that, Ibn Jamaʿa treated another important group, the religious scholars (*ʿulamaʾ*). He listed the main offices that he associated with upholding the *shariʿa*.[101] In his conception, the scholars were in charge of 'preserving and transmitting it [the *shariʿa*], they are the authority in [determining] what is permitted and forbidden according to it, and its application'.[102] Accordingly, they controlled part of the process of *tahrir* and had the power to draft and pass laws. Furthermore, Ibn Jamaʿa listed five administrative offices entrusted with the preservation of the *shariʿa*. These five posts secured the scholars a further role in the executive process of *tadbir* through the judiciary and administration. Within this listing, the author advocated a precise division of labour between judgeship, jurisconsultship, market inspection, teaching and supervision of charitable endowments; additionally, he enumerated the conditions for assuming every post, and delimited the scope of market inspection, probably influenced by the late Ayyubid treatise, *al-ʿIqd al-farid*.[103] Consequently, and under the rubric of upholding *shariʿa*, Ibn Jamaʿa thus secured a further division of judicial and administrative labour and the participation of the *ʿulamaʾ* in issuing and administering ordinances of government.

This part of the *Tahrir*, additionally, included a section that resembled an administrative manual of finances and taxation.[104] The precision, abridgment

---

[100] Ibn Jamaʿa, *Tahrir*, 80.

[101] Ibid., 87–93; section five is titled, *Regarding the Preservation of the Rules of the Shariʿa and the Procedures for Proper Appointments Related to It*. Refer to Rosenthal, *Political Thought*, 48–9, for a related discussion.

[102] Ibn Jamaʿa, *Tahrir*, 87.

[103] Refer to Chapter 4, 140–1, for a discussion on Ibn Talha's *al-ʿIqd al-farid*; in all likelihood Ibn Jamaʿa was influenced by this work as his list of the *shariʿa*-related offices is identical to Ibn Talha's with one difference: teaching.

[104] Section seven of Ibn Jamaʿa, *Tahrir*, 98–117; refer to section three of the *Mukhtasar*.

and lucidity of this discussion suggested an attempt to codify the Islamic laws and rules related to public spending and taxation. What really mattered in this discussion, which was based on earlier treatises, was Ibn Jamaʿa's concise and organised style and that he consistently presented the opinions of other *madhhabs*.[105] This section fits well with the following one on the rules of war. It could easily have been integrated into it.

The codification of the rules of war

After discussing his conception of political authority, the main offices and the administration, Ibn Jamaʿa turned his focus to codifying the rules of war. In the remaining seven sections of the *Tahrir*, he consolidated earlier discussions on war, booty, truce, rebellion and the *dhimma*. Such a systematic arrangement of topics was novel and it is no exaggeration to claim that it inaugurated a new field within Islamic political thought. This codification of the rules of war should be understood within the context of Ibn Jamaʿa's salient concern for the rule of law as exhibited throughout the *Tahrir*.

This codification covered situations that arose in wartime or its aftermath. Ibn Jamaʿa intended to regulate the conduct of Muslims during and after war based on earlier precedents and in accordance with the *shariʿa*, and to treat legal issues that appeared in situations of war. This included topics such as the comportment of armies, the justification for war, the rules of collecting and distributing the spoils of war, the treatment of captives and civilians, the guidelines for conducting a truce, the law of rebellion that deals with the justification for rebellion and the treatment of Muslim rebels, and the treatment of non-Muslims (*dhimmis*). As is typical in his writing, Ibn Jamaʿa consistently presented the opinions of other *madhhabs*. Within the context of his effort to organise every aspect of the exercise of power and his concern for the rule of law, these last sections of the *Tahrir* resembled a rulebook to regulate conduct during war and its aftermath.

---

105 Ibn Jamaʿa's eclectic use of legal opinions – similar to other earlier Shafiʿi political treatises – can be contrasted, for instance, with Hanbali treatises that often only quoted their own sources. Refer to Nimrod Hurvitz, *Competing Texts: The Relationship Between al-Mawardi's and Abu Ya'la's al-Ahkam al-Sultaniyya* (Cambridge, MA: ILSP, Harvard Law School, 2007), 28; Hurvitz noted, 'Al-Mawardi . . . aspires to present an open-ended description of legal options. Abu Yaʿla, on the other hand, relies almost solely on the Hanbali school . . .'

The discussion was based on a rich corpus of cases and precedents. These cases were not novel, there were ample examples in earlier Islamic legal works. Ibn Jamaʿa's original arrangement of them signalled his move towards the codification of the rules of war.[106] Section eleven deals with the various types of war according to the *shariʿa*, and its different rules, for instance, the need for the consent of the sultan and parents before participating in war, or the permissibility of *dhimmis*' participation in Muslim armies.[107] In section twelve, Ibn Jamaʿa referred to, 'all the rules of conduct during war' (*jamiʿ adab al-harb*).[108] These rules laid down, for instance, that it was not permissible to fight people who had not been invited into Islam. Furthermore, the author reiterated the distinction between pagans and those to whom the poll tax (*jizya*) applied. Additionally, this codification included a collection of specific situations: who represented a legitimate target for fighting; the case of having a non-believer father or relative; the case of a blind man who was involved in providing military advice to the enemy; women were not to be fought against unless they struck first; the safety of the enemy's envoys; the permissible means of force during a siege; the treatment of animals; firing arrows at an enemy who used Muslim prisoners as shields and other such cases.

Subsequently, Ibn Jamaʿa discussed booty and truce. Throughout sections thirteen and fourteen, he examined what was considered lawful booty (*ghanima*), its rules, the proper ways of distributing it, and listed various opinions of the four *madhhab*s on these issues.[109] Furthermore, in section fifteen Ibn Jamaʿa treated the prerogative of concluding and abrogating a truce, its lawful terms and conditions, its expiration, and what amounted to a violation of a truce.[110] Likewise, he presented the lawful conditions, duration and terms of safe conduct (*aman*), and even reproduced the wording of such a document.[111]

---

106 Some are based on al-Mawardi and Abu Yaʿla, prophetic tradition, and various juristic works as noted by the editor of the *Tahrir*.

107 Section eleven, *Tahrir*, 152–69. Ibn Jamaʿa refers to the *Mustanad* on 162, thus confirming the chronological order of his works.

108 Section twelve, ibid., 170–87.

109 Sections thirteen and fourteen, ibid., 188–215, 216–30.

110 Section fifteen titled, *On Truce and Safe Conduct and the [Lawful] Rules of Safe Conduct*, ibid., 231–8.

111 For instance, Ibn Jamaʿa noted that an *aman* could not be accorded under duress or to a spy, and that even the *imam* could not abrogate an *aman*; ibid., 237.

The treatment of the rules of war also covered the law of rebellion.[112] Ibn Jamaʿa provided a thorough classification of rebels: 'If a powerful group of Muslims broke away from the *imam* with the intention of overthrowing him or renouncing his authority, or rejected one of his due rights by showing a different interpretation (*taʾwil*), and he could only bring them back [to obey him] by fighting them, then they are the rebels (*bughat*).'[113] Consequently, groups who lacked one of the two necessary conditions – different interpretation (*taʾwil*) and military power (*shawka*) – were not to be considered as rebels. As chief judge during the transition from Baybars al-Jashankir to al-Nasir Muhammad, Ibn Jamaʿa was involved in such classification.

The *Tahrir* treated the sultan's lawful options when dealing with rebellion. The sultan should first 'attempt to bring the rebels back to obedience through dialogue or by remedying their grievances'.[114] The sultan should resort to fighting them only until they return to obedience if these initial efforts fail. Ibn Jamaʿa stressed that rebels 'should not be considered unbelievers but mutineers who held erroneous opinions'.[115] The *Tahrir*'s concern for the rule of law extended to the rebels' judicial and fiscal structures: court rulings and taxation in rebel-held territory were considered lawful and, as such, were upheld.

Ibn Jamaʿa's 'moral classification' of Muslim rebels entailed legal protection.[116] He stipulated stringent rules dictating the treatment of captured rebels. As soon as they returned to obedience or ceased to threaten the realm, imprisoned rebels should be released with their women, children and slaves.[117] Moreover, Ibn Jamaʿa treated various legal opinions on the permissibility of

---

112 Section sixteen titled, *Regarding Fighting Muslim Rebels*, *Tahrir*, 239–47. For a similar discussion refer to section five of al-Mawardi, *Ahkam*, 79–83. Refer to Mohamad El-Merheb, '"There Is No Just Ruler at This Time!" Political Censure in Pre-Modern Islamic Juristic Discourses', in K. Kellermann, A. Plassmann and C. Schwermann (eds), *Criticising the Ruler in Pre-Modern Societies: Possibilities, Chances, and Methods* (Göttingen, Bonn University Press, 2019), 349–76.

113 Ibn Jamaʿa, *Tahrir*, 240.

114 El-Merheb, 'Political Censure', 370.

115 Ibid.; *Tahrir*, 240.

116 El-Merheb, 'Political Censure', 370. I borrowed this term from the seminal book of Khaled Abou el Fadl on the law of rebellion and its repercussions, *Rebellion and Violence in Islamic Law* (Cambridge: Cambridge University Press, 2001), p. 286.

117 The editor of the *Tahrir* makes very useful references to al-Mawardi, Abu Yaʿla and various other sources. For instance, compare with section five of al-Mawardi, *Ahkam*, 79–83, on whether rebels should be fought while retreating.

using weapons of indiscriminate destruction (*ma yaʿimmu atharuh*) when fighting rebels, including flooding, fire and mangonels.[118] Although rooted in earlier juristic discourses and established precedents, the *Tahrir*'s codification of the rules of war – especially its systematised and consistent treatment of the law of rebellion – is better understood within the context of Ibn Jamaʿa's call for the rule of law.[119]

Finally, the *Tahrir* treated the protected people (*dhimma*) contract.[120] Although this was not a novel topic, Ibn Jamaʿa's discussion was marked by its detail and organisation within the rubric of the rules of war. This discussion, taken in the context of the *Tahrir*, not only stressed the obligation to the *dhimmis*, but equally their rights under the wider concern for the rule of law.

The Praxis of Ibn Jamaʿa's Political Thought

There was a reciprocal influence between Ibn Jamaʿa's thought and his career, which I refer to here as the praxis of his political thought. He developed his ideas not only by synthesising earlier works of political thought, but, more significantly, throughout a career that shaped his thought. Conversely, Ibn Jamaʿa's political thought influenced political developments. As mentioned above, Ibn Jamaʿa found himself involved in the removal of Kitbugha, the renewal of the oath of allegiance to Baybars al-Jashankir, and, more perilously, in the events that led to the third reign of al-Nasir Muhammad. As the Shafiʿi chief judge, it was Ibn Jamaʿa's job to attest or renounce oaths of allegiance, letters of confirmation, delegations, dismissals and resignations. His involvement influenced his synthesis of Shafiʿi thought in the *Tahrir*; in turn his thought influenced events in the political sphere.

This praxis can be discerned in the appointment and delegation letters exchanged between the ʿAbbasid caliph and Mamluk sultan, which Ibn Jamaʿa was involved in drafting. Such letters were more than formulaic exchanges, rather, the result of a complex and negotiated constitutional process. This is attested to by the chronicle *Tarikh al-salatin wa-al-ʿasakir* (*The History of Sultans and Military Commanders*), authored by the prominent secretary

---

[118] El-Merheb, 'Political Censure', 370.

[119] Ibid.

[120] Section seventeen titled *Regarding the dhimma Contract and its Provisions*, *Tahrir*, 248–63.

Shafiʿ Ibn ʿAli (d. 730/1330).[121] This work revealed the complex process of drafting such letters, which involved a considerable contribution by the judiciary and the chancery and in which Ibn Jamaʿa, Shafiʿ Ibn ʿAli and other experts participated. Furthermore, this process was negotiated among sultan, caliph, jurists, judges, secretaries and *amirs*, albeit with differing degrees of influence. By examining these letters, we can see how Ibn Jamaʿa's political thought was put into practice in early Mamluk political history.

Tarikh al-salatin takes us into the corridors of power that Ibn Jamaʿa walked and enables us to see at close range his constitutional contribution when power changed hands. The work attests to the importance of dismissal, appointment and delegation letters during the events that surrounded the fall of Baybars al-Jashankir and the third reinstatement of al-Nasir Muhammad.[122] According to Shafiʿ Ibn ʿAli, when Baybars al-Jashankir felt that the return of al-Nasir was imminent, he 'turned to the judges to seek a legal opinion against our lord the sultan [al-Nasir] regarding his [alleged] self-dismissal from rule', which was provided by some jurists.[123] Moreover, Baybars al-Jashankir – at the behest of these jurists – turned to caliph al-Mustakfi bi-Allah. The caliph invalidated the sultanate of al-Nasir on the basis of a legal opinion (*fatwa*), which he pronounced in an annulment in a public letter and from the pulpit. This letter confirmed Baybars al-Jashankir as the lawful sultan and announced the caliph's intent to join him in battle against al-Nasir.[124] However, when al-Nasir entered Cairo and regained the seat of the sultanate, the caliph needed to exonerate himself. He claimed that he had confessed earlier to chief judge Ibn Jamaʿa that he was under duress when

---

121 I am very grateful to Gowaart Van Den Bossche for bringing this important source to my attention. Gowaart, furthermore, successfully identified the author as Shafiʿ Ibn ʿAli. The *Tarikh al-salatin* title is found on the manuscript and must be a later addition; the actual title is unknown, although Shafiʿ Ibn ʿAli does refer to it as *Sirat al-Malik al-Nasir Muhammad*. Refer to Gowaart Van Den Bossche, 'Literarisierung Reconsidered in the Context of Sultanic Biography: The Case of Shāfiʿ b. ʿAlī's Sīrat al-Nāṣir Muḥammad (BnF MS Arabe 1705)', in Jo Van Steenbergen and Maya Termonia (eds), *New Readings in Arabic Historiography from Late Medieval Egypt and Syria* (Leiden: Brill, 2021), 466–89.

122 These events are corroborated by Ibn al-Dawadari, *Kanz*, 9:177–185 and especially 184–5.

123 Shafiʿ Ibn ʿAli, *Tarikh al-salatin wa-al-ʿasakir*, MS Bibliothèque nationale de France, Paris, Arabe 1705, fol. 89 a & b. Refer to fn. 125, below.

124 Ibid., fol. 95a. Furthermore, refer to fol. 90a, where it says that al-Nasir assured his soldiers that 'there will no bloodshed among Muslims', which suggests that the caliph's letter was a source of concern as it provided legal ground for war against al-Nasir.

he had issued the letter of annulment.[125] Later, the caliph, witnessed by all the chief judges of Egypt and Syria, attested 'willingly and voluntarily' that the rightful sultan was al-Nasir Muhammad and that the earlier opinion he had uttered under duress against the sultan was invalid.[126] At this point, the judges (*al-hukkam*) – including Ibn Jamaʿa – endorsed the lawfulness of the sultanate of al-Nasir.[127] Subsequently, the judges and the jurists convened in the absence of the sultan in order to examine and confirm his appointment by the caliph. They agreed 'after careful inspection and examination that [al-Nasir's appointment] is confirmed in the finest manner'.[128] Ibn Jamaʿa was at the centre of this process, which was carefully crafted so as to appear to be transparent and impartial. Finally, Shafiʿ Ibn ʿAli produced the content of the appointment (*taqlid*), which included the 'renewed oath (*ʿahd*) from the commander of the believers [caliph] to our lord the sultan' and annulled the earlier *fatwa*.[129]

Although military power was undoubtedly the decisive factor in appointing a new sultan, what followed was, as this example shows, a negotiated process of confirmation in which the scholars and administrators commanded a reasonable degree of influence. This was a process of legitimation that was based on reciprocal delegations and appointments between caliph, judges and sultan, which were drafted and orchestrated by leading judges and secretaries. Shafiʿ Ibn ʿAli related that the chief judges 'asked our lord the sultan to confirm and renew their appointments to bring bliss upon bliss and so that they can be effective in implementing the law; the sultan confirmed their appointments in the presence of the commander of the believers in the best lawful manner and they [the judges] accepted this rightful appointment and clear delegation'.[130] Shafiʿ Ibn ʿAli explained that he had personally drafted

125 Ibid., fol. 95a–96b. According to al-Maqrizi, when al-Nasir Muhammad entered Cairo, he addressed Ibn Jamaʿa, '"Qadi! How can you issue a legal opinion [allowing] Muslims to fight me?" So he [Ibn Jamaʿa] replied, "God forbid! The *fatwa* was simply based on the content of the enquiry of the one who requested it (*al-mustafti*)."' Al-Maqrizi, *Suluk*, 2:444; see also Ibn Taghribirdi, *Nujum*, 9:7–8.

126 There is an interesting gloss on the margin of the MS: 'By God he is not the commander of the faithful but he is as free as a chained monkey . . .' in *Tarikh al-salatin wa-al-ʿasakir*, fol. 95b.

127 Ibid., fol.95b.

128 Ibid., fol. 96a.

129 Ibid., fol. 97.

130 Ibid., fol. 96a–b.

the appointment letters of the judges and enclosed them within the renewed 'covenant' by the caliph to the sultan.[131] Given the efforts put into it, this procedure of reciprocal appointment and legitimation seems to have been taken relatively seriously. Although it was not a case of appointment in return for legitimation, the judges felt influential enough to ask the victorious sultan to confirm their jobs.

Shafiʿ Ibn ʿAli carefully differentiated between appointment (*taqlid*) and delegation (*tafwid*), and highlighted the complex process of drafting both. The sultan's appointment by the caliph was based on a special form of delegation, the same delegation of the vizierate (*tafwid muwazara*) that was cited in the *Tahrir* and discussed above. The *taqlid* letter mentioned that both sultan and caliph acted as:

> counterparts in mutual cooperation and assistance (*mutakatifin, mutawazinin, mutaʿadidin*) in the presence of the chief judges of the Muslims in Egypt and Syria, of those absent and those present, and the prominent *amirs* who loosen and bind (*umaraʾ al-hall wa-al-ʿaqd*), and those experts who made this delegation impeccable, and the commander of the faithful renounced what he was forced to declare and he renewed the delegation of the vizierate (*tafwid muwazara*) to our lord the sultan . . .[132]

The author boasted about the role of chancery experts, under his supervision, in securing their sultan an 'impeccable' form of delegation, one that could not be questioned in the future.

Shafiʿ Ibn ʿAli explained that the authorities granted under this type of delegation of the vizierate included 'all the authorities (*wilayat*) that exist under the roots of piety', indicating the full authorities of the *imam* but within the limitations of the *shariʿa*.[133] Furthermore, the author detailed the constitutional process of drafting the delegation. First, the chief judges 'attested to the delegation and executed it', meaning that the judiciary ratified it. In the second step of the process, as Shafiʿ Ibn ʿAli explained, the caliph took the delegation to the chancery (*diwan al-inshaʾ wa-al-mukatabat*) to

[131] Ibid.
[132] Ibid., fol. 103b.
[133] Ibid., fol. 104a.

'draft' the appointment (*taqlid*).[134] At this point, and in a sophisticated division of labour to complete this constitutional process, the experts of the administration drafted the final text of the appointment based on the choice of delegation that had been ratified by the judges.

Shafiʿ Ibn ʿAli produced the content of the appointment:

> [The commander of the believers] has delegated what falls under the duties and authorities of his caliphate and *imamate* [in Arabic both *khilafatuhu* and *imamatuhu*] from: attending [to his subjects]; augmented acts of justice; charity and enquiry [about the subjects' conditions]; raising armies; coining his [the sultan's] magnanimous name along with the name of the commander of faithful on the *dirham* and the *dinar*; assigning duties and dealing with the crooked; raising soldiers and sacrificing himself in fighting the enemies of God; bestowing benevolently; appointing judges and governors and selecting competent regents; raising lawful taxes and spending them on their right ends, and repossessing them from the usurper; attending to the frontiers; carrying out the prescribed punishments; protecting the lands of Islam; assisting the troubled; striving to reclaim the [corruptly] seized money whether it is one *dirham* or thousands; acting in justice equally to an *amir* or a common person; attending to the plaintiff; following constantly in his rulings the book [Qur'an] and the *sunna*; and appointing the proper commander to his soldiers . . .[135]

This constitutional process and the ensuing appointment (*taqlid*) was an example of the praxis of Ibn Jamaʿa's thought. There are several indications that this was indeed a case of putting the *Tahrir*'s tripartite conception of *imam*, caliph and sultan into practice. First, as chief judge Ibn Jamaʿa was at the heart of this process of selecting the type of delegation and drafting the appointment. Secondly, the duties of the sultan as listed in this appointment are nearly identical to the *imam*'s duties as stipulated in the *Tahrir* and the *Mukhtasar*. Thirdly, and most importantly, Ibn Jamaʿa's mark on this process was clear in the way it distinguished between the authorities of caliph and *imam*: this distinction between '*khilafatuhu*' and '*imamatuhu*' within

[134] Ibid., fol. 104a & b.

[135] Ibid., fol. 104b–105a.

the delegation of power and the appointment letter is a trademark of the *Tahrir*. As mentioned above, within this tripartite conception the coercive sultan might be *imam* in the absence or presence of a caliph. The caliph, on the other hand, was the Qurashi commander of the believers as was, in this case, the nominal ʿAbbasid caliph of Cairo. Once the sultan seizes power his delegation becomes effective and he becomes the *imam*. By securing for the sultan the delegation of both offices, caliph and *imam*, Ibn Jamaʿa sealed the delegation and the appointment impeccably; the eventuality of the caliph al-Mustakfi issuing a future *fatwa* against al-Nasir Muhammad in favour of another wielder of power (like Baybars al-Jashankir) was no longer possible constitutionally as he had relinquished his caliphal (i.e., his legitimating) authority. As such, Ibn Jamaʿa not only secured the full powers of the *imam* for the sultan, but also any legitimating authority of the caliph. As per the *Tahrir*'s conception of political authority, this was an instance of the caliphate being unnecessary. Ibn Jamaʿa was by this time a qualified expert in the political, judicial and administrative spheres of the Mamluk sultanate and capable of navigating such a complex process between caliph, jurists, judges, secretaries and influential *amir*s.

The constitutional ideals of the rule of law, limited government and delegation of power were reflected in the choice of the renewed delegation (*tafwid muwazara*). This type of delegation, which was carefully selected by Ibn Jamaʿa and other judges, jurists and chancery secretaries, guaranteed, as explained in the *Tahrir*, the full delegation of the *imam*'s powers to the sultan in Egypt and Syria despite the presence of a recognised caliph. Among the various delegations mentioned in the *Tahrir*, this selection suited best the interests of the sultan and, concurrently, the various concerns that the powerful stakeholders may have harboured. It allowed the judges, chancery secretaries and the professionalised administration to participate in the process of confirming the sultan. The final version of the caliphal appointment (*taqlid*) mentioned a specific form of delegation (*tafwid*) according to which the caliph, if he wished to, could no longer revoke his appointment to the sultan. This may have not been a unique case in the early Mamluk period, but it is the best-documented case to be found hitherto owing to meticulous record-keeping by Shafiʿ Ibn ʿAli.

Conclusion

Ibn Jamaʿa's career and political thought is edifying as to the development of pre-modern Islamic practicable conceptions of the rule of law. His theory was not a mere repetition of earlier political texts, but one shaped by his prominent career and extensive experience in judicial and administrative branches of government, which in turn influenced events in the political sphere. As such, this chapter has shown that Islamic political thought was not written 'post-mortem' or as a simple justification for established political realities; rather, this thought was at the heart of unfolding political events in what is here termed praxis of political thought. While military force was the decisive factor in attaining political power, there still existed a negotiated constitutional process that rulers seem to have respected and that regulated some aspects of public life.

Ibn Jamaʿa presented a Shafiʿi strain of political thought that resembled a proto-constitution or an official *madhhab* of the state. Within his all-encompassing *Tahrir*, the author upheld the ideals of the rule of law, limited government and delegation of power. Ibn Jamaʿa relied on a long Shafiʿi political tradition that included names like al-Mawardi, al-Juwayni, al-Ghazali and others in order to provide his own conception of the rule of law. He used Shafiʿi legal reasoning and juristic conceptions to provide a new system of checks and balances to limit the ruler's discretionary exercise of power. As such, Ibn Jamaʿa argued for a creative tripartite conception of political authorities: *imam*, caliph and *sultan*. Furthermore, and within this concern for the rule of law, he provided a novel approach to the rules of war in Islam. The *Tahrir* also highlighted a concern for limited government by promoting the professionalised judiciary and administration and a detailed treatment of various senior offices including viziers, *amir*s, judges, market inspectors and others. This aimed at securing, as far as was possible, the interests of the populace, the smooth running of government, and the just dispensing of justice outside the discretionary power of the ruling elites and independently of their struggles. Moreover, the *Tahrir*'s theory of delegation aimed at guaranteeing a resilient and legitimate transfer of powers to various sultanic, political, judicial and administrative authorities. Through this theory, Ibn Jamaʿa attempted to guarantee delegation of powers and the proper functioning of government in every eventuality. The *Tahrir*'s theory of delegation manifested as praxis during the events that led to the third reign of al-Nasir Muhammad Ibn Qalawun.

This synthesis by Ibn Jamaʿa is the most articulate expression of Shafiʿi political thought available to us. It resembles an official *madhhab* of the state, a proto-constitution that aimed to provide answers to every aspect of public life: political authority, main offices and functions, justice, administration and taxation, and even the rules of war. Later thinkers saw it in exactly this way. For instance, and as discussed in Chapter 5, subsequent Shafiʿi jurists like al-Subki understood it well and remembered it as the golden age of Shafiʿi political thought.[136]

A contextualist reading of Islamic political thought in texts such as the *Tahrir* shows that there are no 'perennial' conceptions of political authority in Islam. This contextual study of the development and crystallisation of Ibn Jamaʿa's ideas has made it possible to explicate the originality of his thought despite his heavy reliance on earlier authors like al-Mawardi, al-Juwayni and al-Ghazali. Without such a contextual reading of the *Tahrir*, this research would have missed Ibn Jamaʿa's constitutional concerns and been misled into repeating the erroneous assumption that it was another unrefined repetition of the theory of the caliphate.

[136] Al-Subki, *Muʿid al-niʿam wa-mubid al-niqam*, ed. Muhammad ʿAli al-Najjar, Abu Zayd Shalabi and Muhammad Abu al-ʿUyun (Cairo: Maktabat al-Khanji, 1993), 13–21. After mentioning the caliph, al-Subki states that the sultan is the greatest *imam* (*al-imam al-aʿzam*) (16). Consequently, Ibn Jamaʿa's tripartite view is reiterated by al-Subki, who considers the sultan to be the most effective – but not the only – form of *imamate* while still mentioning the caliph.

3

Sufi Political Thought

The present chapter covers the Sufi contribution to thirteenth-century Islamic political thought from the Syro-Egyptian lands. It treats Sufi conceptions of political authority, the Sufi concern for moderating the exercise of power, and the intellectual and socio-political milieu in which these ideas emerged. This chapter will highlight how the Sufis theorised for the legitimacy of the coercive power of the sultans, how they upheld the case for the rule of law using their own proprietary political language, which benefited from a mystical and Islamised system of ethics, and how they were active participants in the political sphere of the Mamluk sultanate. Throughout this discussion, a caveat is warranted on the use of the 'Sufi' epithet: it is appropriate only within very detailed historical, geographical and sometimes individual contexts that will be defined below.

A fresh analysis of the still unpublished treatise titled *Misbah al-hidaya fi tariq al-imama* (*The Guiding Lamp to the Path of the Imamate*) shows that there was a *distinctly* Sufi strain of political thought during the early Mamluk period.[1] It is considered here as distinctly Sufi since it was presented by its anonymous author to his dedicatee as a uniquely Sufi conception of the imamate and the ideal of the rule of law. By scrutinising how the author of the treatise strived to reflect this Sufi distinctiveness, several aims are achieved in parallel, including tracing the roots and influences of this Sufi treatise; examining the intellectual milieu within which its author flourished; delimiting the contours of the Sufi political theory that was proposed in this treatise; and identifying its links to other *madhhabs* and intellectual currents.

[1] Unknown, *Misbah al-hidaya fi tariq al-imama*, MS Bodleian Library, Oxford, OR. 579. First brought to light by Madelung in his 'Treatise on the Imamate'.

Furthermore, I will highlight the remarkable agency of the mysterious author of the treatise in moulding his work in order to achieve his aims towards the dedicatee and to present the *Misbah* as a distinctly Sufi work.

The *Misbah* is a Mamluk Sufi attempt to conceptualise political authority and make the case for the rule of law in a distinctly Sufi fashion. It was authored at a point in Islamic history when Sufi thought was burgeoning in the central, eastern and western parts of the Islamic world and when the political context of the Syro-Egyptian lands stimulated the elaboration of several sometimes competing strains of political thought. The disciples of great Sufi figures like Najm al-Din Kobra (d. 617/1220), Shihab al-Din ʿUmar al-Suhrawardi (632/1234), Ibn ʿArabi (d. 638/1240), Abu al-Hasan al-Shadhili (d. 656/1258), Jalal al-Din al-Rumi (d. 672/1273) and Ahmad al-Badawi (d. 674/1276) spread throughout the Islamic world and permeated all social groups. It is in this flourishing world of Sufism that our mysterious author produced and dedicated the *Misbah* to sultan Baybars. As such, this distinctly Sufi work of political thought was the manifestation of a political context that encouraged the production of political thought and, similarly, the result of a Sufi intellectual context that witnessed great advances in speculative Sufism. Accordingly, there are important conclusions that will be drawn here regarding the main tenets of the author's political theory and his agency in using the sources he relied upon, in addition to some assumptions made about his personal ideology, education and social milieu.

The general question of Sufi political ideas still warrants further investigation, despite the significant advances made recently in the study of Sufism. There is still much work to be done to place Sufi conceptions of political authority within wider Islamic political thought; hopefully this monograph will offer a contribution to this end. In particular, no research has yet been done that places Sufi political ideas on a par with the political thought expressed by the jurists of the four *madhhab*s or the authors of mirrors for princes and administrative manuals. Sufi political opinion has thus far not been considered a serious contributor to the existing strains of Islamic political thought that existed in the Ayyubid and Mamluk periods, so scholarship has not yet made an attempt to link treatises that are, in the view of this book, closely connected. There are two main reasons for the lack of such research and the failure to place Sufi political ideas in this wider framework. First, *madhhab*-based political thought has not been studied hitherto. Secondly, until the authoritative and long-overdue work of Nathan Hofer on thirteenth-century Sufism in Egypt and Huseyin Yilmaz's recent monograph on mystical influences on Ottoman political thought, Sufi political opinion – and Sufism more generally – was incorrectly regarded as a completely opposite category to that of the jurists.[2] This chapter will complement Hofer's research by proposing that the production of treatises of political thought was another 'Sufi thing' that contributed to the popularisation of Sufism.[3] Likewise, this chapter relates to Yilmaz's work as it highlights an earlier, pre-Ottoman precedent where the imamate was packaged in mystical and moral language that was relevant to the early Mamluk context. More will be said about both seminal monographs below.

It is imperative to underline the commonality between Sufi and the jurists' political thought. The political theory advanced by Sufi treatises such as the *Misbah* was deeply rooted in and complementary to the successive political works of al-Mawardi, al-Juwayni, al-Ghazali and others. Historically, and unlike the jurists, the Sufis did not provide much theory because, in principle, they were supposed to maintain a distance from politics and the corruptive effects of associating with power and authority. Furthermore, some of them did not subscribe to the idea of political leaders being solely of Qurashi descent, but rather adopted an idea closer to the heavenly mandate of power. Nevertheless, Sufis were visibly and consistently at the heart of Islamic political life and closely associated and involved with rulers, as is evident in the case of the ʿAbbasid caliph al-Nasir li-Din-Allah (r. 575/1180–622/1225) and his close adviser al-Suhrawardi (539/1144/5–632/1234). Furthermore, scholarly generalisations about the Sufis adopting Turkic notions of the heavenly mandate of power to Islam are compelling and sometimes accurate. However, such ideas did in many respects complement the theories of Sunni jurists. In this notion of heavenly mandate, the Sufis overlapped with al-Mawardi's theory on usurpation (*imarat al-istila*ʾ), and the successive and uninterrupted line of later Shafiʿi political ideas of al-Juwayni, al-Ghazali and Ibn Jamaʿa regarding the requirement for the sultan. This should not

[2] Hofer, *The Popularisation of Sufism*; Huseyin Yilmaz, *Caliphate Redefined: The Mystical Turn in Ottoman Political Thought* (Princeton, NJ: Princeton University Press, 2017).

[3] Hofer, *The Popularisation of Sufism*, 10–11, 13.

come as a surprise; these Shafiʿi jurists were Sufis. Likewise, 'political' Sufis, including al-Suhrawardi and Najm al-Din Daya Razi (573/1177–654/1256), were Sunni and Ashʿari, and al-Suhrawardi was Shafiʿi too. This will become clearer with the analysis of this Sufi political text. First, the spheres of Sufis, jurists and scholars should be demarcated.

The Sufis and the Production of Political Thought

The latest advances in the study of Sufism have dispelled the ingrained misunderstanding of the relation between Sufis and jurists. Thanks to these advances, it is now possible to also argue how interrelated the two groups were in the production of political thought and to show that both categories emerged from common intellectual and social milieux. Until recently, the study of Sufism, not only in the Ayyubid and Mamluk context, was blurred by a serious impediment to understanding the popularisation of Sufism. Before the publication of Hofer's monograph, *The Popularisation of Sufism in Ayyubid and Mamluk Egypt, 1173–1325,* the advance of Sufism was often considered a spiritual or mystical popular reaction to the legalism of normative Islam as represented by the jurists. Only al-Ghazali (d. 505/1111), it was thought, succeeded in bringing the two supposedly opposite sides closer. Hofer refuted, very convincingly, three main misconceptions in this narrative, 'that the Sufis were socially and culturally distinct from the jurists; that the social formation of the jurists preceded that of the Sufis; and that non-Sufi Islam is inadequate to the religious needs of the populace'.[4] Indeed, the popularisation of Sufism permeated all levels of society, 'elite and non-elite alike'.[5] Often jurists were Sufis, as in the case of Ibn Jamaʿa, and, as evident throughout this book, this was also frequently the case among authors of treatises of political thought during the thirteenth century.

In the context of the late Ayyubid and early Mamluk period, being Sufi meant different things. Sufism in Cairo and Damascus during the thirteenth century reflected this diversity. In the case of Cairo, Hofer's study portrayed very distinct kinds of Sufi. A simple look into the differences between the state-sponsored Sufis of Saʿid al-Suʿada *khanqah*, the Shadhili brotherhood

4 Hofer, *The Popularisation of Sufism*, 7.

5 Ibid., 6.

patronised by Ayyubid and Mamluk rulers, and the Sufis of Upper Egypt, who were hostile to the state, reflected how complicated and diverse Egyptian Sufism was; Hofer noted that, 'The [Sufi] epithet only makes sense within very specific historical, social and political contexts.'[6] Similarly, the situation of Sufism in Damascus reflected an equally diverse world of Sufi groups.[7] Despite the 'ascetic' and 'mystical' aspects of Sufi groups, some Damascene Sufis were clearly close to the highest circles of power. In Syria as much as in Egypt, the Sufi epithet held many different meanings.

The banu Hamawiyya, a renowned Sufi Damascene family, reflected this diversity. The life and career of some members of this family, the offices and political roles they assumed, and their political writings epitomised the interrelatedness between Syro-Egyptian politics, Sufism and the production of political thought. This prominent Damascene family reflected how the two categories of Sufis and jurists were in no way mutually exclusive. Furthermore, it showed how both categories were closely entangled with the sphere of rulers, administrators and statesmen. Most significantly, a member of this extended Damascene Sufi family authored a work of advice literature in the thirteenth century that has come down to us. The treatise, titled *Kitab al-Siyasa al-mulukiyya* (*The Book of Kingly Rulership*), was authored by Taj al-Din Abu Muhammad ʿAbd Allah b. Muhammad b. ʿUmar b. ʿAli b. Muhammad al-Sarakhsi al-Dimashqi al-Shafiʿi Ibn Hamawiyya (d. 642/1244), and most likely dedicated to the Ayyubid sultan al-Malik al-Kamil.[8] Although this text was not concerned with presenting uniquely Sufi ideas, like the *Misbah* did, it was valuable as it attested to the production of political thought by a Sufi who was also a statesman and a jurist.[9]

---

6 Ibid., 25.

7 Louis Pouzet, *Damas au VIIe–XIIIe siècle: vie et structures religieuses d'une métropole islamique* (Beirut: Dar el-Machreq, 1991), 207–43.

8 On the dedication to al-Kamil refer to Sibt Ibn al-Jawzi, *Mirʾat al-zaman fi tarikh al-aʿyan*, ed. Salman Al-Juburi, vol. 22 (Beirut: Dar al-Kutub al-ʿIlmiya, 2013), 384. His date of birth is 572/1177 according to Sibt Ibn al-Jawzi, or – and this is less likely – 566/1170 according to al-Dhahabi, *Siyar aʿlam al-nubalaʾ*, ed. Shuʿayb al-Arnaʾut, 25 vols (Beirut: Muʾassasat al-Risalah, 1991), 23:96–7. Refer to Abu Shama, *Tarajim rijal al-qarnayn al-sadis wa-al-sabiʿ al-maʿruf bi al-dhayl ʿala al-rawdatayn*, ed. ʿIzzat al-ʿAttar al-Husayni (Beirut: Dar al-Jil, 1974), 174.

9 Ibn Hamawiyya, *Kitab al-Siyasa al-mulukiyya*, MS Topkapi, Istanbul, TSMK A. 1116. I am grateful to Murat Sonmez, to the staff of Topkapi Palace directorate, and especially to Esra Müyesseroglu for all the support they provide to researchers, which made it possible for me to locate this manuscript.

The case of the banu Hamawiyya shows that Sufis operated at the heart of Syro-Egyptian political authority. This family of Sufi and Shafiʿi jurists played an important role in the politics of the late Ayyubid period and became central to Ayyubid dynastic life. Not all the banu Hamawiyya led an ascetic life, which led Louis Pouzet to observe that the banu Hamawiyya, 'semblait peu compatible avec les exigences d'une vie à base de renoncement et d'humilité'; they were nevertheless Sufi and represented an active and influential strain of Syro-Egyptian Sufism.[10] The first member of this family to settle in Damascus from Khurasan, when he was appointed inspector of the Sufi institutions in Syria by Nur al-Din Zangi (r. 541/1146–569/1174), was ʿImad al-Din Abu al-Fath ʿUmar b. ʿAli Ibn Hamawiyya al-Juwayni (d. 577/1181).[11] He then became head of the Sufis in Damascus (*shaykh al-shuyukh*); after his death, his family dominated this position for a century.[12] ʿImad al-Din ʿUmar had two sons. The first was Sadr al-Din Abu al-Hasan Muhammad (543/1148–617/1220), who was very close to the Ayyubid sultan, al-Kamil. The post then fell to Sadr al-Din's sons, of which he had four and who were often referred to as *Awlad al-Shaykh*. They enjoyed distinguished careers as statesmen and three of them occupied the position of *shaykh al-shuyukh*.[13] No doubt the most distinguished of the *Awlad al-Shaykh* was Fakhr al-Din Yusuf (580/1184–647/1250), who served sultan al-Kamil as an emissary to the caliph and as an ambassador to Frederick II Hohenstaufen (1194–1250); some sources claim he befriended the emperor and exchanged letters with him, and that Frederick II even complained to Fakhr al-Din about the Pope.[14] The second son of Imad al-Din ʿUmar was Taj al-Din Abu Muhammad ʿAbdallah, who was a bit more adventurous. He served the Almohads in Morocco and, upon his return to Damascus, succeeded his brother as *shaykh al-shuyukh*. Taj al-Din was a 'scholar in law, hadith, mysticism, medicine, geometry, and history, he was the author of

---

10 Pouzet, *Damas au VIIe–XIIIe siècle*, 213; for more on the Sufism of *Awlad al-Shaykh* refer to Hofer, 'Office of the "Chief Sufi"', 25.

11 Anne-Marie Eddé, 'Awlād Al-Shaykh', *EI*[3]; Hofer, 'Office of the "Chief Sufi"', 12.

12 For more on the post of *shaykh al-shuyukh* refer to Hofer, 'Office of the "Chief Sufi"'.

13 Ibid., 19, 21; 'Only Fakhr al-Dīn Yūsuf was not attached to any religious office, despite being trained as an ʿ*ālim*'; only one of them occupied the position according to Eddé, 'Awlād Al-Shaykh'.

14 Mohamad El-Merheb, 'Louis IX in Medieval Arabic Sources: The Saint, the King, and the Sicilian Connection', *Al-Masāq* 28(3) (2016): 285.

several works';[15] based on my examination of his hitherto unstudied political treatise, I add Arabic philosophy to the list.

Taj al-Din Ibn Hamawiyya's *al-Siyasa al-mulukiyya* is a typical specimen of Arabic gnomologia.[16] The treatise consists of collections of aphorisms and anecdotes mostly transmitted from or attributed to the Greek philosophers, as is characteristic of this popular genre of Arabic advice literature, which adopted and developed its Hellenistic prototype.[17] Despite facing the usual challenging issues of transmission, sources and cross-influences, especially as Taj al-Din Ibn Hamawiyya freely quoted, omitted and reshaped his sources, it is nonetheless possible to ascertain *al-Siyasa al-mulukiyya*'s overlap with Ayyubid masterpieces such as *Lubab al-Adab* (*The Kernels of Refinement*) of Usama Ibn Munqidh (d. 584/1188) and the *ʿUyun al-anbaʾ fi tabaqat al-atibbaʾ* (*The Best Accounts of the Classes of Physicians*) of Ibn Abi Usaybiʿa (b. after 590/1193, d. 668/1269–70).[18] Such works of the Ayyubid period, especially those by Ibn Abi Usaybiʿa, seem to have valued the knowledge of the Greek philosophers and considered their wisdom as essential.[19] Like its Ayyubid counterparts, it is also evident that *al-Siyasa al-mulukiyya* greatly benefited from the *Mukhtar al-hikam wa-mahasin al-kalim* (*A Collection of Wise Maxims and Beneficial Words*; 440/1048–9), which was authored by the Arab philosopher al-Mubashshir Ibn Fatik, who transmitted and attributed to the Greek philosophers and 'the learned men of the past' such as 'Seth, Hermes, Pythagoras, Plato, Aristotle, Alexander, Galen, and Luqmān'.[20] This founding work was translated in medieval Europe between

[15] Eddé, 'Awlād Al-Shaykh'.

[16] Perhaps this explains why *al-Siyasa al-mulukiyya* is sometimes wrongly listed in the catalogues as a work of Plato.

[17] Refer to the seminal study of Dimitri Gutas, *Greek Wisdom Literature in Arabic Translation: A Study of the Graeco-Arabic Gnomologia* (New Haven, CT: American Oriental Society, 1975). Refer also to Marlow, 'Advice and Advice Literature', *EI*[3].

[18] For more on these texts, refer to Paul M. Cobb, 'Usāma Ibn Munqidh's Lubāb Al-Ādāb (The Kernels of Refinement): Autobiographical and Historical Excerpts', *Al-Masāq* 18(1) (2006): 67–8; Emilie Savage-Smith et al. (eds), *A Literary History of Medicine: The 'Uyūn Al-Anbā' Fī ṭabaqāt Al-Aṭibbā', of Ibn Abīuṣaybi'ah*, Handbook of Oriental Studies. Section One, Near and Middle East, 5 vols (Leiden: Brill, 2020), 1:134.

[19] Savage-Smith et al., *A Literary History of Medicine*, refer especially to ch. 7, Simon Swain, 'The Greek Chapters and Galen'.

[20] Refer to Marlow, 'Advice and Advice Literature', *EI*[3]. See also the useful introduction by 'Abd al-Rahman Badawi in Mubashshir Ibn Fatik, *Mukhtar al-hikam wa-mahasin al-kalim* (Beirut: al-Mu'assasa al-'Arabiya li-al-Dirasat wa-al-Nashr, 1980).

the thirteenth and late fifteenth centuries into Spanish, Latin, French, Occitan and English.

These findings render *al-Siyasa al-mulukiyya* of great value to the study of the history of Sufi political thought.[21] This text offers desiderata of evidence related to the production of political thought by Sufis in the central lands of Islam and to its incubating intellectual and socio-political milieu. First, and most importantly, *al-Siyasa al-mulukiyya*, unlike the *Misbah*, was not a Sufi text per se but a work of political advice authored by a statesman who was, similarly, a chief Sufi. Its author thrived before 1244, that is, three or four decades before the *Misbah* was written. Consequently, it attests to a lively engagement of Sufis in writing works of political thought concurrently with the surge in Shafiʿi political writing that characterised the thirteenth century. Secondly, *al-Siyasa al-mulukiyya* provides, along with the *Misbah*, proof of the importance of the central lands of Islam in the production of political thought by Sufi authors who were influenced, one way or another, by Graeco-Arabic philosophy. As such, it allows Sufi ethical systems of moderating the exercise of power to be linked to Islamised Hellenistic political concepts, as I shall demonstrate below. Thirdly, it shows that the rise of political thought written by Sufis preceded the Mamluks and, as such, was pertinent to the development of Sufism within the wider context of the late ʿAbbasid world. Fourthly, by pinning down a work of political thought to a specific Sufi author, Taj al-Din, about whom and whose family the sources spell much out, we are rewarded with an unprecedented appreciation of the milieu within which the production of this thought took place. Based on what we know about Taj al-Din and the banu Hamawiyya, one can draw the following preliminary depiction: it was a staunchly Sufi, Shafiʿi and Ashʿari milieu with strong personal and professional ties to the Islamic East, and in the case of Taj al-Din to the Islamic West.[22] This sketch concurs with Hofer's conclusions on the typical profile of the holder of the office of *shaykh al-shuyukh* as originating from 'typically Iraq or Khurasan' and primarily 'being a jurist,

[21] Ibn Hamawiyya, *al-Siyasa al-mulukiyya*.

[22] Interestingly, such findings fit perfectly with the profile Julie Scott Meisami proposed for the unknown author of the *Bahr al-fawaʾid* (*Sea of Precious Virtues*), an anonymous Persian treatise composed in Syria in the mid-twelfth century. Scott Meisami noted, 'he was a Sunnī, an Ashʿarī, and an adherent of the Shāfiʿī legal school' and probably a religious scholar brought from the East to Syria in Scott Meisami, *The Sea of Precious Virtues*, xii.

having trained in Shāfiʿi jurisprudence and Ashʿari theology'.[23] Fifthly, and lastly, through the life of its author, *al-Siyasa al-mulukiyya* provides direct evidence of the interrelatedness of political Ashʿari Sufism in Syria, Egypt, Iraq, Khurasan, Anatolia, the Maghrib and beyond.

The banu Hamawiyya offer one final precious clue to the study of the history of Islamic political thought. The family's social networks demonstrate the solid links between the Sufi milieu that produced political thought during the thirteenth century back to the Ashʿari theologians and Shafiʿi jurists Imam al-Haramayn al-Juwayni and al-Ghazali. This conclusion will be confirmed subsequently by textual analysis of the *Misbah*, but I shall highlight it here in terms of social networks.[24] The grandfather of ʿImad al-Din ʿUmar b. Hamawiyya, the first *shaykh al-shuyukh* in Syria, was Abu ʿAbd Allah Muhammad al-Juwayni (d. 530/1135), a renowned Sufi in Khurasan and Iraq. Most importantly, he was a student of Imam al-Haramayn al-Juwayni. Furthermore, ʿImad al-Din's father, Najm al-Din Abu al-Hasan ʿAli (d. 539/1144), was a Sufi who studied under al-Ghazali. These strong ties between the banu Hamawiyya and al-Juwayni and al-Ghazali may have prompted Nur al-Din to appoint ʿImad al-Din as his chief Sufi; Hofer concluded that this 'Ashʿari/Shāfiʿi/Ghazāli background would become the *sine qua non* for the office of the Chief Sufi under the Ayyubids and early Mamluks'.[25] As such, the banu Hamawiyya came to epitomise the flourishing of Syro-Egyptian Ashʿari–Shafiʿi Sufism and, moreover, highlighted the strong links between the production of Sufi political thought and both al-Juwayni and al-Ghazali. This conclusion will be reaffirmed below when the sources and influences of the *Misbah* are identified.

Sufism and Politics

The case of the banu Hamawiyya was not an isolated instance, the Sufis played important roles throughout the political history of the late ʿAbbasid period. This family is just one of numerous cases that confirm the interrelatedness between politics and Sufism, which preceded the Hamawiyyas and continued well after them. I argued above for the need to analyse the

---

[23] Hofer, 'Office of the "Chief Sufi"', 1.

[24] Ibid., 12–13, for a detailed discussion of these networks.

[25] Ibid., 13.

rise of Sufi political thought within a wider late ʿAbbasid context because this period displayed striking cases of powerful Sufis playing a role in defining the political ideology of the late caliphs of Baghdad and, later, exerting political influence on the Mamluk ruling elite. This seemed like a foreseeable development in ʿAbbasid history. Sufism had played a pivotal role and came to pervade all groups and strata of Islamic society. The political elites and the *ʿulamaʾ* embraced Sufism, so did the common people in urban centres and remote villages, craftsmen and guildsmen, slaves and destitute social groups, and most notably soldiers. This contributed to the development of Sufi institutions like *khanqah*s, *zawiya*s and *ribat*s, which in turn further increased the political influence of Sufis. Not only did Sufism benefit from the patronage of rulers and the elites, it also played a role in politics and, in later ʿAbbasid times, came to contribute to and even helped to shape the ideology of the caliphate. I will detail below two selected cases of Sufi political influence that elucidate this wider late ʿAbbasid context.

The most notable instance was the relationship between the ʿAbbasid caliph al-Nasir li-Din Allah and the famous Sufi, Abu Hafs ʿUmar al-Suhrawardi.[26] Al-Nasir, intent on reviving the weakened ʿAbbasid caliphate by reshaping it as the spiritual and political focus of the Islamic world, found in al-Suhrawardi an able theorist and ally who could achieve this task. With this in mind, the caliph supported and personally joined a strain of *futuwwa* that was heavily infused with Sufism.[27] Under this arrangement, al-Suhrawardi provided the ideological foundations for the caliph's enterprise by envisioning a unification of *futuwwa* with Sufism (*tasawwuf*); although it must be noted here that the nature of al-Suhrawardi's ideology and political theory are still a topic of scholarly debate.[28] Additionally, al-Suhrawardi

[26] I rely here on Angelika Hartmann, 'Al-Suhrawardī' and 'al-Nāṣir Li-Dīn Allāh', in *EI²* and benefit from the seminal study of Erik S. Ohlander, *Sufism in an Age of Transition: 'Umar Al-Suhrawardī and the Rise of the Islamic Mystical Brotherhoods*, Islamic History and Civilization: Studies and Texts, vol. 71 (Leiden: Brill, 2008).

[27] Ibid. For a related reading, refer to the two recent articles by Salah Natij, ‚Murūʾa: Soucis et Interrogations éthiques Dans La Culture Arabe Classique (1ere Partie)', *Studia Islamica* 112 (2017): 206–63; (2e Partie), *Studia Islamica* 113 (2018): 1–55.

[28] For different opinions on this refer to Hartmann, 'Al-Suhrawardī' and 'al-Nāṣir Li-Dīn Allāh', in *EI²*; Ohlander, *Sufism in an Age of Transition*, 254–9; Mohsen Zakeri, 'From Futuwwa to Mystic Political Thought – The Caliph Al-Nāṣir Li-Dīn Allāh and Abū Ḥafṣ Suhrawardī's Theory of Government', in Shahrokh Raei (ed.), *Islamic Alternatives: Non-Mainstream Religion in Persianate*

posited that the *futuwwa* was part of Sufism and, later, advanced a political theory in which he harmonised the three pillars of *futuwwa*, Sufism and the caliphate.[29] *Futuwwa* continued well into the Mamluk period, yet there were more visible manifestations of Sufi influence on Mamluk politics.

Mamluk sultans, *amirs* and households continued to patronise Sufis and, at times, conceded considerable political power to them. Evidence for Sufi involvement in Mamluk politics and household power struggles is abundant, but I will limit my discussion to two well-studied cases that occurred under sultans Baybars, al-Nasir Muhammad and Baybars al-Jashankir. The first case is the sway that the Sufi *shaykh* Khidr al-Mihrani (d. 676/1277) held over Baybars. The second case is the rivalry between the powerful camp of the Sufi Nasr al-Manbiji (d. 719/1319) and Ibn Taymiyya's allies, which extended from Damascus to Cairo and reflected the active participation of Sufis in the Mamluk households' competition for power. So deep was the Sufi involvement in these Mamluk rivalries that one gets the distorted impression that the competing factions were Sufi and Hanbali rather than the households of Baybars al-Jashankir, *amir* Salar and al-Nasir Muhammad.[30]

I shall start with the case of *shaykh* Khidr al-Mihrani (d. 676/1277). The role he played during Baybars' reign was the paradigm of the distorted perception of Sufi influence: unruly, unerudite and dangerous.[31] Before his service to Baybars, *shaykh* Khidr is said to have led a disreputable and scandalous life. Baybars met Khidr on one of his campaigns, and when the *shaykh*'s predictions of some of the sultan's victories materialised the latter invited him to Egypt. According to another version, the two met when Baybars was still an *amir* and Khidr predicted Baybars' ascent to the throne. Be that as it may, Khidr quickly succeeded in exercising considerable influence on the

---

Societies, Göttinger Orientforschungen. III, Reihe, Iranica 16 (Wiesbaden: Harrassowitz, 2017), 35–9.

29 'Al-Nāṣir Li-Dīn Allāh', *EI*².

30 Ibn Taymiyya did not represent all the Hanbalis and this contention refers to the competition between Ibn Taymiyya and certain Sufi groups and influential Sufis. Furthermore, Hanbalis and Sufis were not mutually exclusive or necessarily in opposition, Hanbali Sufism existed and was also present in the circles around Ibn Taymiyya; refer to Birgit Krawietz, 'Ibn Qayyim Al-Jawzīyah: His Life and Works', *Mamlūk Studies Review* 10(2) (2006): 19–64.

31 For *shaykh* Khidr, I relied on Peter Thorau, *The Lion of Egypt: Sultan Baybars I and the Near East in the Thirteenth Century* (London: Longman, 1995); P.M. Holt, 'An Early Source on Shaykh Khaḍir Al-Mihrānī', *BSOAS* 46 (1983): 33–9.

sultan, who built *zawiyas* for him in Jerusalem, Damascus, Baʿalbak, Hama and Hims.[32] While the actual extent of Khidr's influence on Baybars' political and administrative decisions remains unclear, it was obvious that after several successful prophecies the *shaykh* became important enough to be considered a real threat by the powerful Mamluk *amirs* around the sultan. Furthermore, his crimes and excesses against Christians and Jews in the Syro-Egyptian lands antagonised the leading Muslim scholars, *amirs* and administrators, as they resented him even more for threatening the public order of the realm. In 671/1273, the Mamluk notables struck first and *shaykh* Khidr was accused of 'unnatural sexual intercourse and of adultery' and tried before a special court in Cairo.[33] Realising that the court was about to sentence him to death, Khidr resorted to a last-minute and brilliant manoeuvre: he prophesied that his death would be immediately followed by that of the sultan. The trick worked as the prophecy was taken seriously, and Khidr was eventually sentenced to life imprisonment. Later, he was killed in prison and his final prophecy materialised as the sultan died shortly afterwards. Although most Muslim chroniclers were hostile to Khidr, it is possible to gauge the magnitude of his sway over the sultan from Ibn al-Dawadari's words: 'His conduct throughout the kingdom of the sultan al-Malik al-Zahir was as the conduct of rulers, and his writings were exemplary and incontrovertible in all the Islamic kingdoms under the rule of al-Malik al-Zahir.'[34]

The second case of Sufi political agency could not have been more different. In contradistinction to the first case, which was marked by prophecies, the second instance was more complex and manifested as a hotchpotch of disputes over theology and creed, rivalries among Mamluk households and street demonstrations. It took place during the successive trials (*mihnas*) of Ibn Taymiyya and reflected the ability of Sufis to engage in political machinations at the heart of Mamluk political power. There is no point in repeating the chronology of the events or adding to the valuable existing studies on the *mihnas* of Ibn Taymiyya.[35] Therefore, I will limit my discussion to highlight-

32 Holt, 'Shaykh Khaḍir', 34.
33 Thorau, *The Lion of Egypt*, 225–9.
34 Translation from Holt, 'Shaykh Khaḍir', 35; refer to Ibn al-Dawadari, *Kanz*, 8:222.
35 Although in this section I rely mostly on the recent works of Caterina Bori and Nathan Hofer, there are several other valuable studies on Ibn Taymiyya.

ing the impressive agency of Sufis in cooperating together and influencing the Mamluk judicial process and political sphere. I will show how Sufis cooperated and participated in these events, albeit for different reasons, ranging from disputes on creed and theology, answering for personal offences, and involvement in Mamluk household competition.

During his second reign, sultan al-Nasir Muhammad Ibn Qalawun was still young. Two *amir*s controlled the realm: the powerful head of the sultan's household (*ustadar*) Baybars al-Jashankir, who later acquired the throne; and the powerful *amir* Sayf al-Din Salar (d. 710/1310). The latter was a patron of Ibn Taymiyya, while Baybars al-Jashankir was close to Sufi *shaykh* Nasr al-Manbiji (d. 719/1319). The clash started when Ibn Taymiyya offended Nasr al-Manbiji by attacking Ibn ʿArabi and his famous work *Fusus al-hikam* (*The Bezels of Wisdom*), thereby indirectly questioning the authority and the status of al-Manbiji.[36] By then, Ibn Taymiyya's continual attacks on Sufis, including Ibn ʿArabi, al-Shadhili and Nasr al-Manbiji, had already antagonised Sufi groups in Syria and Egypt. Al-Manbiji joined forces with Karim al-Din al-Amuli, the chief Sufi in Cairo, and the Sufis demonstrated en masse at the citadel of Cairo.[37] According to Hofer, Ibn ʿAtaʾ Allah al-Iskandari (d. 709/1309), the Maliki jurist and powerful Shadhili Sufi, personally led the crowd of Sufis to demonstrate at the citadel against *amir* Salar, the protector of Ibn Taymiyya. Under pressure, Salar passed the case to the chief judge Ibn Jamaʿa, as mentioned briefly in Chapter 2. During the trial, Ibn ʿAtaʾ al-Iskandari raised the issue of Ibn Taymiyya's rejection of the invocation of the Prophet for help (*istighatha*), which Ibn Jamaʿa saw as mere insolence. The Sufis were not satisfied with this ruling. Supported by many jurists and probably by Baybars al-Jashankir, they insisted that Ibn Jamaʿa imprison Ibn Taymiyya since the '*dawla*' required it;[38] Ibn Jamaʿa eventually succumbed,

---

36 Bori, '"The Missing Link', 71–2.

37 Hofer, *The Popularisation of Sufism*, 166–71.

38 Useful here is Jo van Steenbergen's conception of *dawla*, which denoted the political order and legitimate continuity of the *Dawlat al-Atrak*, including its different components such as 'officials, places, customs, apparel and rituals', the '*dawla's* memory', and its institutions and 'formal manifestations'; refer to Jo van Steenbergen, 'Appearances of Dawla and Political Order in Late Medieval Syro-Egypt. The State, Social Theory, and the Political History of the Cairo Sultanate (Thirteenth–Sixteenth Centuries)', in Stephan Conermann (ed.), *History and Society during the Mamluk Period (1250–1517)* (Göttingen, V&R Unipress, 2016), 54–7, 60, 61, 62, 66–8.

saying that prison was for Ibn Taymiyya's 'own good'.[39] Ibn Kathir was convinced that this machination was all the work of Nasr al-Manbiji and noted that the latter was very influential in the sultanate because 'he captivated the mind of al-Jashankir' and other influential individuals while, at the same time, lamenting that sultan al-Nasir Muhammad was powerless.[40]

This was an unprecedented chapter in the mutual history of Sufism and Mamluk politics. Unlike the earlier case of the unruly *shaykh* Khidr, the Sufi role in the successive *mihna*s of Ibn Taymiyya demonstrated impressive sway over the Mamluk political and judicial systems. Sufi *shaykh* Nasr al-Manbiji exercised an indisputably considerable personal influence on Baybars al-Jashankir, the real holder of power in the realm. Moreover, the strong spread of Shadhilism meant that Ibn ʿAtaʾ Allah al-Iskandari could muster and lead a popular Sufi show of force at the citadel of Cairo when needed. Additionally, the cooperation between Karim al-Din al-Amuli, the chief Sufi in Cairo, and Nasr al-Manbiji reflected how the Sufis could act and respond swiftly based on a collective sense of threat. It mattered little whether this was triggered by a dogmatic reaction in defence of Ibn ʿArabi's *Fusus al-hikam*, simply to protect the egos of the Sufi *shaykh*s al-Manbiji and al-Iskandari, or whether it instead reflected the Sufis' deep involvement in the competition between Mamluk households. The Sufis' ability to chase Ibn Taymiyya across Damascus and Cairo and put him on trial more than once, and their ability to influence the Mamluk judiciary by forcing the renowned chief judge Ibn Jamaʿa to reverse his judgement and imprison Ibn Taymiyya was striking.

Misbah al-hidaya: Sufi Political Thought

It is within the above context that I am offering to re-examine *Misbah al-hidaya fi tariq al-imama* (*The Guiding Lamp to the Path of the imama*) as an illustration of Mamluk Sufi political thought. This valuable Sufi political treatise is better understood alongside four preliminary conclusions that can be drawn from the intellectual, social and political context discussed above.

39 Ibn Kathir, *Bidaya*, 16:62–3; Nasr al-Manbiji was the 'personal friend and influential advisor to Baybars al-Jāshnakīr', in Hofer, *The Popularisation of Sufism*, 168. Refer also to Chapter 2, above.

40 Ibn Kathir, *Bidaya*, 16:63; al-Yunini relates a similar story in *Dhayl mirʾat al-zaman*, 2:1174.

A first conclusion is that the Sufis were active in the Ayyubid and Mamluk political spheres, and in some cases were engaged in open political confrontations with other religious, social or political groups. The second conclusion relates to the characteristics of the Sufi milieu that were active in producing political thought, as is evident from the case of *Kitab al-Siyasa al-mulukiyya*. This milieu was formed in the Sunni theological and juristic tradition of the Ashʿaris and the Shafiʿis; it was strongly tied to al-Juwayni and al-Ghazali through social and intellectual networks; it was highly erudite and well versed in the Graeco-Arabic philosophical tradition; it was close to the political power of the late Ayyubid period; and it held strong Sufi, political, and professional ties within the Islamic East and West. Thirdly, this milieu was dissimilar in every conceivable way to the unruly – yet influential – Sufism that was epitomised by *shaykh* Khidr al-Mihrani. A fourth and final conclusion: this milieu was multifaceted in the sense that it could put on a Sufi, Ashʿari, Shafiʿi or even a philosophical appearance, as is evident in the style in which *al-Siyasa al-mulukiyya* was authored. At the risk of pre-empting the conclusion of this chapter, I will show in what follows that the analysis of *Misbah al-hidaya* leads to similar conclusions and that this treatise was the product of the historical and intellectual context described in this paragraph.

It was in 1995 that Wilferd Madelung brought *Misbah al-hidaya* to light and emphasised its relevance to the political thought of the Mamluk period.[41] Although Madelung made some useful observations on the author, the supposed dedicatee, and the Sufi character of the treatise and its content, this section will challenge some of his findings based on new evidence. Most importantly, this section will link the treatise to the wider tradition of Islamic political thought and will show that the *Misbah* was not an isolated case that emerged from nowhere. The investigative work below will identify the sources and influences of the treatise, the background and aims of its author, the likely dedicatee, and will propose new conjectures on its political theory.

A good starting point for this investigation is to revisit the identity of the *Misbah*'s author. Madelung noted the 'Ṣūfī outlook of the author' and suspected he may be none other than *shaykh* Khidr al-Mihrani.[42] Nonetheless,

[41] Madelung, 'A Treatise on the Imamate' first presented at a congress in 1988.
[42] Ibid., 91.

Madelung observed that there were other Sufis in the entourage of Baybars who could have authored the treatise; indeed, there was nothing in the intellectual and literary career of *shaykh* Khidr that suggested he was capable of such writing.[43] Additionally, the attribution of the *Misbah* to Khidr is not tenable for several other reasons. The *Misbah* was authored by a Sufi who held the same level of concern for the rule of law as the other jurists dealt with in this research. Moreover, the *Misbah*'s author exhorted the modest conduct of scholars and the respect of the *shari'a*.[44] Nothing in the unruly life of Khidr indicated any consideration for the rule of law or modesty, neither his flagrant disregard for the *dhimma* code in his treatment of Jews and Christians, nor his personal conduct and pursuit of personal gain and pleasure, which marred his reputation before and during his service under Baybars. There are, of course, no guarantees that the authors of homiletics abide by what they preach. Accordingly, I propose a more convincing refutation, which is that Khidr's influence on his patron was grounded on legitimation by prophecies rather than by the exposition of coherent political thought. Based on all the above reasons, it is perfectly sensible to disregard Khidr as a possible author of the *Misbah*.

There is, similarly, the chief question of the dedicatee of the *Misbah*. The author of the treatise mentioned that he dedicated it to:

> The pillar of Islam and Muslims (*Rukn al-Islam wa-al-muslimin*), the suppressor of infidels and rebels, the one who sets the rituals of justice and benevolence, the demolisher of injustice and oppression, the one who spreads security and safety, the disseminator of generosity and beneficence, and the one who holds the support of God, the seal of his age, al-Sultan al-Malik al-Zahir.[45]

Madelung believed the treatise was dedicated to sultan Baybars as he was the only 'al-Malik az-Ẓāhir who bore the title Rukn ad-Dīn'.[46] Although Madelung's conjecture is plausible, it is important to reflect on it more carefully. While the author of the treatise used '*Rukn al-Islam wa-al-muslimin*', it

---

43 Ibid., 92.
44 Refer to the last section of this chapter on the merits of the Sufis.
45 *Misbah*, fols. 3v–4r.
46 Madelung, 'A Treatise on the Imamate', 91.

cannot be taken as a conclusive reference to the regnal title of Baybars, since it could simply have been a panegyric description of the dedicatee. Therefore, *Rukn al-Din* is not necessarily a rendition of '*Rukn al-Islam wa al-muslimin*' as Madelung suggested. A more useful clue can be found carved on a wooden memorial panel dated from 664/1265 in the National Museum of Damascus. It was completed on the orders of Baybars to commemorate his campaign in Cilicia and placed above the tomb of the Prophet's companion Khalid Ibn al-Walid in Hims.[47] It reads, 'Our Lord al-Sultan al-Malik al-Zahir, the pillar of the world and religion and the sultan of Islam and Muslims (*Rukn al-dunya wa-al-din, wa sultan al-Islam wa-al-muslimin*), the slayer of unbelievers and polytheists, the suppressor of rebels and insurgents.'[48] This panel provides a better indication still that the *Misbah* was indeed dedicated to Baybars. However, it is still not conclusive evidence and, although highly unlikely, future findings may show that the dedicatee of the *Misbah* was another one of the seven Burji Mamluk sultans who bore the title al-Malik al-Zahir.[49]

The *Misbah* did not simply have a Sufi outlook, as Madelung suggested, but was expressed in a *distinctly* Sufi style. The author did not compose the *Misbah* as a political work merely influenced by Sufism, but rather as a Sufi treatise that treated *distinctly* Sufi political thought that he presented as such to his dedicatee and intended audience. The *Misbah* was a political treatise not simply because its author described it as an epistle on the imamate (*risala fi-al-imama*), but since it treated predominantly themes of rulership.[50] Likewise, the *Misbah* was a Sufi work whose content relied on Sufi texts, language and concepts. Most importantly, the author of the *Misbah* strived to present it as a purely and distinctly Sufi work and desired it to be read as such.

In the prologue of the *Misbah*, the author displayed his Sufi colours.[51] He carefully built his case for a distinctly Sufi political thought that was on a par

---

[47] Memorial Panel from the Mosque of Khalid ibn al-Walid, Homs, Syria, 664/1265, National Museum of Damascus, see at: http://islamicart.museumwnf.org/database_item.php?id=object;ISL;sy;Mus01;36;en&cp.

[48] *Mawlana al-Sultan al-Malik al-Zahir rukn al-dunya wa-al-din, wa sultan al-Islam wa-al-muslimin, qatil al-kafara wa-al-mushrikin, qahir al-khawarij wa-al-mutamarridin . . .*

[49] C. E. Bosworth, *The New Islamic Dynasties: A Chronological and Genealogical Manual* (Edinburgh: Edinburgh University Press, 1996), 76–8.

[50] *Misbah*, fol. 2v.

[51] Ibid., fols. 4v–9v.

with the main Islamic intellectual currents. He first stated that the ultimate aim of creation was to attain the awareness and mystical knowledge of God (*maʿrifat al-bari*); the author explained, furthermore, that the duty of worship comes second to this knowledge (*maʿrifa*). These were unmistakable distinguishing signs of the Sufiness of the treatise. Following that, when arguing for the requirement of the imamate, the author presented Sufism as a distinct third school of thought that was equal to Ashʿarism and Muʿtazilism. In order to reach the awareness of God, he said, the Ashʿarites resorted to scripture and revelation and the Muʿtazilites to reason, while the Sufis advocated *tasfiya* (often translated as spiritual purification or refinement).[52] The author of the *Misbah* presented the Sufi way as being equal to the investigation and speculative reasoning (*istidlal* and *nazar*) of both the Ashʿaris and Muʿtazilis, and as an alternative that accepted both revelation and reason. The case for distinctly Sufi political thought was thus firmly defined.

In his attempt to present Sufism as a third alternative to Ashʿarism and Muʿtazilism, the author revealed two valuable clues, one on his sources and the other on political theory. The first clue related to his sources and his agency in using them. The author, I noticed, used al-Mawardi's discussion in *Adab al-dunya wa-al-din* on whether to rely on reason or revelation (*ʿaql* or *sharʿ*) in justifying the requirement for an *imam*.[53] The author of the *Misbah* skilfully modified al-Mawardi's discussion and integrated Sufism into it. Clearly this was not a case of someone simply repeating and collating earlier texts, but rather a highly erudite and able scholar who was capable of selecting, rearranging, modifying and employing earlier political discussions and texts to suit his own purposes. As for the clue concerning his political theory, the author of the *Misbah* revealed that his distinctly Sufi treatise legitimated the forceful seizure of the sultanate. As such, the introduction indicated that this was to be a work of political thought, like others discussed in this book, which was interested in the question of rule under a sultan and in the absence of a 'classical' caliph.

---

52 Madelung, 'A Treatise on the Imamate', 93; Madelung translates *tasfiya* as self-purification.

53 Al-Mawardi, *Adab al-dunya wa-al-din*, ed. Muhammad Karim Rajih (Beirut: Dar Iqraʾ, 1985), 150–1.

Coercive Authority by Right of Necessity

The prologue of the *Misbah* resembled the political language of the jurists in approaching coercive power. Despite the effort made by the author to project distinctly Sufi thought, his discussion on the requirement for the imamate replicated familiar ideas from the juristic political treatises that treated the forceful seizure of power.[54] The author said that there was a necessity for a ruler who could achieve prosperity and run people's religious and mundane affairs (*dinuhum* and *dunyahum*) to uphold the duty of worship. Furthermore, he said that God sent his messengers to invite people to know and worship him. Upon the end of the messengers, this task was entrusted to the ruler who resorts both to investigation and speculative reasoning (*istidlal* and *nazar*) in order to reach the *maʿrifa*, and who also forbids evil and enjoins what is good, brings benefit and suppresses corruption.[55] The author explained that the only one who could achieve this was the pious *imam* (*al-mutadayyin*) and the sultan learned in religious law (*al-mutasharriʿ*) whose existence was a requirement in every land and in every time.[56] The discussion was even more similar to the juristic treatises where it noted that, in the absence of such an *imam*, the forceful ruler, the wielder of coercive power – the sultan (*imam* of *shawka* and *sultan* of *quwwa*) – should be invested. Only then would prosperity and the duties of worship be guaranteed and dissension subside.[57] This resemblance continues when the author states that the imamate can be accorded either by designation from the previous *imam* or by the consensus of the people who loosen and bind (*ahl al-hall wa-al-ʿaqd*).[58] It cannot be accorded to two *imams* at the same age and place. This all bore a striking resemblance to juristic treatises.

The author of the *Misbah* argued for the legitimacy of the coercive sultan. This legitimation was founded on the right of necessity. The author first listed eight stipulations for the imamate, which evidently referred to the sultanate.[59]

[54] Refer to Madelung, 'A Treatise on the Imamate', 93–4.
[55] *Misbah*, fols. 7v, 7r, 8v & 8r.
[56] Ibid., fol. 8v–8r.
[57] Ibid., fols. 8v–9r.
[58] For more on the 'people who loosen and bind' refer to Muhammad Qasim Zaman, 'Ahl al-ḥall wa-l-ʿaqd', *EI*[3].
[59] Essay one titled 'The stipulations for the *imamate*' (*fi sharaʾitiha*) in the *Misbah*, fols. 9v–12r.

According to the *Misbah*'s theory, the *imam* must be: (1) male, as the author noted the *imamate* of women was not valid; (2) judicious (*ʿaqil*) and mature (*baligh*), as madmen and boys were incapable of considering serious matters or managing the affairs of people; (3) free (*hurr*), as a slave was constantly occupied with his duty to serve his master; (4) just (*ʿadl*) as the depraved did not reject unfairness;[60] (5) knowledgeable (*ʿalim*) in religious rulings; (6) well-informed in his ruling duties (*ʿarif*) and command independent abilities to carry out any duties he may have to assume (*kafi*); (7) he need not be from Quraysh; and, finally, (8) the condition of infallibility (*maʿsum*) as per the Shiʿa belief was rejected. The author of the *Misbah* then stated that if no candidate with such requirements was available and a Muslim who commanded military power (*shawka*) arose to assume the imamate, then his tenure became lawful and effective by the right of necessity (*nafadhat imamatuhu li-al-darura*) even if he lacked the quality of knowledge in deriving religious law (*mujtahid*) and even if he displayed immoral conduct (*fasiq*). The author explained that in his time the knowledgeable were absent and the just could rarely be found.

While Madelung was unequivocally correct in assuming that imamate meant sultanate in the *Misbah*, his explanation of the exclusion of the necessity of Qurashi or ʿAlid descent is a major point of diversion with this monograph. Unlike Madelung, I posit that this exclusion was rooted in the Shafiʿi–Ashʿari thought of al-Juwayni and al-Ghazali and, likewise, in the *Misbah*'s concern for moderating the ruler's discretionary power. Madelung considered that on the point of Qurashi descent, 'the author begins to deviate from the traditional positions' of the jurists as 'the requirement of the imam being of Qurayš had been a matter of consensus among Sunnite scholars until the recent overthrow of the ʿAbbāsid caliphate in Baghdad . . .'.[61] Madelung even rejected the idea that al-Juwayni departed from this 'consensus'.[62] As discussed extensively in the Chapter 1, this misconception is rooted in a seri-

---

Refer to Madelung, 'A Treatise on the Imamate', 94, where he noted that the author of the *Misbah* equated the imamate with the sultanate.

60 The notion of *ʿadl* not only refers to justice but also to piety (*waraʿ*); refer to discussion below 106–7.

61 Madelung, 'A Treatise on the Imamate', 95.

62 Refer to Chapter 1, 19–22, above, for a detailed discussion on the 'theory of the caliphate' as an impediment in the history of Islamic political thought.

ous and unremitting impediment to the study of the history of Islamic political thought. Despite the academic mythology of the theory of the caliphate, the current of Sunni jurists that rejected the necessity of lineage to Quraysh had in fact been a powerful, confident and vocal trend in Islamic political thought since the eleventh century. Islamic political thinkers had already developed strong views against the requirement for Qurashi lineage and, furthermore, on the necessity of the caliphate itself – well before the fall of Baghdad and, unsurprisingly, after its fall. One notable earlier example of this was al-Juwayni and later ones were Ibn Jamaʿa and the Damascene Hanafi jurist Najm al-Din al-Tarsusi (d. 758/1357). Furthermore, Madelung's observation that the *Misbah* aimed to refute and discredit the Shiʿa doctrine is untenable because, by the time of Baybars, Shiʿism did not pose a grave threat to the Syro-Egyptian Mamluk centre and since this treatise was not concerned with confessional polemics.[63] The author's obsolete refutations of the necessity for any lineage to ʿAli's sons pointed to the sources and influences of the *Misbah*: the eight stipulations of the imamate, including the refutation of ʿAlid or Qurashi descent, led straight back to al-Juwayni and al-Ghazali. Likewise, the refutation of the requirement for infallibility of the *imam* is an expected feature of a political text such as the *Misbah*, with its deep concern for the moderation of the ruler's discretionary power.

The *Misbah*'s eight requirements are strikingly similar to those proposed by the prominent Shafiʿi–Ashʿari theologian and political thinker al-Juwayni. The similarities with the conditions stipulated in al-Juwayni's *Ghiyath al-umam fi-iltiyath al-zulam* (*Aid to Nations Shrouded in Darkness*) are difficult to miss and demark this treatise as an important influence on the author of the *Misbah*.[64] In the *Ghiyath*, al-Juwayni did not deem it 'reasonable' to assume that the imamate required Qurashi lineage and cast serious doubt on a prophetic saying that 'imams are from Quraysh'.[65] For al-Juwayni, the required qualities of the *imam* were to be male, free, judicious (to possess ʿ*aql*), adult, and brave and gallant. As for the acquired qualities, they included knowledge, which was not limited to religious knowledge as

---

[63] Madelung, 'A Treatise on the Imamate', 95.

[64] Al-Juwayni, *Ghiyath al-umam*, 76–97; ch. 4 of the *Ghiyath* treats the qualities of the *imam*. I benefited from the translation of title from Anjum, 'Political Metaphors', 7.

[65] Al-Juwayni, *Ghiyath al-umam*, 70–82; refer to Chapter 1, 21, above.

al-Juwayni explained. While the candidate did not necessarily need to be a *mujtahid*, piety was an essential acquired quality. Furthermore, al-Juwayni refuted the need for infallibility (*ʿisma*).[66]

What is also striking is the resemblance of the *Misbah* to the works of al-Ghazali. The stipulations he outlines in his *Fadaʾih al-batiniyya wa-fadaʾil al-Mustazhiriyya* (*The Scandals of the Esoterics and the Virtues of the Party of [Caliph] al-Mustazhir*) – known as the *Mustazhiri* – are identical to those in the *Misbah* if just two changes are made: adding *najda* (bravery and undauntedness) and descent from Quraysh to the latter.[67] Carol Hillenbrand summarised the list as follows:

> According to al-Ghazālī, ten qualities are necessary for an Imām if he is fit for his office; six are natural or innate (*khilqiyya*) and cannot be acquired, whilst four may be acquired. In the first category are: adult status, sound intellect, freedom, maleness, descent from Quraysh and good hearing and sight . . . In the second category are four so-called 'acquired' attributes: *najda*, *kifāya*, *ʿilm* and *waraʿ*.[68]

It is important to dwell here on al-Ghazali's notions of *kifaya*, *ʿilm* and *waraʿ*, as I aim to show how the author of the *Misbah* used and re-interpreted them to suit his own purposes. Hillenbrand interpreted al-Ghazali's *kifaya* as 'competence to govern' and the ability to 'order religious and temporal matters'.[69] As for al-Ghazali's *waraʿ*, it meant both piety and justice. Hillenbrand interpreted *waraʿ* as follows, 'It is the very foundation of authority. It is difficult to reconcile *waraʿ* with the exercise of power, but the basis of this is strict adherence to justice. It is noteworthy that al-Ghazālī does not demand that

66 Ibid., 91–7.

67 Al-Ghazali, *al-Mustazhiri (Fadāʾih al-batiniyya)*, ed. ʿAbd al-Rahman Badawi (Kuwait: Dar al-Kutub al-Thaqafiyya, 1964), 179–95. Al-Ghazali's requirements for the imamate are tenfold; one is born with six and four are acquired. The candidate should be mature, rational or sane, have free status, be male, descend from Quraysh, and have good sight and hearing. The acquired qualities are *najda* (undauntedness, bravery, and command and control of the troops), *kifaya* (ability, efficiency, savviness), *waraʿ* (piety and justice) and *ʿilm* (knowledge). Al-Ghazali explains each one in detail.

68 Carole Hillenbrand, 'Islamic Orthodoxy or Realpolitik? Al-Ghazālī's Views on Government', *Iran* 26 (1988): 83. Refer to *al-Mustazhiri*, 185–7. Here *kifaya* refers to many talents, including proper counsel, judicious rule, balance between careful consideration and swift and powerful response, and fast reaction to emerging situations.

69 Hillenbrand, 'Islamic Orthodoxy or Realpolitik?', 83–4; refer to *al-Mustazhiri*, 187–90, where, in addition to piety, *waraʿ* clearly implies justice in its known and generic meaning.

the *imām* be sinless.'[70] As for *'ilm*, it was religious knowledge. Nevertheless, al-Ghazali did not stipulate that the *imam* be a *mujtahid* as he could benefit from the finest advisers and scholars.

Recognising the above-mentioned variances and similarities are essential to understand the *Misbah*'s theory of the sultanate. The author advocated the requirement and legitimacy of coercive authority by working out a meticulous synthesis of the stipulations for the imamate in al-Juwayni's *Ghiyath* and al-Ghazali's *Mustazhiri.* There were similarities with both treatises, yet the reliance on al-Ghazali was greater. As such, the *Misbah*'s use and explanation of the notions of *'adl*, *'arif* and *kafi* overlapped both textually and conceptually with al-Ghazali's notions of *kifaya* and *wara'*. For instance, the *Misbah*'s explanation of the notion of *'adl* (justice) corresponded to a large degree to al-Ghazali's description of *wara'*. Consequently, the required conditions for the *imam* were nearly identical, the only difference being that bravery and undauntedness were missing from the *Misbah*'s list. On the other hand, it was crucial for the *Misbah* to waive the necessity of Qurashi descent and uphold the coercive authority of the sultanate. Accordingly, the *Misbah* inserted al-Juwayni's dismissal of the necessity of descent from Quraysh and used his line of argument on this issue. This crafty synthesis was possible as both al-Juwayni's *Ghiyath* and al-Ghazali's *Mustazhiri* displayed great similarities, though not on the issue of descent from Quraysh. The author of the *Misbah* thus succeeded in buttressing his own theory of the legitimacy of coercive authority by synthesising the work of al-Juwayni and al-Ghazali. He achieved this by adopting ideas from both authors, summarising and rewriting parts of their work in a way that was relevant to his own time, audience and aims.

Ethics, Mysticism and the Rule of Law

After making the case for coercive authority, the *Misbah* treated the rule of law in a distinctly Sufi fashion. The second essay, titled *On the Nature of the Imamate,* provided the author with the opportunity to differentiate his political theory from that of others by adopting a mystical and ethical conceptualisation of the rule of law as opposed to a juristic one.[71] The *Misbah*

[70] Hillenbrand, 'Islamic Orthodoxy or Realpolitik?', 85

[71] *Fi haqiqat al-imama*; *Misbah,* fols.12r–43r.

distinguished its conception of the imamate by curtailing the arbitrary exercise of power using distinctly Sufi ideas that included, among others, a Sufi interpretation of the philosopher king.[72] While the *Misbah* still resembled al-Mawardi, al-Juwayni and al-Ghazali's take on coercive authority, it described the concern for the rule of law in a mystical and moral language that was relevant to the early Mamluk context. Furthermore, in this second essay of the *Misbah*, the author displayed his command of Sufi texts and the Sufi political tradition to achieve his aims.

In order to uphold concern for the rule of law, the *Misbah* relied on two carefully selected texts.[73] The first was al-Mawardi's *Adab al-dunya wa-al-din* (*The Ethics of the World and of Religion*); the second text was *Mirsad al-ʿibad min al-mabdaʾ ila-al-maʿad* (*The Path of God's Bondsmen from Origin to Return*), a near-contemporary compendium of Sufism that was authored by Najm al-Din Daya Razi (573/1177–654/1256), the thirteenth-century Ashʿari–Sufi thinker.[74] Once more, the examination of the *Misbah* will reflect the agency of its author in using, re-arranging and adapting earlier texts, including these two, to suit his aims. For instance, the analysis will show that *Adab al-dunya* was a suitable choice as it treated the moderation of political power without alluding to the institution of the caliphate, which suited the *Misbah*'s legitimation of coercive authority. On the other hand, the *Mirsad* covered systematically the theory, practices and ethics of Sufism, and discussed various professions, including political and judicial offices and how their holders could achieve spiritual reward;[75] therefore, the author of the *Misbah* used it to project Sufi conceptualisation of the rule of law. In an ethical discussion *On the Nature of the Imamate*, there was little need for juristic opinions, legal requirements and stipulations – here the author could now resort to moral, philosophical and mystical ideals, and present an innovative Sufi contribution to the theory of the *imamate*.

---

72 Refer to Lambton, 'Justice in the Medieval Persian Theory of Kingship', 110–11, 114–15.

73 Most likely among several other texts that future research will hopefully identify.

74 This text is influenced by Ibn ʿArabi and al-Suhrawardi; refer to Zakeri, 'From Futuwwa to Mystic Political Thought', 44.

75 Najm al-Din Razi, *The Path of God's Bondsmen from Origin to Return (Merṣād al-ʿibād min al-mabdāʾ ila-al-maʿād): A Sufi Compendium*, trans. Hamid Algar (Delmar, NY: Caravan Books, 1982), 17.

It should be mentioned that the *Misbah*'s Sufi expression of political thought was not a unique occurrence in the history of Islamic political thought. In addition to the above-mentioned case of al-Suhrawardi's caliphal ideology, the Ottoman period saw a more widespread tradition of presenting Sufi conceptions of political authority to rulers. As the recent book by Huseyin Yilmaz has shown, influential Sufis and 'Sufi-minded' *ʿulamaʾ* legitimated Ottoman rule by transforming the caliphate into an expression of cosmic divine power that served as a moral exemplar.[76] This seminal work discussed how 'leading jurists either abstained from writing on the question of the caliphate in normative juristic language or resorted to the mystical philosophy of prominent Sufi intellectuals, such as Ibn Arabi, to reconfigure the caliphate outside the disciplinary confines of Islamic Jurisprudence'.[77] Although the *Misbah* was not concerned with establishing any form of caliphate, it still resembled these later Ottoman treatises in its reliance on Sufi language and tradition to produce political thought. Interestingly, Yilmaz's study confirms that some of the sources and influences of the *Misbah*, including the *Mirsad*, were central to this later Ottoman Sufi-driven political theorisation.[78]

1. Ethics and Practical Philosophy

The Sufi language of the *Misbah* did not lessen the author's concern for the basic tenets of the rule of law. On the contrary, the second essay highlighted the author's attention to the ruler's equability in matters of taxation and spending, administration of justice, public welfare and defence. The author

---

76 Yilmaz, *Caliphate Redefined*, 2.

77 Ibid.

78 Remarkably it was not until 2017 that Yilmaz – a historian of the Ottoman Empire – noted that the *Mirsad* was a popular text from 'Cairo to China' (*Caliphate Redefined*, 29). Madelung missed the heavy influence of the *Misbah*. Furthermore, the *Mirsad* was translated from Persian to English in 1982, but the translator of the *Mirsad* denied that it had had any influence on the Central and African Islamic regions (20–1), which is rather a surprising assumption. Razi also wrote in Arabic the renowned *Manarat al-saʾirin wa maqamat al-taʾirin bi-Allah* (*Light Towers for Those Voyaging to God, and the Stations of Those Flying with God*), another founding Sufi text with important political ideas (refer to the edition of Saʿid ʿAbd al-Fattah, Kuwait: Dar Suʿad al-Subah, 1993). The translator of the *Mirsad* into English, and following him Lambton, mistook the *Manarat* for an Arabic translation of the *Mirsad*. To add to this series of colossal errors, an Arabic translation of the *Mirsad* appeared in 2002, which was completely unaware of the *Misbah* and earlier Arabic translations of the *Mirsad* (*Falsafat al-tasawuf wa-al-daʿwa ila-Allah fi kitab Mirsad al-ʿibad min al-mabdaʾ ila-al-maʿad*, trans. ʿAli Ismaʿil (Cairo: Etrac Publishing, 2002)).

first outlined two types of *imam*: *imam al-din* (of religion) and *imam al-din wa-al-dunya* (of religion and the world).[79] The first was 'the saint who guides along the straight path', 'takes the key of the *shariʿa* with the hand of the Sufi way (*bi-yad al-tariqa*)', spends his time in worship, and is the very personification of compassion.[80] The second kind was, the author explained, 'the highest wish and the form of the imamate that represents its ultimate purpose', which was achieved only by an *imam* who was capable of preserving religion and the proper running of the affairs of people.[81] Following the heavily Sufi-toned opening, the author of the *Misbah* listed the *imam*'s duties of repelling the enemy by *jihad*; defending the lives, properties and sanctities of Muslims; sustaining public welfare and prosperity; ensuring the equitable administration of tax collection and spending; ensuring the impartial dispensing of justice by upholding both the sultanic courts (*mazalim*) and religious rulings (*ahkam*) equally; and establishing legal punishments (*hudud*) without excess or favouritism.[82] The author of the *Misbah* mentioned that only someone who commanded the ability (*qudra*) to enforce could achieve these duties.[83] Here, we clearly see the direct influence of al-Mawardi's *Adab al-dunya* on the *Misbah*, where the author used, verbatim, five of the *Adab*'s seven duties of the *imam*.[84]

As in the work of previous authors, reconciling the realms of religion and the world was fundamental to the *Misbah*'s political theory. In practical terms, this meant the necessity of just rule by the coercive sultan. Therefore, the author of the *Misbah* repeated verbatim from al-Mawardi's *Adab al-dunya*, 'the following keep this world sound: an obeyed religion, a coercive sultan (*sultan qahir*), widespread justice, prevalent safety, abundant prosperity, and widespread hope'.[85] Following that the author continued, based on

79 This concept can also be found in the works of al-Ghazali and al-Juwayni, who mentioned '*al-imama zaʿamat al-din wa-al-dunya*', in *al-Ghiyath*, 85; this concept was also very central to al-Mawardi's *Adab al-dunya*.

80 Madelung, 'A Treatise on the Imamate', 96; *Misbah*, fols. 13r, 12v, 12r.

81 *Misbah*, fol. 13v.

82 '*yusawi bayna ahlayha*'; ibid., fol. 14r & v.

83 Ibid., refer to Madelung, 'A Treatise on the Imamate', 96–7.

84 Al-Mawardi, *Adab al-dunya*, 151; *Misbah*, fol. 14v & r. Refer to Marlow, 'Advice and Advice Literature', *EI*[3], where Marlow states: 'In his *Adab al-dunya wa-l-dīn*, al-Mawardi seeks to indicate the manners appropriate to the two realms of religion and the world.'

85 *Misbah*, fol. 18r; for a similar translation, see Madelung, 'A Treatise on the Imamate', 97. Refer to al-Mawardi, *Adab al-dunya*, 148.

Adab al-dunya, 'The awe of a coercive sultan is capable of averting dissenting aspirations and uniting divided hearts; his dominant power shall deter transgressors, put fear in insubordinate souls, and restrain those who lost their way in rebellion and corruption . . .'[86] Under the coercive sultan, the religious and mundane affairs of Muslims are put in order and, subsequently, justice and fixed legal judgements are upheld, borders are protected, armies are raised, thieves and highway robbers are dealt with, and Friday prayers and religious feasts are upheld.[87] All that was only possible owing to the rule of a just *imam* who commanded coercive power, that is, the sultan.

There were two main reasons behind the choice of al-Mawardi's *Adab al-dunya* rather than, for instance, his *al-Ahkam al-sultaniyya*. The first obvious reason was that in the *Ahkam* the *imam* was the Qurashi caliph, which rendered it unusable for the *Misbah*'s theory of the just coercive sultanate. The second reason was that the language and the methodological reasoning of the *Adab al-dunya* matched the Sufi character of the *Misbah*. Like the two other works of al-Mawardi, *Tashil al-nazar wa-ta'jil al-zafar* and *Qawanin al-wizara*, the *Adab al-dunya* treated the ethical qualities (*akhlaq*) and the governance of the ruler (the vizier in the case of the *Qawanin*) based on a view rooted in 'the sciences of ethics and practical philosophy'.[88] Furthermore, al-Mawardi's *Adab al-dunya* shared with the *Misbah* a concern for proper governance that suited both the world (*dunya*) and religion (*din*).[89] Clearly, the erudite author of the *Misbah* knew his classical political sources very well and used what best suited his theory and aims.

2. Restraint of the Ruler's Power

The author of the *Misbah* further highlighted the rule of law in another distinctly Sufi manner. To achieve this end, he resorted to Sufi texts like the *Mirsad* in order to articulate a Sufi theory of moderation of the exercise of power by the coercive sultan. Heavily influenced by Ibn 'Arabi and al-Suhrawardi, the *Mirsad* was a founding Sufi text that explained the Sufi

[86] *Misbah*, fol. 18r & v; for a useful translation refer to Madelung, 'A Treatise on the Imamate', 97. Refer to al-Mawardi, *Adab al-dunya*, 149.

[87] *Misbah*, fols.18v–19r.

[88] Marlow, 'Advice and Advice Literature', *EI*[3].

[89] Ibid.

doctrine, summarised its elaboration and demonstrated the Islamic roots of Sufism.[90] Most importantly for this research, the *Mirsad* included an important contribution to Islamic political thought 'couched in distinctively Sufi terms', most notably in its fifth part where its author Najm al-Din Razi discussed the conduct of the ruler, vizier, judges and other professions.[91]

The second essay, the largest section of the *Misbah*, was heavily influenced by this founding Ash'ari–Sufi text. From the beginning to the end of this essay, the author used, and re-arranged, passages from Razi's *Mirsad* in an extraordinarily systematic and purposeful manner.[92] Madelung considered that the second essay included a lengthy moral discussion of the *imam*'s conduct in relation to himself, his subjects (*ra'iyya*) or family, and God 'in a fanciful manner with a strong element of Ṣūfī concepts and terminology'.[93] Madelung did not, however, attempt to trace the sources and influences of these Sufi concepts. Yet the near-verbatim use of the *Mirsad* can be spotted right at the beginning of the second essay when the author of the *Misbah* described *imam al-din*. The first chapter of the fifth part of the *Mirsad* titled, *Concerning the Wayfaring of Kings and the Lords of Command* related that 'There are two classes of kings: kings of the world and kings of religion.' As for those who are the kings of religion, it said:

> They have opened the supreme talisman of form with the key of the Law, held in the hand of the Path, and with the eye of the Truth they have contemplated the states and attributes stored and hidden in the depths of their being, like buried treasure and gems. They have penetrated to the mystery of the treasure of 'he who knows his self, knows too his Lord'.[94]

This was, verbatim, how the *Misbah* described *imam al-din*.[95]

As further illustrations of this word-for-word usage, I will highlight two more relevant passages from the *Mirsad* that were used in the *Misbah*. First, what Madelung termed as the fanciful Sufi language of the extended discussion on the *imam*'s conduct in relation to himself, his subjects and God was

---

90 Razi, *God's Bondsmen*, 17. Refer to Zakeri, 'From Futuwwa to Mystic Political Thought', 44.
91 Razi, *God's Bondsmen*, 19.
92 *Misbah*, fols. 12v–43r.
93 Madelung, 'A Treatise on the Imamate', 98.
94 Translation from Razi, *God's Bondsmen*, 396.
95 *Misbah*, fol. 12v–r; identical text.

actually obtained from the second chapter of the fifth part of the *Mirsad*, titled *Concerning the State of Kings and their Conduct toward Each Group of Their Subjects and Their Solicitude for the People.*[96] Secondly, the whole discussion on the passion and anger (*al-hawa*ʾ and *al-ghadab*) that ought to be avoided was entirely based on the sixth chapter of the third part of the *Mirsad* titled, *Concerning the Refinement of the Soul and the Knowledge Thereof.*[97]

The use of earlier Sufi texts was more than just mindless or arbitrary repetition. It was based on a carefully considered inclusion–exclusion strategy that befitted the political theory proposed in the *Misbah*. The author aimed at presenting a distinctly Sufi conception of the rule of law that was, nonetheless, in complete agreement with the political theory that he had already advanced in the prologue and the first essay of his treatise. Since the *Misbah*'s theory was centred on the just sultan who commanded coercive power and whose exercise of power was restrained by a Sufi system of morals and ethics, the author knew perfectly well what passages to include and exclude from earlier texts. For instance, the following passage of the *Mirsad* had to be omitted as it could have indicated support for the institution of the caliphate: 'For kingship over others is the deputyship and vice-regency of God, and second only to prophethood; than it, there is no greater task.'[98] This case of exclusion made perfect sense, as the passage did not fit with the *Misbah*'s conception of political authority. Furthermore, this exclusion–inclusion strategy resembled the above-mentioned careful and selective use of the works of al-Mawardi, al-Juwayni and al-Ghazali.

The *Misbah* upheld the Sufi call for justice, restraint, moderation, benevolence and accountability. Its concern for restraining the exercise of political power was rooted in a system of morals and ethics that was exquisitely presented in earlier Sufi texts. This system was based on an eclectic use of Islamic and other concepts, like the philosopher king, which were by the thirteenth century well integrated into the Islamic intellectual tradition.[99] Inevitably,

---

96 Ibid., starts fol. 16 v & r; translation from Razi, *God's Bondsmen*, starts 411.

97 *Misbah*, fols. 23r–29r; translation from Razi, *God's Bondsmen*, 194.

98 Translation from Razi, *God's Bondsmen*, 412. Yilmaz noted that 'Daye equated the sultanate with the caliphate and attributed to it the same status as prophethood . . .' in *Caliphate Redefined*, 212. The author of the *Misbah* took no chances whatsoever and omitted any reference to the caliphate.

99 Lambton noted of Najm al-Din Razi that, 'He is influenced by the conceptions of the philosopher king but interprets this in terms of Sufism' in 'Justice in the Medieval Persian Theory of Kingship', 110–11. Refer to the above discussion on *al-Siyasa al-mulukiyya*.

parts of the second essay where the author expressed his concern for the rule of law in a Sufi mixture of moral and philosophical ideas resembled homiletic works of political advice. For instance, throughout the discussion of the comportment of the *imam* towards his subjects, the author of the *Misbah* stressed the importance of justice, removing oppression, fairness, aiding the oppressed and the weak, spending alms on the poor and the needy, assisting travellers, honouring the *ʿulamaʾ* by securing their subsistence, and the proper treatment of ascetics and Sufis by attending to their needs and revering their leaders.[100] In achieving this, the author noted that the *imam* would secure both 'the steadiness of his rule in this world and his good rank in the afterlife'.[101] For the *Misbah*, the *imam* was accountable for his deeds on Judgement Day. Moreover, the author warned against the sinful behaviour of the sultan, which would cause strife in the realm; he explained that corrupt advisers and companions in the sultan's service and entourage would lead to sin, oppression and exploitation under the pretext of increasing the treasury's revenues. Accordingly, he cautioned against unlawful taxation, unjust and corrupt confiscation, and oppression and injustice, which would lead to the corruption of the realm and even the end of the rule.[102] Finally, the *Misbah* warned against pride and arrogance.[103] Such was the distinctly Sufi summation of the moderation and restraint of the arbitrary exercise of power.

The Sufi Theory of Delegation

The epilogue of the *Misbah* was essentially a call to the dedicatee of the treatise, in all likeliness sultan Baybars, to secure the primacy of Sufis over the *ʿulamaʾ*, including judges, jurisconsults and sermon-givers.[104] It covered three subjects: the office of the vizier; the conduct of judges; and the etiquette of the *ʿulamaʾ* and Sufi *shaykh*s.[105] Throughout this tripartite discussion, the author of the *Misbah* focused on highlighting the merits of the Sufis in order to present his strain of political thought as the superior one.

[100] *Misbah*, fols. 29r–30v and fols. 31v–32r are, respectively, based verbatim on Razi, *God's Bondsmen*, 413, 414–15.

[101] *Misbah*, fols. 29v, 30v–r, 31r.

[102] Ibid., fols. 33v–35r.

[103] Ibid., fols. 39r–40v.

[104] Ibid., fols. 43r–54r.

[105] Ibid., fols. 43r–v.

The epilogue's discussion on the office of the vizier contained an additional valuable Sufi contribution to Islamic political thought, namely, the lawful delegation of powers from the sultan.[106] Although it was supposed to treat the merits and qualifications of the vizier, this discussion reasserted the *Misbah*'s views on the legitimacy of coercive authority by confirming the sultan as the source of delegation of political, legal and administrative powers. The author of the *Misbah* started his discussion on the vizierate by stating, '*al-saltana tali al-nubuwwa*', that is, the sultanate comes second to prophethood. The author first stated that the 'kingdom is like a tent, and the *wazir* is its pillar', and then stressed the need for the vizier to be just and judicious and that he should possess four qualities: integrity, exaltedness, steadiness and forbearance.[107] By asserting that the sultanate was delegated the authorities of prophethood, the author achieved two critical aims. First, he reasserted the *Misbah*'s position that the sultanate was an all-inclusive and lawful replacement of the caliphate. Secondly, he indirectly posited that the source of delegation of powers to the vizier originated from the sultan – as the lawful successor of prophethood – and not from the caliph.

With this postulation, the *Misbah* sealed artfully its contribution to Islamic political thought. By asserting that the sultan was the lawful source of delegated authorities, the *Misbah* presented a coherent theory that covered the legitimacy of coercive authority – and, accordingly, the dismissal of the need for Qurashi lineage for the imamate – and the Sufi tenets of the rule of law. Hence, the *Misbah* reasserted firmly its conception of political authority as presented in the prologue and first essay. Most importantly, it presented its own contribution to the theory of delegation of powers, which was also a central theme of other treatises as discussed extensively in Chapters 2 and 4 of this book. While the *Misbah*'s contribution to the theory of delegation was not expressed in the most exquisite legal language, it nevertheless addressed successfully two important issues that were probably of concern to Baybars: the nominal caliphate of Cairo; and the source of delegated powers to the viziers, judges, governors and administrative posts.

---

106 Ibid., fols. 44v–46r. Madelung noted the irrelevance of this discussion for the Mamluk period; 'A Treatise on the Imamate', 99.

107 'The minister must also have four qualities like the pole: straightness, loftiness, steadfastness, and endurance'; in Razi, *God's Bondsmen*, 434.

Subsequently, the *Misbah*'s epilogue treated the conduct of judges.[108] Here, the author merged his cherished and uncompromising concern for upholding the rule of law with his theory of delegation. He wrote that there should be one judge, second to the *imam*, in every land in order to avoid chaos and strife. He discerned three types of judge. The first, was qualified to pass rulings and was knowledgeable in jurisprudence, judicious, virtuous, high-minded, of clear conscience, with no desire for the office, impartial in his rulings and with no predisposition to favour the powerful. The second, was the incompetent type who was not suitable for office and, as such, ruled according to his personal whims and accepted bribes; his rulings were not to be accepted. The third, while qualified for office, nevertheless opted to rule improperly, favoured some individuals over rightness, accepted bribes, abused orphans' rights, charitable endowments and mosques, did not support the righteous, hindered the implementation of market inspections and favoured the powerful; accordingly, his judgeship was not valid and he was destined for hell. The sultan should not permit this sort of judgeship or he would be considered an accomplice (*sharikan lahum*) and answer for it on Judgement Day. Accountability (*mu'akhadha*) was a consequence of the theory of delegation of powers; as the lawful source of power, the sultan was accountable for the excesses of his appointees. This was another instance of the uncompromising attitude of thirteenth-century thinkers on upholding the rule of law, at the risk of antagonising their dedicatees.

The Primacy of Sufi Counsel

The epilogue's discussion, moreover, treated the types of knowledge, the different kinds of scholars and their etiquette.[109] Its main aim was to reaffirm the merits of Sufis and their counsel over the other *'ulama'*. The author of the *Misbah* first stated that knowledge (*'ilm*) was the ultimate way to know and be closer to God and went on to discuss the conduct of *'ulama'* who were not judges. He explained in a detailed manner the two kinds of knowledge: the outer and the inner.[110] Outer – or revealed – knowledge was practical knowledge disclosed to the companions of the Prophet and to the *imams*

[108] *Misbah*, fols. 46r–48r; Madelung, 'A Treatise on the Imamate', 99.
[109] *Misbah*, fols. 49v–54r.
[110] Ibid., fols. 49v–50r. Refer to Madelung, 'A Treatise on the Imamate', 100–1.

who followed them; this included the sciences of the Qur'an, the prophetic tradition, exegesis and jurisprudence. Likewise, he explained in great detail the inner or hidden knowledge (*batin*).[111] Subsequently, the author stated that there were three kinds of *'ulama'*. Some commanded outer knowledge, some commanded inner knowledge and others were in command of both.[112] The existence of just a handful from the last group would have filled the world with bliss and virtue. The author reiterated the prophetic saying, 'The *'ulama'* of my community are [like] the prophets of the people of Israel.' Some of the *'ulama'* who commanded the outer knowledge of jurisprudence and prophetic tradition were modest and did not seek the goods of this life, the sultan's favour or the people's approval; they were as such the elite selected by God (*khawass*). However, some amongst them sought wealth, office and approval. Their way was that of argument, controversy, harmfulness, unfairness and falsehood and they ought to be shunned.[113] With this reference to corrupt scholars, the author made his final move to promote the primacy of Sufis.

The *Misbah* concluded in the same way that it started, by promoting Sufism and Sufis. The author's epilogue placed this Sufi treatise as a serious strain of political thought that upheld distinct conceptions of the rule of law and political authority, and pointed out that it was dedicated to the sultan as such. The author passed his final verdict and recommendation to his dedicatee, 'As for those who command inner knowledge, they are the Sufi *shaykhs* (*mashayikh al-tariqa*). They choose isolation, seclusion, and remove themselves from people. They exercise self-restraint and fight the soul and the devil, and follow God and his Messenger. They are immune to hell and are the chosen ones.'[114] The author was thus setting out before Baybars the merits of the Sufis and their counsel: they were so unsullied that their political theory, the one that he advanced in his *Misbah*, was superior to other strains of Islamic political thought.

---

[111] Refer to the *Misbah*, fols. 50r–51v. There is also a valuable classification of Sufi sciences in the *Mirsad*; Razi, *God's Bondsmen*, 446–7. Here the influence of al-Ghazali, Ibn 'Arabi and al-Suhrawardi on both the *Misbah* and *Mirsad* is evident. For a very relevant discussion on the classification of scholars and Sufi sciences refer to Ohlander, *Sufism in an Age of Transition*, 142–8.

[112] *Misbah*, fols. 51v–53v.

[113] Ibid., fols. 51v–53v; Madelung, 'A Treatise on the Imamate', 101. The *Misbah*, fols. 52r–53v, is based verbatim on Razi, *God's Bondsmen*, 448–9, where it was more detailed.

[114] *Misbah*, fols. 53v–54r.

The agency of the *Misbah*'s author in benefiting from the *Mirsad* was also evident in the above postulation. In this instance, there was a central idea in the *Mirsad* that dealt with corrupt Sufis, which the author of the *Misbah* chose to disregard completely:

> Evil scholars, hypocritical ascetics, and mendicant dervishes, who in their greed sell religion for worldly gain, constantly frequent the portals of kings in abjection, and enter the gates of princes and grandees in abasement.[115]

The decision to exclude from the *Misbah* a passage that critiqued corrupt Sufis who frequented rulers highlighted the substantial efforts that the author undertook in his selection and exclusion–inclusion strategies in order to present a distinctly Sufi political theory that was on a par with others.

Conclusion

The author of the *Misbah* succeeded in presenting a coherent Sufi political theory. He expressed his distinctly Sufi theory of a legitimate, coercive and just sultanate based on five tenets. The first, was a conception of the highest political authority that was in harmony with the coercive sultanate argued for by al-Mawardi, al-Juwayni and al-Ghazali. It was also a conception that disregarded the caliphate and the lineage to Quraysh altogether. The author of the *Misbah* achieved this first aim based on a shrewd synthesis of these three thinkers. The second tenet was upholding the rule of law, which the author expressed in a Sufi language that was rooted in the works of al-Mawardi, Najm al-Din Daya Razi, and – through the latter – Ibn ʿArabi and al-Suhrawardi. This was presented to the dedicatee based on a mystical and Islamised system of ethics that included a Sufi conception of the philosopher king. The third tenet of the *Misbah* was its author's success in presenting a distinctly Sufi political theory. Although the *Misbah* was deeply rooted in Ashʿari–Shafiʿi political thought, the author succeeded in making it distinctly Sufi through a careful and artful reworking of works such as the *Adab al-dunya* and the *Mirsad*. The fourth tenet was that the *Misbah* tried to accommodate the concerns of its dedicatee, sultan Baybars. In the discussion of the vizierate, the treatise presented a suitable theory of delegation that fixed the origins of

115 Razi, *God's Bondsmen*, 449.

political authority within the sultanate as the successor of prophethood. This discussion may not have been expressed in the *Misbah* using the finest juristic language, but what mattered most was whether or not it was well received by its dedicatee. The fifth tenet was that the author of the *Misbah* succeeded in presenting his treatise as a serious strain of political thought by highlighting the merits of Sufis over some corrupt scholars.

The agency of the author of the *Misbah* was astonishing. Unfailingly, he demonstrated an informed and artful usage of the works of al-Mawardi, al-Juwayni, al-Ghazali and Najm al-Din Razi.[116] He succeeded in achieving a synthesis between the theories of the coercive sultanate in al-Ghazali's *Mustazhiri* and al-Juwayni's *Ghiyath* by merging the requirements for the *imam* and his duties from both works, while upholding al-Juwayni's views on Qurashi lineage. Furthermore, the careful selection of his sources also served the aims of his theory. For instance, using al-Mawardi's *Adab al-dunya* instead of *al-Ahkam al-sultaniyya* meant that the author could discuss the rule of coercive authority without referring to the caliphate. Additionally, his artful usage of treatises like the *Mirsad* reflected a command of the full original texts. As an illustration, omitting the mention of corrupt Sufis in order to promote Sufis as an impeccable alternative to corrupt scholars was a creative use of his sources. Consequently, the author of the *Misbah* succeeded in presenting Sufism as a source of a coherent political theory while at the same accommodating the concerns of his dedicatee and upholding the concern for the rule of law. The result of this agency was a truly distinct and coherent work of Islamic political thought.

The exposition of the author's Sufi conception of the rule of law differed from other treatises examined in this monograph. The *Misbah* relied on an ethical system of checks and balances to curtail the arbitrary exercise of power by the sultan. This conception was detailed in the second essay, titled *On the Nature of the Imamate*, using distinctly Sufi ideas that included, among others, a Sufi and Islamised interpretation of the philosopher king and relying on a mystical and moral language that was relevant to the *Misbah*'s historical and intellectual context. To achieve his aims, the Sufi author adapted and re-arranged passages from carefully selected texts of the Islamic and Sufi

[116] And probably others; the advance in digital humanities will shed more light on this.

political tradition. In his exquisite ethical discussion of the *imamate*, the author avoided, as much as he possibly could, juristic and legal stipulations and presented an original and distinctly Sufi contribution using moral, philosophical and mystical conceptualisations of the rule of law.

The *Misbah* nevertheless did not present an all-inclusive theory. It avoided treating important aspects that were central to other strains of political thought such as taxation, administrative law and the law of rebellion. In this the *Misbah* was significantly lacking in comparison with other juristic treatises discussed in this book. One explanation for this is that any discussion of the law of rebellion or taxation, for instance, would inevitably rely on the juristic language of the legal schools and, accordingly, dissipate the distinct and independent Sufi character of the *Misbah* for which the author was striving.

Finally, it is now possible to make some assertions and assumptions about the mysterious author of the *Misbah*. He was a self-professed Sufi, who was undoubtedly educated in an Ashʿari – probably Shafiʿi – milieu given his heavy reliance on the works of al-Mawardi, al-Juwayni and al-Ghazali. Based on his use of some of the political and doctrinal concepts of the aforementioned thinkers, it is possible also to ascertain that he was personally an Ashʿari and, in all likeliness, a Shafiʿi. Furthermore, he was well informed about the latest works of Sufism based on his reliance on near-contemporary Sufi texts. A final safe assumption that can be made based on the crafty dissemination of the conceptions of the *imamate* and the delegation of power throughout the *Misbah* is that the author was well experienced in communicating with the ruling military elites of the thirteenth century. The author probably came from a highly literate milieu that was staunchly Sufi–Ashʿari–Shafiʿi; one that was capable of making an artful synthesis of the political theories of al-Mawardi, al-Juwayni and al-Ghazali, and yet present it in an ethical and moral language of the Graeco-Arabic philosophy that resembled the *Kitab al-Siyasa al-mulukiyya*; one that understood and accommodated the worries of the ruling military elites; and one that had strong bonds to scholarly networks throughout the Islamic worlds. Perhaps this work has uncovered more clues that will reveal more of the author's identity in time.

The author of the *Misbah* thus achieved a distinctly Sufi expression of political thought in the early Mamluk period. Consequently, political thought should be considered part of the social and cultural output of Sufism that led to the popularisation of Sufism in the thirteenth century. As Hofer argued, this process of production included doing '"Sufi" things: dressing in certain ways, dancing, chanting, writing treatises, teaching disciples, parading in the streets and so on.'[117] I propose adding to Hofer's list the production of political thought as another 'Sufi thing' that contributed to the popularisation of Sufism in the Mamluk period.

[117] Hofer, *The Popularisation of Sufism*, 13.

4

The Late Ayyubid and Early Mamluk Context: Ibn Talha and al-Qarafi

This chapter argues that the writings of Ibn Talha (d. 652/1254) and al-Qarafi (d. 682/1283 or 684/1285) are emblematic of the production of political thought during the late Ayyubid and early Mamluk period. It reinforces a central tenet of this book, which is that political thought is best interpreted within its narrow historical context, and provides further challenges to the prevalent mythologies and approaches in the field. Authored immediately before and after the destruction of Baghdad by the Mongols, the two works of Ibn Talha and al-Qarafi that are examined here furnish first-hand evidence as to the candid views of Islamic thinkers on the institution of the caliphate. Furthermore, they show that the literary genre of a treatise is only a channel to convey political ideas and conceptions of authority and, accordingly, does not dictate their content. Additionally, the study of these two authors highlights how their immediate social and ideological contexts helped to shape their political postulations. Like others discussed so far in this monograph, Ibn Talha and al-Qarafi did not stray from the period's predominant concern to moderate and limit the exercise of sultanic power.

The previous two chapters highlighted novel and hitherto misinterpreted political themes in Ibn Jamaʿa's *Tahrir* and the anonymous *Misbah*. These two treatises, while sharing family resemblances with earlier Shafiʿi and Ashʿari–Sufi works, expressed new conceptions of political authority and the moderation of the exercise of sultanic power. Ibn Jamaʿa's tripartite conception of political authority ruled out the normative need for the caliphate, upheld the moderation of political power by proposing a proto-constitution that regulated all aspects of public life and empowering the administration, and proposed practicable solutions for the legitimate delegation of power to high-ranking offices of government. Likewise, the unknown Sufi author of the *Misbah* presented a coherent political theory that identified the sultanate as the legitimate heir of prophethood. He, additionally, proposed moderating sultanic power through an ethical system rooted in the *shariʿa* and in Islamised ethical systems often deriving from Graeco-Arabic philosophy. Neither author debated perennial answers. While they dealt with and reinterpreted questions treated by earlier thinkers such as al-Mawardi, their discussions yielded new answers that were relevant to their own contexts. Accordingly, their conceptions of the highest political authority in Islam and the moderation of power were drastically different. The two chapters reflected the creativity of authors of the Mamluk period in selecting from, altering and adapting earlier texts in order to suit their own aims in writing the *Misbah* and the *Tahrir*.

The present chapter seeks to consolidate the findings of the previous two chapters and, accordingly, confirm the methodological and theoretical backdrop of this monograph. In particular, I intend to validate the following two propositions put forward in Chapter 1: (1) there are no perennial answers in Islamic political thought, and – as such – (2) authors only treat concerns and ideas available to them in their empirical world.[1] I argue that one way to achieve these validations is through examining developments in Islamic political thought over narrower chronological intervals.[2] That is, as mentioned in the Introduction, less focus is needed on imagined continuities, and more on short-term and tangible development of political ideas – in this case the period between al-Kamil (d. 635/1237) and Baybars (d. 676/1277). Within this narrower and more meaningful interval, I plan to examine the emergence of political ideas in tandem with major political transformations, while keeping a close eye on the equally relevant intellectual, ideological and social contexts of the authors. This examination will not be limited to the tradition of authoring political advice, but will extend to theological and legal works.

---

[1] There is in fact a third proposition to demonstrate: (3) it is necessary to understand the prevailing conventions of the treatment of the authors' concerns in order to understand their political texts, but this will be discussed in the next chapter.

[2] This is not the same as examining the expansion of an author's ideas over a period of time as with Ibn Jamaʿa in Chapter 2, above.

The commonsensical starting point for tracing nascent political ideas within a narrower chronological context is the study of texts produced around the previous major political transformation. In the Syro-Egyptian lands, the obvious change that comes to mind is the colossal yet relatively well-ordered shift from the Ayyubid to Mamluk sultanate. The transition between these two military patronage states preserved the social and intellectual setting within which Islamic scholars operated and, furthermore, their processes of professionalisation and *adab*isation continued. This transition, likewise, did not alter the blossoming of Syro-Egyptian urban centres like Damascus and especially Cairo as universal hubs for knowledge transmission, despite continuous Frankish and Mongol disturbances. As for the major urban institutions that tied the old and new ruling elites to the civilian elites, such as the citadel, *madrasa*, Sufi hospice, hospital and charitable endowment, they survived the transition and even flourished afterwards.

By studying carefully selected political texts in the context of this late Ayyubid to Mamluk transition, one succeeds in isolating and highlighting nascent political ideas. To that end, this chapter identifies two pertinent texts for close examination: the first originated in Ayyubid northern Syria and the second in early Mamluk Cairo. The first treatise is the *Precious Subjects for the Council of al-Malik al-Nasir* (*Nafaʾis al-ʿanasir li-majalis al-Malik al-Nasir*), more commonly known as *The Unique Necklace for a Content King* (*al-ʿIqd al-farid li-al-malik al-Saʿid*), the title of its later and more popular recension. It was authored by Ibn Talha, a Shafiʿi–Ashʿari judge and legal theoretician, statesman of the Artuqids and late Ayyubids, Sufi and occultist. This work left a strong mark on Ibn Jamaʿa's *Tahrir* in style and content. The second treatise is the more renowned *Book of Perfection in Distinguishing Legal Opinions from Judicial Rulings and the Discretionary Actions of Judges and Rulers* (*al-Ihkam fi tamyiz al-fatawa ʿan al-ahkam wa tasarrufat al-qadi wa al-imam*). Authored by the Maliki–Ashʿari legal theoretician al-Qarafi, this treatise is a work of speculative jurisprudence and law. It contains a valuable contribution to the history of Islamic political thought based on al-Qarafi's novel interpretation of the Prophet's actions.

These two treatises demonstrate that there are no perennial answers in medieval Islamic political thought. They express various political concerns and ideas that were shaped by the intellectual, professional and empirical worlds of their authors: Ibn Talha and al-Qarafi. This chapter challenges the prevailing mythology that the literary genre of a treatise dictated its contents and postulated political ideas in two ways: it shows that Ibn Talha's treatise was based on an amalgamation of literary genres and that political thought can equally be found in works of speculative jurisprudence and law such as al-Qarafi's. Furthermore, this chapter demonstrates how the professional background of Ibn Talha and the immediate non-political concerns of al-Qarafi helped to shape their political discussions. Additionally, the relevance of the emergence of both Ibn Talha and al-Qarafi within the Shafiʿi–Ashʿari intellectual Syro-Egyptian milieu, notwithstanding that the latter was a Maliki jurist, will be treated. Overall, the chapter contests the fallacy that Muslim authors were constantly yearning for the institution of the caliphate. It posits that late Ayyubid and early Mamluk period authors, including Ibn Talha and al-Qarafi, were not interested in restoring the potency of the caliphate – neither before nor after the fall of Baghdad – but rather concerned with continuity, stability, proper running of government and moderating the exercise of coercive power.

Ibn Talha: Taming Sultanic Power

The relevance of Ibn Talha's *al-ʿIqd al-farid* (or *Nafaʾis al-ʿanasir*) extends well beyond its palpable influence on the style and content of Ibn Jamaʿa's *Tahrir*.[3] *Al-ʿIqd al-farid* encapsulates the opulent tradition of advice literature that characterised the late Ayyubid and early Mamluk period. Several features of this treatise make it a genealogical missing link that shows the development of a distinct approach to writing political thought in the thirteenth century. Dedicated to the last effective Ayyubid sultan in Syria and written at the dawn of the Mamluk period, *al-ʿIqd al-farid* attests to the elaboration of a blended genre that merged classical legalistic discussions with other genres of advice literature, including administrative handbooks, mirrors for princes, ethical and homiletic writings, and other didactic works. Such a fusion reaffirms that in the history of Islamic political thought, genre is better studied as a mere vehicle to convey political ideas and not as an end in itself, a point that was stressed in Chapter 1.

[3] This influence was alluded to in Chapter 2, 73, above.

The distinctive thematic and stylistic developments exhibited in *al-ʿIqd al-farid* are linked to the intellectual milieu within which its author emerged. I have argued elsewhere that the intricate background of Ibn Talha was reflected in the variety of subjects and concerns that were covered in his treatise.[4] Like other authors discussed so far in this research, Ibn Talha emerged in the wider Shafiʿi, Ashʿari and Sufi intellectual milieu of the Syro-Egyptian lands. Moreover, he was a litterateur, occultist, diplomat, seasoned statesman and at one point in his career a vizier. Consequently, Ibn Talha's multiple aims in writing *al-ʿIqd al-farid* were shaped by his intellectual and professional background, and his proximity to rulers. These aims ranged from displaying his literary and administrative credentials, educating and entertaining his dedicatees, and – most importantly – moderating their exercise of power. This section hence argues that, like Ibn Jamaʿa and the anonymous Sufi author of the *Misbah* discussed in Chapter 2 and Chapter 3, Ibn Talha aimed at upholding the ideals of the rule of law, limited government, and delegation of power, and the proper and legitimate running of government in the absence of a caliph.

Ibn Talha: Life and Work

Abu Salim Kamal al-Din Ibn Talha al-Nusaybini (582/1186/7–652/1254) was a Shafiʿi legal theoretician (*usuli*) and an expert in the study of divergence between legal schools or disputation (*khilaf*).[5] Ibn Talha was furthermore a litterateur and a statesman who served Ayyubid and Artuqid rulers, participated in diplomatic missions, held the judgeship of his northern Syrian hometown Nusaybin, and served as preacher of the Umayyad Mosque in Damascus.[6] In 648/1250, Ayyubid sultan al-Nasir Salah al-Din Yusuf

[4] Refer to El-Merheb, 'Islamic Political Thought and Professional Mobility'. Although the main focus of this article was on professional mobility rather than political thought, it is inevitable that some parts of this present chapter – including biographical and bibliographical information – are very similar.

[5] Taj al-Din al-Subki, *Tabaqat al-Shafiʿiyya al-kubra*, ed. Mustafa ʿAbd al-Qadir Ahmad ʿAta ʿAta, 6 vols (Beirut: Dar al-Kutub al-ʿIlmiyya, 1999), 4:272–3; al-Safadi, *al-Wafi bi-al-wafayat*, 3:146; Abu Shama, *al-Dhayl ʿala al-rawdatayn*, 188; al-Yafiʿi, *Mirʾat al-jinan wa-ʿibrat al-yaqzan fi maʿrifat ma yuʿtabar min hawadith al-zaman*, 4 vols (Beirut: Dar al-Kutub al-ʿIlmiyya, 1997), 4:99–100; Ibn Taghribirdi, *Nujum*, 7:30.

[6] Stephen Humphreys mentions that Ibn Talha was the preacher of the Umayyad Mosque in *From Saladin to the Mongols: The Ayyubids of Damascus, 1193–1260* (Albany, NY: SUNY Press, 1977), 247. Ibn Taghribirdi uses *mufti* to describe Ibn Talha, in *Nujum*, 17:30.

(r. 634/1237–658/1260) entered Damascus and appointed him vizier; after holding the post for two days, Ibn Talha removed himself and disappeared.[7] It is said that during this period he wore the cotton garment of the Sufis and became an ascetic. Later, he reappeared in Aleppo where he died in 652/1254. Ibn Talha had a passion for the science of letters (*ʿilm al-huruf*) and the science of magic squares (*ʿilm al-awfaq*): the occult sciences of the numerical values of Arabic letters, often applied to verses in the Qurʾan to learn the esoteric significance of creation. Such sciences were often connected to the Sufi belief in the unity of creation (*wahdat al-wujud*), but also associated with the practice of astrology.[8]

Some anecdotes claimed that Ibn Talha predicted the date of his own death on the basis of his study of the letters of a verse recited by a wandering Sufi (*faqir*) in Mount Lebanon.[9] Ibn Talha is said to have later renounced such interests and composed the following verses in retrospect:

> Never trust the prediction of an astrologer; all matters are attributed to God
> A true Muslim should not suppose that planets could influence the occurrence of events.[10]

As this section will show, this intricate background marked his political thought in various ways.

Advice literature was also one of Ibn Talha's fields of enquiry.[11] He dedicated the same treatise to two different rulers under different titles.[12] *Nafaʾis*

---

[7] In 648/1250, al-Nasir Yusuf entered Damascus during a politically volatile situation in Egypt and Syria; Humphreys, *From Saladin to the Mongols*, 306.

[8] During the Mamluk period, this 'science that had formerly been the reserve of small and discreet communities of practitioners' was now being made available to a 'much wider audience of literate and devout readers, as well as Turkish military–political elites'; refer to Noah Gardiner, 'The Occultist Encyclopedism of ʿAbd Al-Raḥmān al-Bisṭāmī', *Mamlūk Studies Review* 20 (2017): 29. For a comprehensive study that covers various aspects of Ibn Talha's occultism, refer to A. C. S. Peacock, 'Politics, Religion and the Occult in the Works of Kamal Al-Din Ibn Talha, a Vizier, 'Alim and Author in Thirteenth-Century Syria', in Carole Hillenbrand (ed.), *Syria in Crusader Times: Conflict and Coexistence* (Edinburgh: Edinburgh University Press, 2020), 34–60.

[9] For a detailed account, refer to al-Yafiʿi, *Mirʾat al-jinan*, 4:99.

[10] Ibn Talha, *al-ʿIqd al-farid li-al-malik al-Saʿid*, ed. Yusuf bin ʿUthman al-Hazim (Riyadh: Ibn al-Azraq Center for Political Studies, 2013), 21.

[11] Refer to El-Merheb, 'Islamic Political Thought and Professional Mobility', 211, for the same discussion.

[12] Peacock, 'Politics, Religion and the Occult', 43.

al-ʿanasir li-majalis al-Malik al-Nasir was dedicated to the Ayyubid sultan al-Nasir Salah al-Din Yusuf and later to the Artuqid ruler of Mardin, al-Saʿid Najm al-Din Ghazi (r. 637/1239–658/1260) as *al-ʿIqd al-farid li-al-malik al-Saʿid*. As clearly established by Andrew Peacock, these two treatises were nearly identical except for some minor differences, such as the dedicatee's name and one passage in the *Nafaʾis* hailing sultan al-Nasir's victory over the Khwarazmians in 644/1246.[13] Peacock also noted that it 'was as *al-ʿIqd al-farid* that the work became popular, surviving in numerous manuscripts'.[14] *Nafaʾis al-ʿanasir* clearly predated *al-ʿIqd al-farid* as Ibn Talha did not trouble himself with removing the Ayyubid sultan's name from the copy he dedicated later to the Artuqid ruler where, for instance, interestingly, he discussed the merit of the Ayyubid sultan's first name, Yusuf, using the numerical values of letters.[15] For ease of reference and as both treatises are nearly identical, the more popular title, *al-ʿIqd al-farid*, will be used in what follows.

I will, nevertheless, refer one final time to *Nafaʾis al-ʿanasir* as a note is warranted on its dedicatee. Sultan al-Nasir Salah al-Din Yusuf's dramatic reign(s) over Aleppo and Damascus between 634/1237 and 658/1260 epitomised every characteristic of the transition from Ayyubid to Mamluk rule.[16] On a political and military level, the Ayyubid sultan was embroiled in early competitions among the *Bahri* Mamluks, and was defeated by Egyptian Mamluk armies in 648/1250, then decisively in 648/1251, and his attempts to take Cairo failed again in 653/1255.[17] Furthermore, al-Nasir paid the ultimate price for the Mamluk victory over the Mongols at ʿAyn Jalut in 658/1260 since, upon hearing the news of his army's humiliating defeat, Hulegu summarily executed him at his court in Tabriz.[18]

---

[13] Ibid., 43.

[14] Ibid. As per Peacock's complaint of the state of available editions, the one to which I had access was unsatisfactory and confusing with no serious effort to ascertain the dedicatee's identity.

[15] Refer to Ibn Talha, *al-ʿIqd al-farid*, 328, 340–1. This suggests that Ibn Talha renounced his interest in *ʿilm al-huruf* after dedicating the book to two rulers or – most likely – that he never did renounce it. Moreover, there seems to be unwarranted confusion regarding the identity of the dedicatee of *al-ʿIqd al-farid* (in fact, *Nafaʾis al-ʿanasir*). One scholar believed the treatise was dedicated to al-Malik al-Saʿid Nasir al-Din Baraka (1260–1280), son of Baybars; refer to the editor's note, in Ibn Nubata, *al-Mukhtar min kitab tadbir al-duwal*, ed. Salwa Qindil (Beirut: al-Abhath li-al-Tarjama wa-al-Nashr wa-al-Tawziʿ, 2006), 79–80.

[16] For more on this sultan, refer to Humphreys, *From Saladin to the Mongols*, 309–63.

[17] Ibid., 315–16, 317–19, 327–8.

[18] Ibid., 357–8.

The Blending of Genres

Ibn Talha's career deeply marked his political thought.[19] I have already mentioned above that his background as judge, Shafiʿi jurist and legal theoretician, staunch Ashʿari–Sufi, statesman and courtier of the Ayyubid and Artuqid sultanates, preacher of the Great Mosque of Damascus, and occultist influenced the thematic and stylistic features of *al-ʿIqd al-farid*. This intricate professional and intellectual background was reflected in the variety of subjects that were covered in *al-ʿIqd al-farid*, which attested to the elaboration of a blended genre during the late Ayyubid and early Mamluk period. In a nutshell, Ibn Talha attempted to cover in one treatise what others achieved in a multitude of works that treated the origins of political authority, the duties and rights of a ruler, senior administrative functions, and the virtues that a ruler should possess.

Al-ʿIqd al-farid resembles a blend of a collection of earlier and subsequent works of political advice. Ibn Talha's treatise merged constitutional and juristic discussions, akin to al-Mawardi's *Ahkam* and Ibn Jamaʿa's *Tahrir*, with a wide range of other genres of advice literature, including administrative and statecraft handbooks such as al-Shayzari's (d. 589/1193) *al-Nahj al-masluk fi siyasat al-muluk* (*The Established Path to the Statecraft of Kings*), dedicated to Salah al-Din (532/1138–589/1193), and al-Subki's *Muʿid al-niʿam*;[20] works referred to as mirrors for princes, such as Ibn al-Haddad's *al-Jawhar al-nafis fi siyasat al-raʾis* (*The Exquisite Kernel of the Ruler's Statecraft*), dedicated to Badr al-Din Luʾluʾ (r. 631/1234–657/1259), ruler of Mosul, and al-ʿAbbasi's (fl. first quarter of eighth/fourteenth century) *Athar al-uwal fi tartib al-duwal* (*Foregoing Examples of Statecraft*), dedicated to Baybars al-Jashankir in 709/1309;[21] Sufi political treatises such as the anonymous *Misbah* discussed

[19] El-Merheb, 'Islamic Political Thought and Professional Mobility', 212 and *passim*.

[20] al-Shayzari, *al-Nahj al-masluk fi siyasat al-muluk*, ed. Muhammad Ismaʿil and Ahmad al-Mazidi (Beirut: Dar al-Kutub al-ʿIlmiyya, 2003).

[21] Ibn al-Haddad, *al-Jawhar al-nafis fi siyasat al-raʾis (649/1251/2)*, ed. Radwan al-Sayyid (Beirut: Dar al-Taliʿa, 1983). Al-ʿAbbasi, *Athar al-uwal fi tartib al-duwal* (Cairo: al-Matbaʿa al-Maymaniyya, 1878); al-ʿAbbasi – also referred to as al-Safadi – was a secretary in the chancery and worked in the postal service. He dedicated other works and poems to at least two other Mamluk sultans, al-ʿAdil Kitbugha and al-Nasir Muhammad, in addition to Abu al-Fidaʾ, the Ayyubid ruler of Hama. Refer to Stefan Leder, 'Sultanic Rule in the Mirror of Medieval Political Literature', in Neguin Yavari and Regula Forster (eds), *Global Medieval: Mirrors*

in Chapter 3, which was probably dedicated to Baybars I; ethical and homiletic writings, such as al-Mawardi's *Tashil al-nazar* and his *Adab al-dunya wa-al-din*, and the anonymous *Bahr al-fawa'id* (*The Sea of Precious Virtues*), composed in mid-twelfth-century Zangid Syria; other forms of courtly didactic works, such as Ibn al-Wahid's (647/1249/50–711/1311/2) *al-Urjuza al-ma'rufa bi-Nisf al-'aysh fi tadbir hadhihi al-hayat* (*The Metric Poem [Titled] Half of One's Life is Based on His Proper Administration*), dedicated to al-Ashraf Khalil Ibn Qalawun;[22] and finally other works such as *Qadah al-dirasa fi manahij al-siyasa* (*The Goblet of Instruction in the Ways of Government*), dedicated to Qalawun (r. 678/1279–689/1290) with no intelligible political theory, which simply intended to gain the sultan's favour.[23] Additionally, Ibn Talha, aimed to entertain at court and impress his dedicatees using his knowledge of the numerical values of letters.[24] These categories are in no way

for Princes Revisited (Cambridge, MA: Harvard University Press, 2015), 93–111, where the title is translated as 'Teachings of the Ancients on the Organization of Dynastic Rule'; and to Maurice A. Pomerantz, 'A Maqāma Collection by a Mamlūk Historian: Al-Maqāmāt al-Ǧalāliyya by al-Ḥasan b. Abī Muḥammad al-Ṣafadī (Fl. First Quarter of the 8th/14th c.)', *Arabica* 61(6) (2014): 631–63; Maurice A. Pomerantz, 'The Play of Genre: A Maqāma of "Ease after Hardship" from the Eighth/Fourteenth Century and its Literary Context', in Maurice A. Pomerantz and Aram A. Shahin (eds), *The Heritage of Arabo-Islamic Learning* (Leiden: Brill, 2015), 461–82. Refer also to the useful introduction by the editor of al-'Abbasi, *Nuzhat al-malik wa-al-mamluk fi mukhtasar sirat man waliya Misr min-al-muluk*, ed. 'Umar 'Abd al-Salam Tadmuri (Sayda and Beirut: al-Maktaba al-'Asriyya, 2003), and 7, 9, 10. Al-'Abbasi may have authored another work of political thought, which was probably dedicated to al-'Adil Kitbugha (14); however, Pomerantz believes it was the same work as *Athar al-uwal* (refer to 'A Maqāma Collection', 634).

22 The author of *Nisf al-'aysh* was a chancery secretary who also held a post in the Hakim Mosque in Cairo; in addition, he was a poet, a renowned calligrapher and a translator. The poem's title is based on a rearrangement of a weak prophetic *hadith*, 'proper administration is half of one's life' (*al-tadbir nisf al-'aysh*). It is available in Leipzig as a beautiful manuscript copied in 697/1297; Ibn al-Wahid, 'Al-Urjuza al-ma'rufa bi-nisf al-'aysh fi tadbir hadhihi al-hayat', MS University Library of Leipzig (1297), Vollers 0553. The quality of the manuscript suggests that it was intended for circulation among the elite, most likely for court use. For more on the poet's biography refer to *Nisf al-'aysh*, ed. 'Adil al-Bakri (al-Mawsil: Matba'at al-Jumhuriyya, 1969), 9–12; Ibn Hajar, *Durar*, 3:453–6; al-Kutubi, *Fawat al-wafayat*, ed. Ihsan 'Abbas, 5 vols (Beirut: Dar Sadir, 1973), 3:390–1; al-Safadi, *al-Wafi bi-al-wafayat*, 3:125–7.

23 *Qadah al-dirasa fi manahij al-siyasa*, MS British Library, Or.1534; the BL manuscript is possibly from the Mamluk period. The work seems to be mostly based on aphorisms, wisdom and anecdotes from earlier texts and anthologies. Its unknown author mentioned that he composed his work 'in the hope that he [the sultan] will accept it and it will become my means of access to him (*wasilati ilayhi*)'. For more on this treatise, refer to Marlow, 'The Way of Viziers', 179.

24 Peacock spotted aspects of this amalgamation and noted, 'To a degree then, one may see Ibn Talha's project as successfully weaving together two disparate strands in the Mirrors for Princes

mutually exclusive and are used here merely to illustrate *al-ʿIqd al-farid*'s blending of genres.[25]

The opening section of *al-ʿIqd al-farid* prepared its audience for the above-mentioned fusion of themes and styles. Here Ibn Talha announced his intent to combine almost every 'expected' mode of presentation and the different generic stylistic and thematic features that characterised other works of advice literature of his age.[26] This section goes on to provide a panoply of examples that illustrate his declared intent. For instance, he included an 'explicit statement of purpose' where he acknowledged the favour bestowed upon him by the sultan and dedicated his work to the latter as a token of appreciation.[27] In this statement of purpose, Ibn Talha urged the sultan to consult this treatise frequently to benefit from its wisdom. Furthermore, the author's use of stylistic techniques like courtly Arabic rhyming prose and the pairing of synonymous words is evident in the opening of *al-ʿIqd al-farid*.[28] That was aided no doubt by the author's intimate knowledge of the writing arts of the chancery.[29] As for literary genres, Ibn Talha's opening indicated that his treatise would resemble mirrors for princes when he declared his intention to treat themes like character traits and virtues (*akhlaq*), passions (*shahawat*), gracious and desirable qualities (*sifat hamida, marghuba*), and disreputable and unpleasant qualities (*sifat madhmuma, qabiha*).[30] Additionally, Ibn Talha mentioned his reliance on the genre of historical example by investigating the lives of great models and kings.[31] He proclaimed, likewise, his attention

tradition, the more homiletic, religiously motivated works with the legalistic and normative'; in 'Politics, Religion and the Occult', 54.

25 For more on some of the treatises mentioned here and the limitations of these classifications, refer to the seminal article by Marlow, 'Advice and Advice Literature', *EI*³.

26 Marlow noted that similar works of advice literature displayed 'expected' and 'generic' features that included the use of stylistic techniques like rhyming prose or pairing of synonymous words, systematic gathering from anthologies, and, most noticeably, the common use of ten chapters divided by usual themes; in 'The Way of Viziers', 177–84. For a similar discussion relevant to the Anatolian context, refer to A. C. S. Peacock, 'Advice for the Sultans of Rum: The "Mirrors for Princes" of Early Thirteenth-Century Anatolia', in Bill Hickman, Gary Leiser and Robert Dankoff (eds), *Turkish Language, Literature, and History: Travellers' Tales, Sultans, and Scholars since the Eighth Century* (Routledge: London, 2016), 276–307.

27 Ibn Talha, *al-ʿIqd al-farid*, 23–4; Marlow, 'The Way of Viziers', 179.

28 For more on this stylistic feature, refer to Marlow, 'The Way of Viziers', 178.

29 Refer to Ibn Talha, *al-ʿIqd al-farid*, 256–64.

30 Ibid., 25–6.

31 Ibid., p. 28. In this *al-ʿIqd al-farid* resembled al-ʿAbbasi's *Athar al-uwal*. The use of carefully

to the importance of holding the proper creeds (*ʿaqaʾid*).[32] Furthermore, he incorporated clear signs of his Sufism as is evident in his reference to gnostics (*ahl al-hidaya wa-al-ʿirfan*) when discussing the passions and virtues of men.[33] The opening thus heralded the amalgamated nature of the treatise.

The chapterisation of *al-ʿIqd al-farid* mirrored Ibn Talha's amalgamation of literary genres of advice literature.[34] The author divided his work into four main sections, the content of which resembled a mirror for princes, followed by a juristic political treatise, an administrative manual spreading over the second and third chapters, and finally an addendum:[35]

1. Noble character and attributes (*al-akhlaq wa-al-sifat*);
2. The sultanate and [the main] functions (*al-saltana wa-al-wilayat*);
3. Law and religious matters (*al-shariʿa wa-al-diyanat*);
4. An addendum consisting of assorted themes.

This structure secured the treatment of nearly all themes of Islamic advice literature, including the virtues and temperament of the ruler often found in mirrors for princes authored by Ashʿari-Sufis; followed by a discussion of the constitutional, legal and religious foundations of the sultanate typical of juridical treatises of Shafiʿi jurists; the main administrative and religious offices found in statecraft manuals of Ayyubid statesmen and judges; and, lastly, a selection of anecdotes that resembled mere *adab* works and aimed to instruct and entertain the ruler and his court, and reflect the author's varied literary and administrative proficiencies, and his occultism. In the following discussion, I address Ibn Talha's various aims in writing *al-ʿIqd al-farid* by looking at the four thematic sections in turn.

---

selected precedents and anecdotes from the Ayyubid period is also evident in Ibn Nubata's work, which was dedicated to an Ayyubid prince; refer to *al-Mukhtar min kitab tadbir al-duwal*, 104–6, 107, 118–19, 153–4, 163–4, 215.

32 Ibn Talha, *al-ʿIqd al-farid*, 28. The author includes a strong anti-anthropomorphism paragraph on 53. For more on this discourse refer to discussion and fn. 38, below.

33 Ibid., 25. This was reminiscent of the *Misbah* where the author displayed his Sufi colours in the prologue; refer to 'Misbah al-hidaya', fols. 4–9 as discussed in Chapter 3.

34 Refer to El-Merheb, 'Islamic Political Thought and Professional Mobility', 213 for the same discussion.

35 Ibn Talha, *al-ʿIqd al-farid*, 28.

Moderation of Power by Ethics

The first section (or foundation) of *al-ʿIqd al-farid* reads like works that are commonly referred to as mirrors for princes. This is manifest in its structure, content, sources and the author's ideological influences. In terms of structure, the first foundation resembles a standalone mirror featuring the usual ten subsections as per the customary literary practice of the time.[36] Ibn Talha listed the following ten subsections:[37]

1. On reason as a basis for the right creed of monotheism and the required religious duties;
2. On the praise of forbearance and caution and the disparagement of trepidation and hastiness;
3. On the praise of gratitude and the disparagement of ingratitude;
4. On the bliss of counsel and the dispraise of shunning it;
5. On justice and equity and the dispraise of injustice and unfairness;
6. On agreement and collaboration and the dispraise of divergence and disagreement;
7. On trustworthiness and the dispraise of betrayal;
8. On vigilance and resourcefulness and the dispraise of hesitation and negligence;
9. On forgiveness, beneficence and relief for the destitute;
10. On honesty and the dispraise of deceit.

Ibn Talha thus adhered to the global tradition of Islamic advice literature of the thirteenth and fourteenth centuries and treated its expected themes, including the merits of justice, consultation, liberality and moderation. Furthermore, the mirror for princes embedded in *al-ʿIqd al-farid* is edifying with regard to Ibn Talha's sources and his professional, theological and intellectual background. It confirms that he was an *adab*ised jurist who relished writing in high chancery language, and that he was acquainted with court interests and etiquette. This section also reflects that he was an ardent

[36] Refer Marlow, 'The Way of Viziers', 177–84.
[37] Ibn Talha, *al-ʿIqd al-farid*, 29.

Ash'ari, Shafi'i and Sufi, as is evident from his sources and deployment of particular parables and discussions. For instance, Ibn Talha's Sufism and Ash'arism were apparent when he quoted al-Qushayri (d. 465/1072) and included a paragraph laden with anti-anthropomorphism evocative of the Shafi'i–Ash'ari rhetoric directed against traditionalist Hanbalis in thirteenth-century Damascus.[38] In terms of sources, the indications that Ibn Talha benefited from al-Mawardi's works are easy to discern. To name one, *al-'Iqd al-farid*'s first subsection on reason, in its treatment of instinctive and acquired reason, relied on the first section of al-Mawardi's *Adab al-dunya* titled *Regarding the Merits of Reason and the Dispraise of Passion.*[39]

Coercive Power: Legitimacy, Necessity and Justice

The second section of *al-'Iqd al-farid* focused on the sultanate and the main offices of the government. Here Ibn Talha treated the themes of the need for the sultanate and the divine legitimacy of the sultan, the moderation of the exercise of power, and the main governmental appointments and, as such, delegation of power. Although this section resembled, structurally and thematically, classical juristic and constitutional treatises such as al-Mawardi's *Ahkam*, it displayed a strong Sufi flavour and reflected – in a very original way – the author's late Ayyubid context and his own political concerns and aims. Ibn Talha divided it into two subsections as follows:[40]

1. The sultanate, the qualities of the chosen sultan, and what is required to uphold its provisions;
2. The [principal] offices that administer the realm and control the affairs of the state, and the description of various supervisory ranks.

---

[38] For al-Qushayri's quotations refer to Ibn Talha, *al-'Iqd al-farid*, 71. For more on the debate on divine attributes and its context refer to al-Subki, *Tabaqat*, 4:360–8; Konrad Hirschler, 'Pre-Eighteenth-Century Traditions of Revivalism: Damascus in the Thirteenth Century', *BSOAS* 68(2) (2005): 197, 201, 202, 213; George Makdisi, 'Ash'arī and the Ash'arites in Islamic Religious History I', *Studia Islamica* 17 (1962): 44–67; Pouzet, *Damas au VIIe–XIIIe siècle*, 88–93; and Chapter 5, 168–73, below.

[39] Al-Mawardi, *Adab al-dunya*, 6–33.

[40] Ibn Talha, *al-'Iqd al-farid*, 231–76.

Like juristic treatises, the second section started with an extensive discussion on the need for the sultan.[41] The first subsection listed several rationalisations for the sultanate that stressed the divine legitimacy of the coercive sultan and alluded to what was expected from him in return. Ibn Talha's proposed formula was simple: the divine legitimacy of the sultan's coercive power was respected and its longevity guaranteed in exchange for upholding the right creed, tending to the interests of the populace and moderating the exercise of power. Ibn Talha stated that: the sultanate was a divine secret (*sirr min asrar al-rububiyya*); the sultan was needed to 'tend to the people of God, protect the land of God, guard the religion of God, uphold the prescribed legal punishments (*hudud*) of God, and safeguard the laws of God'; the sultan was sanctioned (*irtadahu*) by God for this task and, as such, total obedience was due to him; and he was the reflection of God on earth.[42] The sultan thus became a necessity since without him, the author explained, there was no safety, no ritual prayer, no cultivation of land, no trade, no craftsmanship and no transmission of knowledge.[43] In return, God required the sultan to uphold the true creed and the rightful Sufi way (*tariqa*), maintain virtuous conduct, achieve honourable deeds, and be effective and dedicated in carrying out his duties.[44]

Although *al-ʿIqd al-farid* resembled a juristic treatise, Ibn Talha's conception of supreme political authority was essentially a Sufi one. As with the *Misbah* discussed in Chapter 3, *al-ʿIqd al-farid*'s theory of legitimacy and delegation posited that the sultan was the heir of prophethood and, as such, was fully delegated with caliphal authorities that were moderated by an eclectic ethical system partially rooted in the *shariʿa*. As the ruler's comportment and virtues were central to this ethical system, Ibn Talha reminded his audience that the first section of his treatise had already emphasised the need to cultivate noble traits and that he had felt compelled to reiterate some of the traits pertinent to the sultan.[45] Following that, Ibn Talha treated the

41 Refer to El-Merheb, 'Islamic Political Thought and Professional Mobility', 214–16; the discussion in this section is more detailed and brings to light further aspects of Ibn Talha's thought.

42 Ibn Talha, *al-ʿIqd al-farid*, 235–6. I use reflection instead of shadow as a more meaningful translation that was suggested to me by Suzanne Ruggi.

43 Ibid., 236.

44 Ibid.; Ibn Talha proclaims subsequently that the sultan is the vice-regent of God (see 246, 248).

45 Ibid., 236–8.

primacy of the rank of prophethood (*nubuwwa*) and stated that its holders commanded the highest and noblest traits. The author then mentioned that since the sultanate was, similarly, among the elevated positions, the sultan's self-management (*siyasat al-nafs*) was a prerequisite to running the affairs of his subjects. By making this rather blatant insinuation that the sultanate was in the same rank as prophethood, Ibn Talha connected the two and suggested that the sultanate was second to prophethood and its legitimate heir in a way that was reminiscent of the *Misbah*.[46] As per the Sufi model of the *Misbah*, the moderation of the exercise of power by the sultan can be achieved through an ethical system that had roots within and outside the *shariʿa*; this becomes clear in the author's treatment of the ten duties of the sultan.

Ibn Talha then discussed the qualities of the chosen sultan and listed the traits that must be avoided.[47] This discussion and, more generally, the ethical system proposed by *al-ʿIqd al-farid* were influenced by works on ethical qualities, including al-Mawardi's *Tashil al-nazar*.[48] Arrogance (*kibar*), pride (*ʿajab*), vanity (*ghurur*), avarice (*shihh*) and deceit (*kadhib*) were five dangerous attributes that the sultan should not exhibit. There were very similar discussions in the *Tashil*, especially on arrogance and pride. Furthermore, Ibn Talha mentioned the need for the sultan to be a careful listener, to measure his words, avoid rage and obstinacy, be discreet, allot and manage his time efficiently, use capable aides and deputies, and seek advice. He made some further suggestions, some of which seem to derive verbatim from the *Tashil*.[49]

In the next subsection, *al-ʿIqd al-farid* treated the ten duties required of the ruler in a very original fashion. The stylistic features of this list look like

---

[46] Ibid., 237. The *Misbah* attempted a similar stratagem, albeit in a less oblique fashion: its author altered the words of Najm al-Din Razi to equate the sultanate with the caliphate, considering it the heir to prophethood; refer to Chapter 3, 112–16.

[47] With such similarities between the two treatises, it makes sense that the sources of and influences upon *al-ʿIqd al-farid* are similar to those of the *Misbah*.

[48] The five traits are discussed in Ibn Talha, *al-ʿIqd al-farid*, 238–42. Refer to al-Mawardi, *Tashil al-nazar wa taʿjil al-zafar fi akhlaq al-malik wa-siyasat al-mulk*, ed. Hasan al-Saʿati and Muhyi Hilal al-Sarhan (Beirut: Dar al-Nahda, 1981), 50–2, where al-Mawardi treated arrogance (*kibar*) and pride (*ʿajab*). For further similar discussions refer to 67–70, 112–14.

[49] Ibn Talha, *al-ʿIqd al-farid*, 242–3. For more similarities with al-Mawardi refer to *Tashil al-nazar* for a discussion on rage, 72–3, on obstinacy, 75, and especially on the merits of being discreet, 89–93. Ibn Talha sometimes resorted to thematic treatment and made it difficult to spot this reuse, as it was not always verbatim. It is also possible that both works benefited from the same sources.

those proposed in al-Mawardi's *Ahkam* and Ibn Jama'a's *Tahrir*, yet they mirror Ibn Talha's life and career and echo his own concerns as a courtier, statesman and judge of the late Ayyubid period. Elements of the author's professional background are manifest in the following original list:[50]

1. To protect the lands of Islam from external threats by retaining *amir*s and armies, and maintaining readiness and vigilance to deter the enemy.
2. To inspect the frontier posts and fortifications by appointing the right governors and guardians, and by maintaining and arming the frontier posts.
3. To uphold sultanic justice (*al-siyasat*[51]) in order to repel the corrupt and the aggressors so that people can safely earn their livelihood and benefit from safe travel on the road.
4. To uphold legally prescribed punishments (*hudud*) as they deter criminal and unjust acts and result in protecting lives and wealth. These fixed punishments should never be susceptible to intercession.
5. To uphold the *shari'a* and abide by it. The sultan should tend to the affairs of scholars, jurists and judges who uphold the *shari'a*. Furthermore, Ibn Talha stated that the sultan should carefully appoint 'righteous judges to end disagreements, preserve money and rights from loss', and that the latter could be achieved by deterring the 'greedy' and setting proper contracts for each individual situation.
6. To arrange appropriate land grants (*iqta'*) for *amir*s and soldiers based on their service and contribution.
7. To manage properly various expenditures and the collection of revenues, and to achieve this efficiently and equitably by being just and fair as this is the greatest assurance against wastage.
8. To commission capable and trustworthy functionaries and advisers.
9. To dedicate time to sit in on *mazalim* (sultanic or non-*shari'a* courts) in order to expose injustice and uphold the 'duties of reason and justice' so that grievances are resolved.[52]

---

[50] Ibn Talha, *al-'Iqd al-farid*, 246–8.

[51] For more on *siyasa*, refer to the discussion in Chapter 1, 44–5, above, and to Rapoport, 'Royal Justice and Religious Law'.

[52] This seems again to be a call for empowering sultanic justice. Further research is needed on the

10. To be constantly informed about various circumstances in the realm through spies and emissaries in order to be able to act swiftly.

Ibn Talha ended this discussion by stating that the sultan was the 'deputy of God' in tending to his people and managing their affairs.

In summary, Ibn Talha's treatment of the ten duties required of the ruler was quite unique, since it transformed a classical juristic discussion that was supposed to remind the sultan of his obligations into one that reinforced his divine rights, political and judicial powers, and aimed to prolong his rule. The essence of Ibn Talha's conception and legitimation of supreme Islamic political authority was that of an Ashʿari–Sufi, Shafiʿi judge and legal theoretician, courtier and professional statesman of the late Ayyubid period. This is apparent in that Ibn Talha does not refer to the list as ten 'duties', but rather as ten 'matters' that required the sultan's attention as they were 'pivotal' to running the realm.[53] Furthermore, the longevity of the sultanate appeared to be one of the author's main concerns; Ibn Talha stated that should the sultan observe these rules in his various decisions, he would secure the preservation of his dominion (*hama hawzat mamlakatihi*).[54] Ibn Talha's discussion also reflected a tendency to assert additional sultanic powers in the judicial sphere by upholding the role of *mazalim* courts, as the third and ninth duties called for the need for swift sultanic justice in the realm. Most noticeably, Ibn Talha reinforced the divine origin of the sultan's legitimacy by mentioning that the sultan 'was bequeathed by God the bliss of the sultanate', and was God's 'deputy in protecting the realm and attending to the people', and vice-regent (*inna al-sultan naʾib Allah fi khaliqatihi*).[55] Nevertheless, the sultan's exercise of power was to be moderated by the requirement to 'uphold the *shariʿa* and abide by it', good governance, the need to be just and equitable, and reliance on capable and trustworthy assistants as clearly stipulated in clauses five to nine. As discussed in Chapter 1, conceiving the use of the *shariʿa* here as the 'rule of

inclusion of the 'duty of reason' in conjunction with justice while discussing the merits of sultanic and non-religious courts.

[53] Ibn Talha mentioned '*madar qutb al-saltana*' in *al-ʿIqd al-farid*, 246.

[54] Ibid., 248.

[55] Ibid., 246, 248.

law' can be useful in explaining the author's concern for the *shari'a* and his encouragement of the sultan to sit on the *mazalim* courts.[56]

Administration, Delegation and the Shari'a

The administrative manual within *al-'Iqd al-farid*, which spreads over the second and third sections, borrowed heavily from the works of al-Mawardi. Yet Ibn Talha's systematic, purposeful and skilful modifications reflected his background in the administration of the Ayyubids and the Artuqids and suited his dedicatee, the sultan. He first treated the principal functions (*wilayat*) of the state in the second subsection of the second foundation.[57] *Al-'Iqd al-farid* proposed that any appointee for senior public office should have four qualities: knowledge, piety, competence and trustworthiness. Ibn Talha discussed five main ranks of appointments: viziers; the chancery of the state (*diwan al-insha'*); the inspectorate of the army (*diwan al-jaysh*); the state treasury (*diwan al-amwal*); and the rest of the sultan's retinue. The discussion of the etymology of vizierate (*wizara*) pointed clearly to al-Mawardi's *Qawanin al-wizara* and, more significantly, the *Ahkam*.[58] Likewise, this influence was manifest in the discussion of the vizierate of full delegation (*wizarat al-tafwid*) and special delegation (*al-tanfidh*); but these were not mere repetitions since Ibn Talha carefully adapted relevant texts of al-Mawardi's *Ahkam* to the Ayyubid and Artuqid contexts by removing any reference to the caliph and restricting the discussion to the sultan.[59] As such, permissible delegations to these senior offices derived from the sultan as the sole origin of legitimate power. Similarly, Ibn Talha's discussion of the inspectorate of the army was based on passages from al-Mawardi's *Ahkam*.[60] As for the author's interest in *diwan al-insha'*, it reflected his personal administrative background and his adherence to the writing style of the chancery, as is apparent throughout the treatise. Ibn Talha's notable conciseness and organised style throughout his treatment of the state treasury, which listed

56 Refer to Chapter 1, 44–5, above.

57 Ibn Talha, *al-'Iqd al-farid*, 251–76.

58 Ibid., 251–3. Refer to al-Mawardi, *Qawanin al-wizara wa-siyasat al-mulk*, ed. Radwan al-Sayyid (Beirut: Dar al-Tali'a, 1979), 137–8; and his *Ahkam*, 2: 30–1. For instance, note the commonality in relating caliph al-Ma'mun's criteria for selecting his vizier.

59 Refer to Ibn Talha, *al-'Iqd al-farid*, 254–6; al-Mawardi, *Ahkam*, 2:34–5.

60 Ibn Talha, *al-'Iqd al-farid*, 264–70; al-Mawardi, *Ahkam*, 2:259–84.

the provenance of funds coming into the treasury, resembled the style of Ibn Jamaʿa's later *Tahrir*.

The third section treated *shariʿa*-related appointments and was, accordingly, a continuation of the administrative manual within *al-ʿIqd al-farid*. Ibn Talha, himself a Shafiʿi jurist and judge in his Syrian hometown Nusaybin, delimited the scope of four religious functions: the muftiship (*fitya*); judgeship (*qadaʾ*); market inspection (*hisba*); and supervision of charitable endowments (*wilayat al-awqaf*).[61] As the author explained, this section covered the necessary qualifications for appointees to the above-mentioned offices.[62] Moreover, this section clarified the scope of each of these functions and Ibn Talha even narrated, in the case of the judgeship, ten relevant anecdotes from the ʿAbbasid era that exemplified the finest conduct of judges. For Ibn Talha, the ruler and his regents were accountable on Judgement Day for appointing unqualified candidates to these offices. Like the Sufi *Misbah*, accountability (*muʾakhadha*) in *al-ʿIqd al-farid* is a consequence of the delegation of power.[63]

Notwithstanding his genuine attachment to the *shariʿa* as supreme knowledge and at the core of his conceptualisation of the rule of law, Ibn Talha still envisaged the exercise of administrative and political power as being relatively independent from the religious offices related to the *shariʿa*.[64] Despite its opening, which extolled the merits of the *shariʿa* and the vital role of scholars and rulers in preserving and upholding it, the third section seems to delimit the contours of the religious offices in running the government. By isolating his section on *shariʿa*-related administrative functions from the preceding discussions on the sultanate and the main political and administrative offices of government, and taken within the context of the tendency to sanction sultanic justice, as is evident in the above-discussed ten duties required of the sultan, Ibn Talha was practically restricting the influence of the religious offices on the ruler's discretionary injunctions in the political and administrative sphere.

---

61 Ibn Talha, *al-ʿIqd al-farid*, 279–306. There are verbatim similarities with Ibn Jamaʿa's *Tahrir* here that will be discussed subsequently.

62 Ibid., 280.

63 Ibid. Refer to Chapter 3, 116, above.

64 For instance, Ibn Talha mentioned that knowledge (*ʿilm*) was first and foremost the knowledge of *shariʿa*; in *al-ʿIqd al-farid*, 309.

This section, furthermore, underlines the significance of *al-ʿIqd al-farid* in the genealogy of medieval Islamic political thought. It provides evidence as to its author's standing in the chain of Shafiʿi political writers between al-Mawardi and Ibn Jamaʿa. Ibn Talha was influenced by al-Mawardi's works and left his mark on Ibn Jamaʿa. The reliance on al-Mawardi's *Ahkam* was evident in several passages of this section of *al-ʿIqd al-farid*, including, for instance, the discussion of the judgeship.[65] This was also manifest in Ibn Talha's treatment of the muftiship (*fitya*) and market inspection (*hisba*), which was also largely based on the *Ahkam*.[66] On the other hand, there existed in this third section of *al-ʿIqd al-farid* indisputable resemblances to the later writing of Ibn Jamaʿa, especially with the fifth section of the *Tahrir*.[67] Both sections discussed in almost the same words the merits of the *shariʿa*, the role of scholars and rulers in upholding it, and listed the functions associated with its preservation.[68] The similarities included the same list of *shariʿa*-related offices: judgeship, muftiship, market inspection, and supervision of charitable endowments; Ibn Jamaʿa added teaching to the list, whereas Ibn Talha highlighted similarly the importance of 'instituting teaching positions in *madrasas* where the rulings of the *shariʿa* are preserved'.[69] The resemblances between the two works extended to content, themes and even to style with both authors' tendency for abridgement and meticulous organisation. *Al-ʿIqd al-farid*'s direct influence on Ibn Jamaʿa is thus too profound to dismiss.

The fourth and final section (foundation) of *al-ʿIqd al-farid* is an addendum authored by Ibn Talha the courtier, litterateur and occultist. It reads like a work of *adab* designed to educate, entertain at court and to impress the dedicatee.[70] In this section, Ibn Talha included uncomplicated problems of mathematics, fiddly legal cases and an assortment of prayers (*duʿaʾ*) for

---

65 Ibid., 281–5. This discussion was based on an abridgment of al-Mawardi's text in the *Ahkam*, 2:88–101, which additionally resembled the genre of *adab al-qadi*.

66 The discussion of the office of the *hisba* is very detailed in the *Ahkam*; refer to 2:315–39.

67 Chapter 5 titled *Fi hifz al-awdaʿ al-sharʿiyya wa qawaʿid manasibiha al-murdiyya* (*Regarding the Preservation of the Rules of the Shariʿa and the Proper Foundations for its Related Appointments*), in Ibn Jamaʿa, *Tahrir*, 87–93.

68 Refer to the discussion in Chapter 2, 73, where those functions were five in the case of Ibn Jamaʿa: judgeship, *iftaʾ*, *hisba*, teaching and *nazar* in *awqaf*.

69 Ibn Talha, *al-ʿIqd al-farid*, 280.

70 Peacock considered it as the 'most distinctive section of al-'Iqd al-farid' in 'Politics, Religion and the Occult', 49. Refer to El-Merheb, 'Islamic Political Thought and Professional Mobility', 217.

his dedicatee, which he introduced in the rhyming prose used by chancery secretaries.[71] The author included, moreover, an additional collection of aphorisms and parables that related to earlier caliphs on the need to be just, to accept and seek advice, to abide by the teachings of the Qur'an and to fear God, also highlighting the merits of self-restraint, honesty, equability, piety, compassion and accountability.[72] Throughout this section, Ibn Talha left some strong clues as to his occultism, such as the above-mentioned use of numerical values of letters to highlight the merits of sultan al-Nasir's first name, Yusuf.[73]

A Genealogical Missing Link?

Composed at the dawn of the Mamluk period, *al-ʿIqd al-farid* (or *Nafaʾis al-ʿanasir*) holds an important place in the genealogy of pre-modern Islamic political thought. Situated at the intersection between earlier works like the *Ahkam* and later ones like the *Tahrir, al-ʿIqd al-farid* is a significant text that fills another gap in the study of the history of Islamic political thought. *Al-ʿIqd al-farid* captured the main thematic and stylistic features of various political writings of its own period, used passages of earlier texts and skilfully adapted them for its own aims, and influenced later major works of the period. Most importantly, the study of this treatise's genre(s), literary styles, thematic organisation, and the author's background and his conceptualisation of political authority provide clear insights into this period's approach to the rule of law, delegation of power and limited government.

Ibn Talha's professional mobility, varied intellectual interests and political concerns were reflected in *al-ʿIqd al-farid* in a mixed genre that merged classical normative treatises with other modes of advice literature, including mirrors for princes, administrative and statecraft manuals, Sufi and ethical writings, and homiletic works.[74] On the one hand, Ibn Talha treated themes of advice literature often expressed in mirrors for princes, and Sufi and ethical writings, including justice, consultation, forbearance, compassion and generosity; the author even upheld the mirrors' concern for the longevity of

71 Ibn Talha, *al-ʿIqd al-farid*, 342–6.
72 Ibid., 347–65.
73 Refer to fn. 15, above.
74 Refer to El-Merheb, 'Islamic Political Thought and Professional Mobility', 218.

his patron's reign and their entertaining *adab* style, which was strengthened by his occultism. On the other hand, *al-ʿIqd al-farid* reflected the concern of juridical treatises for the need for the sultan, his duties, the origin of his authority and its limitations, albeit with a strong Sufi flavour. The fusion of genres was equally apparent in the administrative themes that *al-ʿIqd al-farid* treated, like the ranks of main offices, their jurisdiction and the qualities required of their appointees. This fusion may account for why *al-ʿIqd al-farid* was such a popular work, influencing later thinkers in style and content including Ibn Jamaʿa.

Al-ʿIqd al-farid does not fit any prevalent classification of genre of Islamic political thought, thus buttressing a central argument of this monograph. Being itself an amalgamation of genres, this treatise is testimony to the case – put forward in Chapter 1 – that the scholarly emphasis on studying genres to 'read' texts of Islamic political thought is founded on a dangerously misleading mythology. Given the mix of genres and themes in this treatise, one wonders as to the usefulness of the classifications of scholars like Lambton and Crone, who contrasted juristic treatises to texts they classified as medieval mirrors for princes and other works of political advice literature as a methodology for interpreting Islamic political thought. This mythology often resulted in missing out on the political ideas posited in these political texts and a lack of understanding of the ideological and intellectual networks of their authors, and – as Skinner puts it – their 'empirical beliefs'.[75]

Al-ʿIqd al-farid reflected Ibn Talha's intellectual and ideological leanings. His Ashʿari, Shafiʿi and Sufi background helped to shape the treatise in several ways. Ibn Talha's references to al-Qushayri and al-Ghazali, and his heavy reliance on other Shafiʿi sources including al-Mawardi, were mere indicators of his complex chains of allegiance.[76] In addition, and as already noted, Ibn Talha expressed the strong anti-anthropomorphist views that prevailed within some Shafiʿi–Ashʿari circles in Syria and Egypt; this will be discussed in Chapter 5 in the context of the Ashʿari–Shafiʿi clash with traditionalist Hanbalis in Damascus during the thirteenth century. Moreover, Ibn Talha's Shafiʿi background left its mark on *al-ʿIqd al-farid*'s treatment

[75] Skinner, 'Motives, Intentions and the Interpretation of Texts', 407.

[76] For further evidence on the influence of al-Ghazali refer to Ibn Talha, *al-ʿIqd al-farid*, 356–7.

of constitutional themes, which were generally of great interest to the Shafiʿi strain of political thought, including the concern for securing continuity and stability, curtailing the exercise of power by the sultan, and securing legitimate delegation to the high-ranking offices.

Yet Ibn Talha's use of sources and influences such as al-Mawardi's material was not solely dictated by their adherence to the same *madhhab*. Ibn Talha clearly enjoyed a profound acquaintance with al-Mawardi's various works and commanded a systematic ability to use, alter and adapt passages from this material in order to serve the aims of *al-ʿIqd al-farid*.[77] The use of al-Mawardi made perfect sense as his writings accommodated the multifaceted and varied interests of Ibn Talha. The *Ahkam*'s style and themes inspired the juridical treatise within *al-ʿIqd al-farid* and its constitutional concerns and administrative outlook. Moreover, al-Mawardi's other works like *Qawanin al-wizara*, *Tashil al-nazar* and *Adab al-dunya*, provided a desirable ethical system to moderate the sultan's exercise of power. This was a system rooted in but in no way limited to the *shariʿa*. Such a system did not contradict *al-ʿIqd al-farid*'s other concerns, including the longevity of the sultan's rule, securing extra sultanic powers in areas like justice and defence, and the ruler's practice of an archetypical statecraft. Nonetheless, as shown above, Ibn Talha had at times to resort to reworking al-Mawardi's texts in order to avoid any reference to the caliph as per his consistently sultanic-centred approach throughout his treatise.

Al-ʿIqd al-farid was not simply a panegyric work or an attempt to demonstrate the literary and administrative credentials of Ibn Talha. It expressed a clear theory of delegation, attempted to delimit political and administrative spheres from the religious sphere, and upheld the concern for the rule of law and limited government, three political themes that will now be addressed in turn. First, *al-ʿIqd al-farid*'s theory of delegation of power envisioned the sultan as the successor of prophethood and the person in whom the powers of the caliphate were vested. Ibn Talha stated unequivocally that the sultan was the vice-regent of God (*inna al-sultan naʾib-Allah fi khaliqatihi*).[78] Secondly, one of *al-ʿIqd al-farid*'s aims was to delimit religious functions to

[77] Although he often relied on al-Mawardi's works without acknowledging them, Ibn Talha did refer to al-Mawardi directly and to one of his works, *al-Hawi fi-al-fatawa*; ibid., 309.

[78] Ibn Talha, *al-ʿIqd al-farid*, 248.

prevent their intrusion into some aspects of the political and administrative spheres. This was evident in the way Ibn Talha fostered the importance of the sultan's participation in the non-religious courts (*mazalim*, *siyasat*) as one of the ten duties required of the ruler. However, this stance was neither rooted in disapproval towards the *shari'a* nor intended to grant a free hand to the sultan. Thirdly, the ideals of the rule of law and limited government are apparent as Ibn Talha, in his own words, aimed at 'taming [sultanic] actions or injunctions'.[79] In addition to the central role of the *shari'a* in 'taming' power, this could be achieved through the sultan's exercise of self-control, avoiding anger, being discreet and secretive in his actions, appointing the knowledgeable, and rejecting favouritism and nepotism.[80]

As for limited government, it is an expected ideal to an administrator and statesman of Ibn Talha's calibre. He penned a system that envisaged the sultan's supervision as 'broad, holistic, and non-specific' (*nazar kulli ijmali ghayr tafsili*).[81] Professional and administrative posts – from low-ranking supervisory appointments to the vizierate – were best delegated based on qualification; Ibn Talha noted, 'supervision of detailed matters is delegated to those appointed and invested by the sultan in line with each individual's expertise'.[82] The same drive for granularising the tasks of the highest political authority of Islam can also be found in the contemporary Maliki legal texts of al-Qarafi, albeit in a more theoretical fashion, as will be discussed in the following section of this chapter.

Al-Qarafi: the Granularisation of the Prophet's Authorities

Although political thought can frequently be found in pre-modern Islamic legal texts, it is rarely conveyed with such far-reaching constitutional consequences as in the treatise of the Maliki jurist Shihab al-Din Ahmad al-Qarafi (626/1228–682/1283 or 684/1285) titled *al-Ihkam fi Tamyiz al-fatawa 'an al-ahkam wa-tasarrufat al-qadi wa-al-imam* (*The Book of Perfection in Distinguishing Legal Opinions from Judicial Rulings and the Discretionary*

[79] Ibid., 237.

[80] Ibid., 243, 244, 246, 247, 254. Similar to Sufi treatises, the moderation of the ruler was achieved by an ethical and moral system with some of its roots in the *shari'a*.

[81] Ibid., 251.

[82] Ibid.

Actions of Judges and Rulers).[83] Although it was not authored to advance a specific political theory, but rather as a work situated at the 'intersection' of speculative jurisprudence (*usul al-fiqh*) and substantive law (*furu' al-fiqh*),[84] the *Tamyiz* provides formidable normative contributions to Islamic constitutional thought, especially on the limitation of the exercise of power, the theory of delegation and the origins of legitimate authority. As will be discussed in this section, this is the result of the *Tamyiz*'s methodical endeavour to normalise the relationship between speculative jurisprudence, human application of divine law, and the political institutions and judicial system of the late Ayyubid and early Mamluk period. As such, this section treats an unintended contribution to the history of Islamic political thought, yet a very relevant one to this monograph.[85]

As in previous chapters, it is first necessary to reiterate the caveat on the use of epithets. Maliki political thought in this case strictly refers to the political thought of al-Qarafi as expressed in his *Tamyiz* and is limited to the context of the *madhhab*'s presence in the Syro-Egyptian lands during the late Ayyubid and early Mamluk period. The term does not here represent the rich and thriving Maliki political thought tradition of Islamic Iberia and the rest of the Muslim West, which regrettably cannot be covered here as it is not of direct relevance. The renowned works *Siraj al-muluk* (*The [Guiding] Lamp for Rulers*) and *Bada'i' al-sulk fi taba'i' al-mulk* (*The Exquisite Path to the Modes of Kingship*) of al-Turtushi (d. 520/1126) and Ibn al-Azraq (d. 896/1491), respectively, were only two titles among a thriving and prolific Western tradition of political thought that existed in the middle period.

83 My translation of the title benefits from those of Sherman Jackson, *The Book of Perfection in Distinguishing Legal Responsa from Judicial Decisions and the Discretionary Actions of Judges and Caliphs*, and Fadel, *The Criterion for Distinguishing Legal Opinions from Judicial Rulings and the Administrative Acts of Judges and the Rulers*. As per Jackson's title, I believe *tasarrufat* is best translated as 'discretionary actions', and as per Fadel's, I think *imam* refers to ruler or head of state rather than caliph.

84 Refer to the translator's introduction in al-Qarafi and Fadel, *The Criterion for Distinguishing Legal Opinions from Judicial Rulings and the Administrative Acts of Judges and Rulers*, 2, 4.

85 As in the case of Ibn Jama'a, it is often necessary to examine more than one treatise to fully grasp the political thought expressed by a jurist. I found al-Qarafi's *Furuq* ('Distinctions', full title is *Anwar al-buruq fi anwa' al-furuq*) useful to elucidate aspects of some ideas expressed in the *Tamyiz*.

The *Tamyiz* was authored in a period of great tension between the Maliki and Shafiʿi *madhhabs*. As such, al-Qarafi's constitutional ideas show how competition among the legal schools contributed to the production of political thought.[86] The *Tamyiz*'s discourse was written at the time of sultan Baybars' legal reforms, when the policies of the Shafiʿi chief judge antagonised the sultan, the leading Mamluk *amirs*, and the jurists and judges of other *madhhabs*. Chief judge Taj al-Din Ibn Bint al-Aʿazz (d. 665/1267) refused to enforce the rulings of his deputy judges and, later, judges of other *madhhabs* whenever they contradicted the views of his Shafiʿi *madhhab*. Sherman Jackson noted, 'It was apparently during this conflict, incidentally, that al-Qarafi wrote his *Tamyiz*, as a scholarly protest against exclusivism within the judiciary and as a legal argument affirming the inviolable status of all Sunni *madhhabs*.'[87] For al-Qarafi, the *madhhab* demarcated the relationship between government and community, and this idea endowed his legal protest with a constitutional significance.[88]

As such, it is only reasonable to consider the *Tamyiz* – among other things – as a sweeping Maliki challenge to the legal dominance of Shafiʿism which led to the development of a new expression of political thought. The attempt by al-Qarafi to contest the exclusivist legal policies of the Shafiʿi chief judge of Cairo, Ibn Bint al-Aʿazz, resulted in far-reaching constitutional ideas about restraining the ruler's exercise of power and an innovative conception of political authority in Islam based on the granularisation of the Prophet's authorities. Yet al-Qarafi did not seek to substitute for Shafiʿi dominance, merely to co-exist alongside it while securing a minimal level of legal independence. This was due to the conditions of the Maliki school in the Syro-Egyptian context, as it enjoyed a weaker presence in both the state administration and demographically.

In a seminal article, Jackson covered the impact of al-Qarafi's thought on the caliph's authority by formulating a novel interpretation of the Prophet's actions.[89] This article was later followed by an authoritative monograph that

86 As Sherman Jackson puts it, 'In a sense, it constitutes the triggering device that set off his thinking about constitutional issues overall', in *Islamic Law and the State*, 67.

87 Ibid., 52.

88 Ibid., 72.

89 Sherman A. Jackson, 'From Prophetic Actions to Constitutional Theory: A Novel Chapter in Medieval Muslim Jurisprudence', *International Journal of Middle East Studies* 25(1) (1993): 71–90.

treated al-Qarafi's jurisprudence and highlighted its constitutional influence as a pioneering work in the history of Islamic political thought.[90] The following discussion largely builds on both works to situate al-Qarafi's efforts within the constitutional concern of other Syro-Egyptian jurists discussed in this monograph for the rule of law, limited government and delegation of power in the absence of an effective caliph.

The conflict between *madhhab*s may not have been the only reason behind authoring the *Tamyiz* and the absence of scholarly consensus on this matter must be noted here. For example, without denying its contributions to Islamic political thought, Mohammad H. Fadel downplayed the political context of the treatise and the role of the Maliki–Shafiʿi competition, and considered this treatise primarily a response to standing debates within the Islamic legal framework.[91] For Fadel, preventing the powerful Shafiʿi school 'from using its politically privileged position within the state to impose its own doctrines' was not that high on al-Qarafi's agenda.[92] Rather, the fundamental aim was to guarantee the unassailability of a judge's rulings against challenges from other judges and – especially – *mufti*s. Nonetheless, Fadel still acknowledged that this treatise resulted in 'a significant normative limitation on the powers of the caliph'.[93] For our purposes, what matters most is that, when it comes to its contribution to Islamic constitutional thought, the *Tamyiz* has the same merits in both Jackson and Fadel's interpretations and, moreover, both scholars agree on its author's influences.

Whereas al-Qarafi's education was comparable to any Shafiʿi jurist, his career differed drastically. Although he was a Maliki jurist, al-Qarafi was the product of the same intellectual milieu that produced the thirteenth-century political thought discussed in Chapters 2, 3 and 5. An Ashʿari and a legal theoretician, al-Qarafi studied with several well-known Shafiʿi teachers and was deeply impressed by one of them, ʿIzz al-Din Ibn ʿAbd al-Salam (d. 660/1262) – a key figure in Chapter 5 of this book.[94] Furthermore, he

[90] Jackson, *Islamic Law and the State*.
[91] Fadel, in *Criterion*, 10–11.
[92] Ibid., 43.
[93] Ibid., 44.
[94] Jackson, *Islamic Law and the State*, 3, 5–9. Refer to the editor's useful notes, at 21–9 in al-Qarafi, *al-Ihkam fi tamyiz al-fatawa ʿan al-ahkam wa tasarrufat al-qadi wa-al-imam*, ed. Abu Ghudda

studied with Shams al-Din al-Khusrushahi (d. 652/1254), the prominent Shafiʿi legal theoretician and rationalist theologian. Through him, al-Qarafi was deeply influenced by the Shafiʿi–Ashʿari theologian and philosopher Fakhr al-Din al-Razi (d. 606/1209).[95] On the other hand, unlike his typical Shafiʿi peers, al-Qarafi only held teaching posts in Cairo and never held a chief or deputy judgeship or senior administrative post.[96] Al-Qarafi's educational background and the challenges he faced in his professional career no doubt marked his political thought.

During the thirteenth century, competition among *madhhab*s could easily transmute into constitutional discourses. In order to gain the advantageous unofficial status of preferred legal school or official law of the state, the *madhhab*s extended their contest from the strictly legal domain into the domains of public and constitutional law. These legal schools, who by now had witnessed a 'settling down' from groups loosely gathered around broad legal and theological concepts into better-defined corporate units held together by normative legal conformity (*taqlid*), were competing for salaried offices and for power.[97] In such a context, the 'preferred' *madhhab* of a ruler or dynasty enjoyed immense powers by amassing religious, legal and administrative offices, influencing political edicts, and conferring legitimacy and authority to their doctrines and legal rulings. Thus, for lesser schools like the one to which al-Qarafi' belonged, whenever a Muslim government endorsed and executed a specific interpretation of the law by one of the dominant

---

(Aleppo and Beirut: Maktab al-Matbuʿat al-Islamiyya and Dar al-Bashaʾir al-Islamiyya, 1995). Likewise, Fadel noted that al-Qarafi's 'relationship to Shāfiʿī scholarship was largely a result of his interest in theoretical jurisprudence, comparative law, and theology, not a lack of commitment to Mālikī doctrine'; in *Criterion*, 9. For a valuable study on Ibn ʿAbd al-Salam's formative influence on al-Qarafi, refer to Mariam Sheibani, 'Innovation, Influence, and Borrowing in Mamluk-Era Legal Maxim Collections: The Case of Ibn ʿAbd al-Salām and al-Qarāfī', *Journal of the American Oriental Society* 140(4) (2020): 927–54.

95 Jackson, *Islamic Law and the State*, 7.

96 Ibid., 14–15.

97 For a more detailed discussion on this process refer to Jackson, *Islamic Law and the State*, xx, xxi, 225–8. Fadel's explanation is, likewise, useful here, 'Lurking beneath the visible institutions of Islamic law during this period was the *madhhab*, traditionally rendered as "school of law", in the sense not of a physical structure, but rather as a doctrinal school of law, constituted by a common approach to the study of the law, and, even more important, a shared commitment to a particular set of authoritative legal texts and materials that constituted the foundational views of the school in question'; in *Criterion*, 7.

madhhabs the law became an 'avenue to tyranny'.[98] It is within this wider legal and political context that the *Tamyiz*'s interpretation of prophetic actions is examined in what follows, irrespective of whether or not competition among *madhhabs* was the main or only motivation of al-Qarafi.

The *Tamyiz* posed a number of questions, two of which had far-reaching constitutional consequences. Beyond their immediate legal relevance, al-Qarafi's answers to these questions highlighted his conception of supreme political authority in Islam, and his concern for the rule of law, limited government and delegation of power. The first was question four: '[now that] the difference between jurisconsult (*mufti*) and judge (*hakim*) has been clarified, what is the difference between them and the head of state (*imam*) in his discretionary injunctions (*tasarrufat*)?'[99] The second was question twenty-five: 'What is the difference between the Prophet acting in his capacity as mufti and conveyer of the Message (*muballigh*) and his acting in his capacity as judge, and then as head of state (imam)? Are his actions in each of these capacities all of equal effect on the shari'a . . .?'[100] Based on the *Tamyiz*'s answers to these questions, Jackson explained that al-Qarafi distinguished the Prophet's actions and utterances according to four different aspects of his function: the messenger of God (*rasul*); the jurisconsult whose legal opinions were binding only because he was the Prophet; the judge who issued judicial rulings (*ahkam*); and the head of state who enjoined discretionary injunctions. After the Prophet's death, these functions were passed on to, or rather were distributed – granularised – among the scholars, jurisconsults, judges, and caliphs and rulers.[101] Al-Qarafi explained that non-prophetic legal opinions were non-binding while rulings passed by judges were binding.[102] As for the caliph, his functions incorporated judgeship and (non-binding) lawmaking,

[98] Jackson, *Islamic Law and the State*, xxi, xxiii, xxiv. As mentioned above, this view is not espoused by Fadel; refer to *Criterion*, 43.

[99] My translation; al-Qarafi, *Tamyiz*, 46–57. Refer to *Criterion*, 66–9, for a full translation of both question and answer.

[100] The translation is taken from Jackson, 'From Prophetic Actions to Constitutional Theory', 73. Refer to *Criterion*, 120–34, for another full translation of both question and answer.

[101] Jackson, 'From Prophetic Actions to Constitutional Theory', 74–6.

[102] Fadel explains in great detail how al-Qarafi establishes in the *Tamyiz* the unassailability of the judicial outcome based on his argument that a judge's ruling is an origination (*insha'*) of a binding rule in the context of a specific legal dispute and, as such, part of God's law; refer to *Criterion*, 13, 16–20, 24–6.

but anything outside these two areas solely fell under his discretionary injunctions and the public interest (*maslaha*).[103]

Despite the apparent focus on the caliphate, the above-mentioned discussions were pertinent to the sultanate of the early Mamluk period. Al-Qarafi's constitutional conception of the highest political authority was centred on the coercive sultan being the wielder of executive power. Referring to a powerless and emblematic caliph – no doubt such as the ʿAbbasid caliph in Cairo – al-Qarafi stated that, 'the *imam* who has not been conferred the general administration of the state (*al-siyasa al-ʿamma*) was only called *imam* figuratively and the discussion here is about (*al-haqaʾiq*)', that is, about the core duties of the function of the *imam*.[104] Later in the *Tamyiz*, al-Qarafi explained that the *imam*'s core duties (*haqaʾiq*) included the distribution of revenues, spending the treasury's money on the public interest, upholding prescribed legal punishments, raising armies, fighting rebels, distribution of land grants and so forth, which essentially resembled other juristic discussions of the duties of the *imam*.[105] According to al-Qarafi, any caliph who was not capable of administering these core duties was only called *imam* figuratively and was no longer a true caliph. Consequently, al-Qarafi considered that the ruler who administered the core duties of the office of the *imamate* (*haqaʾiq*) was the coercive sultan.[106] Like the caliph, the latter had no authority over lawmaking.

Al-Qarafi's discussion of these matters brought about three direct consequences within the early Mamluk political context, especially following the arrival of the nominal ʿAbbasid caliph in Cairo. I believe these were the three main aims of the author's discourse and they all focused on securing the independence of his *madhhab* in interpreting the law. The first was that the ʿAbbasid caliph of Cairo who was confirmed by Baybars was not to be considered an effective *imam* since he held no real executive power and could not

---

103 Al-Qarafi, *Tamyiz*, 56; Jackson, 'From Prophetic Actions to Constitutional Theory', 76–7.

104 My translation of '*amma imam lam tufawwad ilayhi al-siyasa al-ʿamma fa-ghayr maʿqul illa ʿala sabil itlaq al-imama ʿalayhi majazan, wa-al-kalam innama huwa fi-al-haqaʾiq*'; al-Qarafi, *Tamyiz*, 105.

105 Ibid., 108.

106 Regarding al-Qarafi's definition of imam, Jackson states, 'Later, in al-*Furūq* he uses the term imam more explicitly to refer to the sultan', in *Islamic Law and the State*, 195; refer to al-Qarafi, *al-Furuq*, ed. ʿUmar Hasan al-Qayyam, 4 vols (Beirut: Muʾassasat al-Risala, 2003), 2:403–13.

enjoin any discretionary injunctions; accordingly, the Cairo caliph had no authority in lawmaking and in issuing legal opinions, and, therefore, no legal authority whatsoever over al-Qarafi's Maliki *mahdhab*.[107] Secondly, within al-Qarafi's conception of the office of the *imamate*, any legal authority that a coercive wielder of power like sultan Baybars may have enjoyed was, likewise, not authoritative over the Maliki *mahdhab*. Thirdly, in a post-prophetic age any legal opinion was not binding and, accordingly, other dominant schools, like the Shafiʿi one, could not enforce their interpretation of the law or their legal opinions over others. As such, al-Qarafi maintained that there should be no single or official interpretation of the law: not by the caliph, not by the sultan and not by any dominant *madhhab*. Al-Qarafi's staunch resistance against the domination of the Shafiʿi *madhhab* highlighted what was really at stake in the competition for an official law of the Mamluk state: adopting a single interpretation of the law, that is, an official one, could lead to tyranny especially since the state was the enforcer of the law. Jackson explained:

> As such, if in determining which interpretation of the law is to be imposed on the Community the state or its government is assigned or assumes the role of final arbiter, then those who disagree with government must inevitably find themselves in the position of having to acquiesce not only in the face of legal interpretations with which they disagree but also in the face of government's claim to the right to carry law and legal sanctions into whatever areas of life it sees fit.[108]

Al-Qarafi's main and immediate aims in formulating his ideas were probably centred on securing the independence of his *madhhab* in interpreting the law, in addition to answering other longstanding legal questions, yet the spirit of his discussion was, intentionally or not, constitutional.

In his response to question thirty-three, the constitutional dimension was evident in al-Qarafi's treatment of judicial rulings, which extended from rigorous law into politics and administration. His exhaustive treatment of

[107] Jackson, *Islamic Law and the State*, 16; Jackson, 'From Prophetic Actions to Constitutional Theory', 81–2. Al-Qarafi wrote the *Tamyiz* before 660/1262, motivated by the arrival of the ʿAbbasid caliph in Cairo in 659/1261, whose authority al-Qarafi perceived as a threat to the weaker Maliki school.

[108] Jackson, *Islamic Law and the State*, xxiii–xxiv.

judicial, administrative and political authorities that were eligible to issue rulings (*hukm*) highlighted his views on the rule of law, limited government and the delegation of authority in one single coherent discussion. Al-Qarafi discussed fifteen public functions (*wilaya*) that were eligible to issue a judicial ruling to varying degrees.[109] The discussion ranged from the highest office, the caliphate (*al-imama al-kubra*), to the lowest, which was, according to al-Qarafi, arbitration (*tahkim*).[110] The caliphate had the broad capacity to issue rulings in all matters ranging from personal status issues to the public administration of the state. Al-Qarafi considered that a fully delegated vizier (*wazir al-tafwid*) was similarly eligible to pass such broad rulings.[111] The third rank was the full emirate (*wilayat al-imara*), which al-Qarafi explained was like 'kings [serving] with caliphs' and probably referred to the sultans of the author's lifetime. Interestingly, the holder of this type of emirate – that is, the sultan – had the capacity to judge (*ahliyat al-qada'*) and al-Qarafi did not stipulate a delegation from the caliph for this. On the other hand, special types of *amir*, in charge of a province, for instance, could issue legal rulings only if they were delegated by the *imam*. Furthermore, al-Qarafi discussed the offices of army commander, chief judgeship, sultanic or non-*shari'a* courts (*mazalim*), and deputy judges (*nuwwab*), whose functions, he believed, entailed various degrees of eligibility to pass judicial rulings.[112] Al-Qarafi bestowed to market inspection (*hisba*) the eligibility to pass rulings – understood here as mere executive or administrative decisions – on specific matters related to its competence such as the maintenance of roads and public spaces. According to al-Qarafi, the market inspector (*muhtasib*) could not issue or execute legal rulings on matters of marriage or civil and criminal matters.[113] Unlike the judge, the market inspector was able to examine cases that had not been raised or reported to him, while the former could deal only

[109] My interpretation; al-Qarafi, *Tamyiz*, 162–76. For another full translation of question and answer refer to *Criterion*, 174–82.

[110] This discussion is reminiscent of al-Subki's *Mu'id al-ni'am* in terms of ranking the *wilayat* as discussed in Chapter 5, 188–90. Fadel, similarly, noted that al-Subki 'adopted wholesale al-Qarāfī's distinction between prophetic actions'; *Criterion*, 54.

[111] Fadel highlighted some similarities with al-Mawardi's *Ahkam*; refer to *Criterion*, 9.

[112] Refer to the editor's useful notes on the difference between *mazalim* and *qada'* in al-Qarafi's thought, *Tamyiz*, 168.

[113] For more on *mu'amalat* refer to Jackson, *Islamic Law and the State*, 197.

with cases that had been brought to his court. Al-Qarafi also discussed other 'restricted functions' (*wilayat juz'iyya*) that could deal only with specific matters that were delegated by judges, such as, for instance, following up on marriage and divorce contracts. Other limited functions that were not eligible to issue a judicial ruling included estimation or surveying activities requested by a judge, distribution of booty, supervision of spending, distribution of alms, secretarial tasks and translation. As such, the above discussion extended from the strictly legal domain into the constitutional aims of the rule of law, limited government, and delegation of powers by deciding which authorities enjoyed what powers and their limitations, and the means by which such powers were delegated. Al-Qarafi indirectly proposed a division of religious, administrative and judicial powers among various authorities, including political ones.

As previously stated, the constitutional consequences of certain legal discussions were far-reaching. Effectively, al-Qarafi split the powers of the caliph into three: executive, legislative and judicial.[114] The author's conception of discretionary injunctions (*tasarrufat*) essentially denoted the executive power of the caliph, which was passed to rulers such as the Syro-Egyptian sultans. This power included the general administration of the state (*al-siyasa al-ʿamma*) and the *Tamyiz* detailed the *imam*'s duties in distributing wealth, preserving order, attending to the public interest and welfare, handling defence, and administering matters related to the ruling elites such as land grants. These were all executive and distinctively non-religious duties that could be transferred to the sultan as the wielder of coercive power. The law moderated the exercise of these executive powers. For that, and to avoid tyranny, a pristine legislative process was required. As such, lawmaking, that is, the interpretation of the law, was the duty of jurisconsults. Should they wish to, the caliph or the sultan could interpret the law alongside other *muftis* of the four *madhhabs*, while conceding that all legal opinions became non-binding after the death of the Prophet. This resulted in securing the

[114] Despite his different position on the role of conflict between legal schools, Fadel agrees with this interpretation. He highlights 'the importance of al-Qarāfī's functional understanding of the Prophet Muḥammad's mission and how that understanding in turn structured and limited the various powers of public officials in the Ayyūbid-Mamlūk polity of which al-Qarāfī was a part'; in *Criterion*, 44.

independence of the four *madhhabs* in interpreting the law, which in turn protected their role in the process of lawmaking. Accordingly, al-Qarafi's conception of legislative power upheld the rule of law by guaranteeing diversity in interpreting the law. Finally, there was judicial power, which was discussed in detail in the above paragraph. Though it was focused only on the eligibility to pass legal rulings, al-Qarafi's conception of the judiciary denoted again a division of legal, administrative and political duties that upheld the ideal of limited government and the legitimate delegation of power as defined in this book.

Being one of the 'non-establishment' scholars, al-Qarafi's works differed in some aspects from other political treatises.[115] There were various areas of political thought that the *Tamyiz* did not cover, or did so incidentally. This should not be viewed as a limitation of the *Tamyiz* since al-Qarafi did not author a political treatise per se, or dedicate his work to rulers in order to gain more power and offices for his *madhhab*, or to advance Malikism as an official law of the state. The *Tamyiz* was authored in a different style and with different aims than, for instance, the *Tahrir* of Ibn Jamaʿa, *al-ʿIqd al-farid* of Ibn Talha and *Misbah* of the unknown Sufi author. Al-Qarafi merely hoped to maintain legal diversity in interpreting the law and the independence of his *madhhab* against the dominant Shafiʿi school, in addition to securing the unassailability of judicial outcomes and responding to fundamental issues within the Islamic legal framework. The constitutional consequences of these discussions were simply formidable.

---

[115] Jackson, *Islamic Law and the State*, xxii–xxiii.

5

Mamluk Historiography as a Form of Political Thought

In addition to juristic treatises, legal texts and other forms of advice literature, Mamluk historiography merits close examination.[1] Political thought of the Mamluk period should be studied in conjunction with the historical writing of the fourteenth century; more specifically, the two works of the Shafiʿi jurist Taj al-Din al-Subki (d. 771/1370), *Tabaqat al-Shafiʿiyya al-kubra* (*The Great Shafiʿi Biographical Dictionary*) and *Muʿid al-niʿam wa-mubid al-niqam* (*The Restorer of Favours and the Restrainer of Chastisements*) should be 'read' as political texts.[2] This chapter argues that al-Subki was memorialising and resuscitating the Shafiʿi strain of political thought by dedicating an exhaustive biography to the jurist ʿAbd al-ʿAziz Ibn ʿAbd al-Salam (d. 660/1262) in the *Tabaqat*.[3] This biography preserved the concern within Shafiʿi thought for upholding the rule of law in a sequence of anecdotes that covered Ibn ʿAbd al-Salam's activism. Additionally, Ibn ʿAbd al-Salam's biography underlines how competition between *madhhab*s was

[1] To complete this chapter, I greatly benefited from Tayeb El-Hibri's book, *Reinterpreting Islamic Historiography: Hārūn al-Rashīd and the Narrative of the ʿAbbasid Caliphate*, Cambridge Studies in Islamic Civilization (New York: Cambridge University Press, 1999), and a collection of works by J. G. A. Pocock, including: 'Historiography as a Form of Political Thought', *History of European Ideas* 37(1) (2011): 1–6 (which clearly influenced this chapter's title); 'The Reconstruction of Discourse'; 'The Politics of Historiography', *Historical Research* 78(199) (2005): 1–14; and ch. 11, 'The Historian as Political Actor in Polity, Society and Academy', in *Political Thought and History*.

[2] For a discussion on 'reading' Islamic political thought, refer to Chapter 1, 29–46.

[3] This argument was first presented in a talk titled '"Les Lieux de Mémoire" of the 13th-Century Shafiʿi Political Thought in Late Medieval Arabic Historiography' during the Fourth Conference of the School of Mamluk Studies at the American University of Beirut in May 2017.

a major stimulus behind the production of political thought in this period. Lastly, this chapter covers in brief the ideal of limited government within the Shafiʿi strain of political thought as preserved in the later work of al-Subki, the *Muʿid*.

Studying Mamluk historiography as a form of political thought fits the methodological considerations discussed in Chapter 1. This book maintains that the prerequisites to interpreting thirteenth- and fourteenth-century political treatises, such as Ibn Jamaʿa's *Tahrir* for instance, are to unlock: the political languages of the authors' period; the languages of the prevalent intellectual discourses of their time; their repertoires of political and ethical ideas; the juristic and theological backgrounds of their works; their doctrinal affiliations and loyalties; the social, intellectual, professional and political networks within which they emerged, operated and flourished; and the social and political concerns presented by their immediate and previous historical contexts. A meticulous study of Ibn ʿAbd al-Salam's biography in the *Tabaqat* will provide the required answers to these methodological questions and is the aim of this chapter.

In sum, I will use the remembrance of Ibn ʿAbd al-Salam to interpret thirteenth- and fourteenth-century Shafiʿi political thought. I will first briefly examine Ibn ʿAbd al-Salam's intellectual background, career and activism, and then focus on how al-Subki's aims in writing Ibn ʿAbd al-Salam's biography in the *Tabaqat* were dictated by his loyalty to the Shafiʿi *madhhab* and his staunchly Ashʿari doctrinal affiliation. As such, this chapter presents the remembrance of Ibn ʿAbd al-Salam as an archetypal Shafiʿi model that al-Subki evoked to counter perceived threats against his *madhhab* and to uphold the cherished ideal of the rule of law. Following that, the biography will be closely examined to unlock the political language of the thirteenth century as preserved in the *Tabaqat* by relying, in parallel, on chronicles contemporary to Ibn ʿAbd al-Salam. This endeavour can be achieved only with knowledge of the major intellectual discourse of the period between rationalists and traditionalists, which manifested in inter-*madhhab* and intra-*madhhab* competition between Shafiʿis and Hanbali traditionalists, and between Shafiʿi–Ashʿaris and Shafiʿi traditionalists. This, in turn, reflects how *madhhab* competition became entangled with the production of political thought. This inquiry will then situate this Shafiʿi strain of political thought within a long Shafiʿi and Shafiʿi–Ashʿari tradition that includes the contributions of al-Mawardi, al-Juwayni, al-Ghazali, Ibn ʿAbd al-Salam and Ibn Jamaʿa, as skilfully portrayed by al-Subki. Subsequently, the biography will be 'read' as a text of political thought by focusing on five selected anecdotes that highlight specific political themes, all of which are related to the rule of law as defined in this book, including the moderation of the exercise of power, political legitimation and protection of the populace.

Al-Subki's Biography of Ibn ʿAbd al-Salam

ʿAbd al-ʿAziz Ibn ʿAbd al-Salam al-Sulami (577 /8/1181/2–660/1262), to whom the sources fondly refer as Ibn ʿAbd al-Salam or ʿIzz al-Din, was the leading Shafiʿi authority in Egypt and Syria of his generation and a renowned jurisconsult.[4] His reputation, as 'sultan of the scholars' (*sultan al-ʿulamaʾ*), stems first from his activism, which manifested as protecting the populace and intransigence towards the ruling elites, and, secondly, his contributions to Islamic legal theory, especially the importance and scope of *maslaha* (common good).[5] Among his most prominent teachers were the renowned Shafiʿi scholar ʿAbd al-Samad al-Harastani (d. 614/1217), Shafiʿi–Ashʿari theologian Fakhr al-Din Ibn ʿAsakir (d. 620/1223), and the Shafiʿi–Ashʿari theologian Sayf al-Din al-Amidi (d. 631/1233), the leading scholar of theology and speculative jurisprudence who was renowned for his knowledge of the 'rational sciences' (*ʿaqliyyat*).[6] Ibn ʿAbd al-Salam's

---

[4] In addition to primary sources, I used for this summary: E. Chaumont, 'Al-Sulamī', *EI*²; Jackson, *Islamic Law and the State*, 9–14; Daniella Talmon-Heller and Raquel Ukeles, 'The Lure of a Controversial Prayer: Ṣalāt Al-Raghāʾib (the Prayer of Great Rewards) in Medieval Arabic Texts and from a Socio-Legal Perspective', *Der Islam* 89(1/2 (2012): 141–66; Daniella Talmon-Heller, 'Muslim Martyrdom and Quest for Martyrdom in the Crusading Period', *Al-Masāq* 14(2) (2002): 131–9; El-Merheb, 'Political Censure', 358–67; Mariam Sheibani's recent study, 'Islamic Law in an Age of Crisis and Consolidation: ʿIzz al-Din Ibn ʿAbd al-Salām and the Ethical Turn in Medieval Islamic Law', PhD thesis, University of Chicago, 2018, ch.1. ProQuest (10841014).

[5] al-Subki, *Tabaqat*, 4:357. Ibn ʿAbd al-Salam's reputation is generally linked to 'his militancy placed exclusively at the service of the community' and 'to his independence in dealing with political authorities', rather than his works or thought; in 'al-Sulamī', *EI*² *Islam*. See El-Merheb, 'Political Censure', 359. Refer to Sheibani, 'Islamic Law in an Age of Crisis', 4, 6–7. Sheibani's valuable thesis fills a crucial gap in our knowledge of the development of the Shafiʿi school in Damascus between the fifth/eleventh and eighth/fourteenth centuries; it is the only study that deals systematically with Ibn ʿAbd al-Salam's legal and theological production.

[6] Al-Subki, *Tabaqat*, 4:354. Refer to Suleiman A. Mourad, 'Ibn ʿAsākir and family', *EI*³; Bernard G. Weiss, 'Sayf al-Dīn al-Āmidī', *EI*³.

Shafiʿi–Ashʿari theological affiliation led him to clash with Ayyubid sultan al-Ashraf Musa (d. 635/1237) and the Hanbali traditionalists of Damascus. Moreover, his career in Damascus is associated with an attempt to abolish what he perceived to be ritual innovations like *salat al-raghaʾib* (the prayer of great rewards).[7] Ibn ʿAbd al-Salam is eulogised in various biographical dictionaries and chronicles for opposing an alliance that the Ayyubid sultan of Damascus, al-Salih Ismaʿil (d. 648/1251), entered into with the Franks in 638/1240 against the sultan's own nephew, sultan al-Salih Ayyub (d. 647/1249) of Cairo.[8] In consequence, al-Salih Ismaʾil imprisoned Ibn ʿAbd al-Salam, who upon his release left immediately for Egypt. In Cairo, al-Salih Ayyub appointed him as *khatib* and judge. Soon Ibn ʿAbd al-Salam's intransigence led him into all sorts of confrontations with the emerging political and military elites in Cairo. Paradoxically, when he resigned his official posts his status as a leading religious authority seems to have increased, not just amongst the *ʿulamaʾ* but also within the political elites and the wider populace of Egypt. In this non-official capacity, Ibn ʿAbd al-Salam was involved in major events, including preparations for war against the Mongols in 658/1260, the legitimation of sultan Baybars, and the confirmation and oath of allegiance (*bayʿa*) of the first ʿAbbasid caliph in Cairo in 659/1261.

The eventful life and career of Ibn ʿAbd al-Salam turned him into the archetypal Shafiʿi champion. His biography, as written by contemporary sources and as later remembered by al-Subki, became a repertoire of political acts and themes that served as a prototype for later Shafiʿi scholars' engagement in the political sphere. As such, the biography of Ibn ʿAbd al-Salam recorded in al-Subki's *Tabaqat* should be read as a political text intended specifically for the remembrance, preservation and revival of the Shafiʿi political thought of the late Ayyubid and Mamluk period. The main political themes preserved by the remembrance of Ibn ʿAbd al-Salam in the *Tabaqat* are closely linked to the Shafiʿi conception of the rule of law. This led to a later documented case of emulation and remembrance by praxis of Ibn ʿAbd al-Salam by the chief judge of Cairo, Ibn Daqiq al-ʿId (625/1228–702/1302), as will be discussed below.

---

[7] Talmon-Heller and Ukeles, 'The Lure of a Controversial Prayer', 141–66.

[8] Humphreys, *From Saladin to the Mongols*, 266–9.

One can now begin to see how Mamluk historical writing, on the one hand, and the politics and political thought of this period, on the other, are closely interrelated. The biographical dictionary of al-Subki celebrates the participation of Ibn ʿAbd al-Salam in the political sphere, often by recounting very carefully crafted anecdotes where the jurist seems to be performing his duties as dictated by the Shafiʿi political thought of the treatises. There is, in the *Tabaqat*, an intentional process of remembrance and preservation of these anecdotes in an attempt to breathe more life into Shafiʿi thought than political treatises allowed for. This makes the biography's anecdotes beneficial for, and sometimes a prerequisite to, comprehending the political thought articulated in Shafiʿi political treatises. As such, this entry in a fourteenth-century biographical dictionary is essential to explicate a political treatise like Ibn Jamaʿa's *Tahrir*, which is the synthesis of Shafiʿi political thought, as discussed in Chapter 2. Likewise, the influence of such political treatises, including Ibn Jamaʿa's *Tahrir* but also other much earlier Shafiʿi political texts, seem to have marked later Mamluk historical writing, as will become evident below from the analysis of Ibn ʿAbd al-Salam's biography in the *Tabaqat*. In sum, one has to look beyond the political treatises and traditional texts in order to understand their meaning and influence in contemporaneous society; this is why the study of carefully selected sources like Ibn ʿAbd al-Salam's biography in the *Tabaqat* is crucial to understand the politics and political thought in the late Ayyubid and Mamluk society.[9]

The Politics of al-Subki's Historiography

The author of the *Tabaqat*, Taj al-Din ʿAbd al-Wahab al-Subki (727/9/1327/9–771/1370) was a Shafiʿi chief judge and a devoted Ashʿari author.[10] Al-Subki was educated in a staunchly Shafiʿi–Ashʿari environment that shaped his career and thought. He was the son of Taqi al-Din al-Subki (683/1284–756/1355), who was chief judge and *khatib* of the Grand Umayyad Mosque of Damascus. Taqi al-Din is best known for playing an

[9] I find the following question raised by J. G. A. Pocock's question very relevant here, 'what kind of political society must we presuppose that will produce written histories and consider them a way of debating its structure and that of political society in general; what manner of "histories" will these be, and what meanings will we be attaching to the words "history" and "politics" when we discuss them?', in 'Historiography as a Form of Political Thought', 1.

[10] Schacht and Bosworth, 'al-Subkī', *EI*².

important role in the main intellectual rift of the period, as he spearheaded the Shafiʿi–Ashʿari response to the traditionalism of Ibn Taymiyya and his students in both theology and jurisprudence. Taqi al-Din authored fierce polemical works against Ibn Taymiyya, including *al-Rasaʾil al-Subkiyya fi al-radd ʿala Ibn Taymiyya wa-tilmidhihi Ibn Qayyim al-Jawziyya* (*al-Subki's Responses to Ibn Taymiyya and His Student Ibn Qayyim al-Jawziyya*).[11] As for his son, Taj al-Din, he studied in Cairo and Damascus, and later became teacher and preacher in the latter. Nominated by his father, he was appointed judge in 756/1354. Taj al-Din continued his father's efforts against "anthropomorphists", a pejorative description often used for anti-Ashʿari Hanbali and Shafiʿi traditionalists.[12]

All was not well for al-Subki and his camp around the time he authored his *Tabaqat*. Gone were the golden days of Nizam al-Mulk and Salah al-Din, when Shafiʿi dominance went unchecked. Baybars' legal reforms of 665/1267 may have not ended the Shafiʿi pre-eminence in Syria and Egypt, but they nonetheless set a trend of slow but steady deterioration for the Shafiʿi *madhhab*. Moreover, the rise of Hanafism became irreversible and, more worrying for al-Subki personally, Hanbali traditionalism was making some gains inside the Shafiʿi *madhhab*. Since al-Subki's chief adversaries were the Hanbali-traditionalists and their Shafiʿi sympathisers, he must have lamented their success in drawing prominent Shafiʿi names in Damascus into their camp, including al-Birzali (d. 739/ 1339), al-Mizzi (742 /1341), al-Dhahabi (d. 748 / 1348) and Ibn Kathir (d. 774 / 1373).[13] Indeed the heavy Ashʿari polemic in the *Tabaqat* was an indication that al-Subki may have felt he "was apparently swimming against the tide".[14] The situation worsened further still and al-Subki was dismissed from all his posts and imprisoned in 769/1368 for 80 days.[15] Ibn Hajar's later account of this affair suggested that

11 Caterina Bori, 'The Collection and Edition of Ibn Taymīyah's Works: Concerns of a Disciple', *Mamlūk Studies Review* 13(2) (2009): 48.

12 Refer to Makdisi's valuable works, 'Ashʿarī and the Ashʿarites' and '"Ṭabaqāt" – Biography: Law and Orthodoxy in Classical Islam', *Islamic Studies* 32(4) (1993): 371–96. Refer also to, 'al-Subkī', *EI²*.

13 Makdisi, 'Ashʿarī and the Ashʿarites', 59, 79.

14 'Al-Subkī', *EI²*.

15 Al-Subki supposedly completed his *Tabaqat* in 766, three years before his imprisonment; refer to another edition of the *Tabaqat*, eds. al-Tanahi and al-Hulu, 10 vols (Cairo: Matbaʿat ʿIsa al-Babi al-Halabi wa-Shurakah, 1964), 1:27.

al-Subki's enemies had fabricated a case of tax embezzlement, as he related that the superintendent of orphans (*nazir al-aytam*) was "expected" to testify that some collected taxes had fallen into al-Subki's hands.[16] These turbulent times were for Taj al-Din al-Subki and his *madhhab* fundamental to the way the author set about authoring his magnum opus *Tabaqat al-Shafiʿiyya al-kubra* (*The Great Shafiʿi Biographical Dictionary*).

It is within this context that Ibn ʿAbd al-Salam's biography should be examined. The *Tabaqat*'s remembrance of Ibn ʿAbd al-Salam is rooted in the main intellectual discourse of the period and constitutes an integral part of al-Subki's view that Shafiʿism and Ashʿarism were irreplaceable in the political sphere. The *Tabaqat* is thus a product of 'the internecine struggle between traditionalists and rationalists within the Shafiʿite *madhhab*'.[17] Grasping this defining feature of the *Tabaqat* is essential for any subsequent effort to unlock the languages of the main intellectual and political discourses of the thirteenth and fourteenth centuries based on the biography of Ibn ʿAbd al-Salam. Furthermore, the *Tabaqat* comprises a history of the Ashʿari movement and the Shafiʿi golden age and its glorious names, like al-Juwayni, al-Ghazali, Nizam al-Mulk and Salah al-Din.[18] Likewise, such a comprehensive remembrance of Ibn ʿAbd al-Salam is partly a memorial to this golden age when Shafiʿism and Ashʿarism played a leading role in the public sphere.

Although al-Subki provided the first comprehensive biography of Ibn ʿAbd al-Salam, contemporary sources of the thirteenth century are also very beneficial to gain an insight into his life. The chronicles of Ibn Wasil (604/1208–697/1298), Abu Shama (599/1203–665/1268), al-Yunini (640/1242–726/1326) and Ibn ʿAbd al-Zahir (620/1223–692/1292) pro-

[16] Ibn Hajar, *Durar*, 2: 425–8. One explanation is that the Subkis' constant opposition to Ibn Taymiyya and his 'powerful faction' put Taj al-Din in jail since the Hanbali chief judge who sentenced him was Ibn Qadi al-Jabal (d.771), one of Ibn Taymiyya's students; refer to the editors' introduction in *Muʿid al-niʿam wa-mubid al-niqam*, "ز". I am grateful to Yossef Rapoport for bringing to my attention that this view is not supported by secondary literature, which generally does not see a posthumous powerful Taymiyyan faction; refer to Caterina Bori, 'Ibn Taymiyya (14th to 17th Century): Transregional Spaces of Reading and Reception', *The Muslim World* 108(1) (2018): 87–123.

[17] Makdisi, '"Ṭabaqāt" – Biography', 383.

[18] Makdisi argued that the *Tabaqat* commanded a universal legacy on Islamic history as it influenced the history of the Ashʿari movement and the 'orthodox victory'; in 'Ashʿarī and the Ashʿarites', 38–9.

vide ample information on Ibn ʿAbd al-Salam.[19] These authors had direct contact with Ibn ʿAbd al-Salam: they either studied with him, or obtained an *ijaza* (licence to teach or retransmit) from him, or witnessed key events of his life that they later reported. Such a blend of contemporary primary sources is robust enough to corroborate the historicity of al-Subki's later and more comprehensive account of Ibn ʿAbd al-Salam's life. Moreover, these sources will aid the evaluation and understanding of Ibn ʿAbd al-Salam's acts in both the religious and political spheres of his time.

As useful as these four contemporary sources are, this chapter does not aim to establish whether al-Subki's historiography is fact or fiction. More useful for our purposes here is gaining an understanding al-Subki's intentions – other than to narrate the actions performed by Ibn ʿAbd al-Salam – and discovering his motives so that the biography can later be read as a text of Islamic political thought. At first glance, this biography in the *Tabaqat* is a typical narrative of the deeds of an exceptional Shafiʿi scholar, but a closer look will show that Ibn ʿAbd al-Salam is portrayed as a political actor whose acts are narrated first and foremost for their archetypal significance to be preserved, remembered and imitated. In this framework where 'the exemplary value of the action outweighed its veracity', the focus of enquiry should be on understanding what made al-Subki consider the actions performed by Ibn ʿAbd al-Salam paradigmatic and worthy of recording, irrespective of whether these deeds actually happened the way the *Tabaqat* reported them.[20] Focusing on this essence draws in 'the politics' of Mamluk historiography and raises the question why the biography was narrated in this manner and, ultimately,

[19] Ibn Wasil, *Mufarrij al-kurub fi akhbar Bani Ayyub (629–645 A.H./1231–1248 A.D.)*, ed. Hasanayn Muhammad Rabiʿ and Saʿid ʿAbd al-Fattah ʿAshur, 5 vols (Cairo: Matbaʿat Dar al-Kutub, 1972); Ibn Wasil, *Die Chronik des ibn Wasil: Ǧamāl ad-Dīn Muḥammad ibn Wāṣil, Mufarriǧ al-Kurūb fī Aḫbār Banī Ayyub: kritische Edition des letzten Teils (646/1248–659/1261) mit Kommentar: Untergang der Ayyubiden und Beginn der Mamlukenherrschaft*, ed. Mohamed Rahim, Arabische Studien, Bd. 6 (Wiesbaden: Harrassowitz, 2010); Abu Shama, *al-Dhayl ʿala al-rawdatayn*; al-Yunini, *Dhayl mirʾat al-zaman*; Ibn ʿAbd al-Zahir, *al-Rawd al-zahir fi sirat al-Malik al-Zahir*, ed. ʿAbd al-ʿAziz al-Khuwaytir (al-Riyad, 1976). For more on Ibn Wasil and Abu Shama refer to Konrad Hirschler, *Medieval Arabic Historiography: Authors as Actors* (London: Routledge, 2006), 18–42; and for al-Yunini refer to Jacqueline Sublet, 'Al-Yūnīnī', *EI*[2]; Donald P. Little, 'Historiography of the Ayyūbid and Mamlūk Epochs', in Carl F. Petry (ed.), *The Cambridge History of Egypt, vol. 1: Islamic Egypt, 640–1517* (Cambridge: Cambridge University Press, 1998), 429–30, and 421 for more on Ibn ʿAbd al-Zahir.

[20] I benefit here from Pocock, 'Historiography as a Form of Political Thought', 2 and *passim*.

how this can help us to understand Islamic political thought of this period.[21]

A Shafiʿi Lieu de Mémoire*?*

Al-Subki's remembrance of Ibn ʿAbd al-Salam is more than a mere entry on a scholar in a Shafiʿi biographical dictionary. Al-Subki's intention was for it to be relevant to the Shafiʿi collective memory as a whole, but it also is exceptional for many other reasons. First, al-Subki was the first author to dedicate a biographical entry to Ibn ʿAbd al-Salam. Furthermore, it was a long biography written in great detail; it is one of the longest entries in the whole *Tabaqat*, exceeded by a few prodigious names of the Shafiʿi *madhhab* like al-Ghazali, al-Juwayni and Taqi al-Din al-Subki, the author's father.[22] It is likewise valuable because al-Subki had access to accounts of Ibn ʿAbd al-Salam's life by his son (Sharaf al-Din ʿAbd al-Latif).[23] Moreover, its value is also clear in that later accounts of Ibn ʿAbd al-Salam in various Shafiʿi biographical dictionaries and chronicles chiefly depend on al-Subki. Additionally, the systematic ascription of miracles (*karamat*) to Ibn ʿAbd al-Salam began with al-Subki.[24] The relevance of this biography clearly extends to the whole *madhhab*.

I found French historian Pierre Nora's concept of *lieux de mémoire* useful to understand al-Subki's aims in preserving Ibn ʿAbd al-Salam memory. Nora's collection titled *Les Lieux de Mémoire* (published in English as *Realms of Memory*) shows how any entity, material or not, can become with time 'a symbolic element of the memorial heritage of any community'.[25] A *lieu de mémoire* can be an archaeological site, a monument, a building, a real or imagined figure, an event, a date or even a literary work. In this case, it is a jurist remembered through an entry, a fairly large one, in a biographical

21 Pocock, 'The Politics of Historiography', 2.

22 The biography of Ibn ʿAbd al-Salam is 32 pages long in al-Subki's, *Tabaqat*, 4:354–86; al-Ghazali's is 120 pages (3:416–536), but this includes an exhaustive bibliography of his works; al-Juwayni's is 41 pages (3:159–200); and Taqi al-Din al-Subki's is 102 pages (5:305–407).

23 Al-Subki, *Tabaqat*, 4:360, 368.

24 Al-Yafiʿi (698/1298–768/1367) wrote probably around the same time as al-Subki and attributed only one 'minor' *karama* to Ibn ʿAbd al-Salam in *Mirʾat al-jinan*, 4:116–20; Al-Yafiʿi was a 'scholar-Ṣūfī' and a 'fervent Ashʿarī' who 'combatted both Muʿtazilī rationalism and Ibn Taymiyya's anthropomorphism' (in E. Geoffroy, 'al-Yāfiʿī', *EI*²).

25 Pierre Nora and Lawrence D. Kritzman (eds), *Realms of Memory: Rethinking the French Past*, European Perspectives (New York: Columbia University Press, 1996).

dictionary. This conception enables one to contemplate how Ibn ʿAbd al-Salam's biography fits with the aim of al-Subki's *Tabaqat* in constructing and preserving the Shafiʿi (more precisely, the Shafiʿi–Ashʿari) collective memory, including its political thought.

There are several features that indicate how Ibn ʿAbd al-Salam is a Shafiʿi *lieu de mémoire* in the *Tabaqat*. These features include al-Subki's 'self-consciousness', his 'will to remember', and his tendency to meticulously reconstitute past events related to this Shafiʿi *lieu de mémoire*.[26] Al-Subki's wilful intention to remember Ibn ʿAbd al-Salam in such a fashion in his *Tabaqat* was intensified by the threats that his Shafiʿi–Ashʿari *madhhab* was enduring. His focus on constructing a Shafiʿi *lieu de mémoire* arose from his mindfulness that the Shafiʿi golden age had practically come to an end. In order to guarantee historical continuity, there was a need, coupled with a will, to preserve for the Shafiʿi memory what was 'worthy of remembrance' in a safeguarded *lieu*.[27] Ibn ʿAbd al-Salam's exemplary life, career and activism made him the ideal choice for this *lieu de memoire*. Al-Subki essentially picked Ibn ʿAbd al-Salam to create a bastion of Shafiʿi identity, which he defended with anecdotes and parables abundant with novel information up to this point in Mamluk historiography; a bastion that the threat he perceived around him moved him to build and defend.[28]

This *lieu de mémoire* served two more critical purposes: it allowed al-Subki to attach himself and his family to Shafiʿi collective memory' and, more importantly, to portray a closely interwoven and uninterrupted line of Shafiʿi thought. In four short, consecutive anecdotes treating the merits of Ibn ʿAbd al-Salam, al-Subki successfully projected the image of a continuous and closely interrelated scholarly milieu stretching from al-Ghazali down to his own time and to his own family.[29] First, he related an anecdote of one of Ibn ʿAbd al-Salam's miracles that he claimed he had heard first-hand from his father Taqi al-Din. Then, he narrated a similar anecdote on the authority of the chief judge Ibn Jamaʿa. Following that, al-Subki mentioned that it

[26] Pierre Nora, 'Between Memory and History: Les Lieux de Mémoire', *Representations* 26 (1989): 7–24, *passim*.
[27] Ibid., 19.
[28] Ibid., 12.
[29] Al-Subki, *Tabaqat*, 4:357.

was Ibn Daqiq al-ʿId who had first named Ibn ʿAbd al-Salam 'the sultan of the scholars'. Finally, he stated that Ibn al-Hajib, the Maliki jurist and grammarian, considered that Ibn ʿAbd al-Salam surpassed al-Ghazali in matters of jurisprudence. Al-Subki hence sketched a continuous and solid milieu of Shafiʿi scholars at the heart of which was Ibn ʿAbd al-Salam, from al-Ghazali to Ibn Daqiq al-ʿId and Ibn Jamaʿa, and ending with the Subkis.

Politics and madhhab*s*

In addition to depicting an unbroken line of Shafiʿi thought, the biography of Ibn ʿAbd al-Salam and, more generally, the *Tabaqat*, highlights the interrelatedness between politics and *madhhab*s. There are various indications that al-Subki saw politics as inseparable from *madhhab* loyalties and doctrinal affiliations.[30] For instance, *madhhab* consideration greatly influenced who did or did not make it into al-Subki's *Tabaqat.* One example is al-Subki's lengthy biography of Salah al-Din who, as a ruler, should not have made it into a work of *Tabaqat* devoted to Shafiʿi scholars.[31] Nonetheless, Salah al-Din was a loyal follower and champion of Shafiʿism and that was sufficient to secure him an entry. On the other hand, Nur al-Din Zangi, despite being referred to by al-Subki as an important champion of Islam on a par with Salah al-Din, Nizam al-Mulk and ʿUmar II, was not granted an entry in the *Tabaqat* owing to his adherence to Hanafism.[32] Remarkably, al-Subki did find a place for Mahmud b. Sebüktigin (r. 388/998–421/1030), sultan of Ghazna.[33] One of the reasons he earned his entry in the *Tabaqat*, as al-Subki explained on the authority of al-Juwayni, was that sultan Mahmud was a Hanafi who converted to Shafiʿism.[34] Al-Subki's tendency to associate politics with *madhhab* and theological affiliations, his interest in treating political themes and his predisposition to earlier Shafiʿi political thinkers resurfaces in his later work, the *Muʿid*, as will be discussed in more detail at the end of this chapter.

30 Al-Subki, *Muʿid al-niʿam*. This work contains various indications that the author was influenced by the political thought of Ibn Jamaʿa as discussed in Chapter 2, 84, and below.

31 Al-Subki, *Tabaqat*, 4:217–38.

32 Ibid., *Tabaqat*, 3:265.

33 Ibid., 3:265–73.

34 Ibid., 3:266.

In the *Tabaqat*, al-Subki made clear his conviction that his *madhhab* was more suitable for conducting politics. As a Shafiʿi 'propagandist',[35] al-Subki contended that any ruler who strayed from the Shafiʿi *madhhab* would simply lose power. He cited the example of Qutuz (r. 657/1259–658/1260), whose sultanate was very brief, despite his illustrious victory against the Mongols, simply because he remained an adherent of the Hanafi *madhhab*.[36] Likewise, Baybars was reprimanded in a dream by Imam al-Shafiʿi himself for having compromised the dominance of Shafiʿism by instituting the legal reform of four chief judges.[37] Baybars later appeared in a scholar's dream admitting that even God did not approve of this legal reform.[38] Following the right *madhhab*, that is, Shafiʿism, leads to successful politics and to the maintenance of rule; any deviation from Shafiʿi dominance leads to dire consequences. As such, the author presented the need for Shafiʿism as the official or preferred *madhhab* of the state by linking adherence to it to ideal and prolonged rule.

As already mentioned, this interrelatedness between *madhhab* and politics in the *Tabaqat* is particularly perceptible in the biography of Ibn ʿAbd al-Salam. The biography preserved a treasure trove of information related to the process of production of Shafiʿi political thought in the late Ayyubid and Mamluk period, the language of its political discourse and its themes, and should, accordingly, be examined as a political text, thus reinforcing the need to examine Mamluk historiography as a form of political thought. By that I am not suggesting that the *Tabaqat*'s biography of Ibn ʿAbd al-Salam is to be treated like Aristotle's *Politics* or al-Mawardi's *Ahkam*. I propose rather that the biography is a political text because the intentions of al-Subki '*in* writing the text' were political, since it was predominantly and consciously treating political themes, and since it promoted a preferred *madhhab* of the state.[39] While earlier obituaries and references to Ibn ʿAbd al-Salam (including Ibn Wasil, Abu Shama, al-Yunini and Ibn ʿAbd al- Zahir) do mention key events of his life, they did so while either treating his personal merits or citing other

---

35 Makdisi argued that al-Subki's work was 'Ashʿarite propaganda'; in 'Ashʿarī and the Ashʿarites', 69.

36 Jorgen S. Nielsen, 'Sultan Al-Ẓāhir Baybars and the Appointment of Four Chief Qāḍīs, 663/1265', *Studia Islamica* 60 (1984): 173.

37 Ibid., 173–4; al-Subki, *Tabaqat*, 4:425.

38 Ibid.; refer to discussion below, 188.

39 Refer to the discussion on Quentin Skinner's methodology, below, and in Chapter 1, above.

events; as such they are not 'political texts'. The subsequent parts of this chapter will identify the main political themes treated in the biography of Ibn ʿAbd al-Salam and link them to the main constitutional concerns of Shafiʿi political thought.

Conventions Preserved

A prerequisite to recovering these political themes is to decode the prevalent conventions of the political discourse of the late Ayyubid and Mamluk period. Here the works of Quentin Skinner and J. G. A. Pocock offer very useful guidelines. Skinner explained:

> My first suggested rule is: focus not just on the text to be interpreted, but on the prevailing conventions governing the treatment of the issues or themes with which that text is concerned. This rule derives from the fact that any writer must standardly be engaged in an intended act of communication. It follows that whatever intentions a given writer may have, they must be conventional intentions in the strong sense that they must be recognizable *as* intentions to uphold some particular position in argument, to contribute in a particular way to the treatment of some particular theme, and so on. It follows in turn that to understand what any given writer may have been *doing in* using some particular concept or argument, we need first of all to grasp the nature and range of things that could recognizably have been done by using that particular concept, in the treatment of that particular theme, at that particular time.[40]

Similarly, Pocock argued that a necessary step to understand a political text is 'to identify the "language" or "vocabulary" with and within which the author operated'.[41] Contextualism thus maintains that 'reading' a political text requires that the reader interpret the shared conventions that the author used and were recognised by its audience as the prevailing conventions that governed the political discourse of the time. I am not suggesting that the conventions preserved in the biography of Ibn ʿAbd al-Salam defined the

---

40 Skinner, 'Motives, Intentions and the Interpretation of Texts', 406. For the same discussion refer to Skinner, *Visions of Politics: Regarding Method*, 1:101–2.

41 Pocock, 'Languages and Their Implications', 25. Also refer to the same author, 'The Reconstruction of Discourse', for a very beneficial and related reading.

meanings of the political text, but rather that understanding them is a necessary step that greatly facilitates the understanding of the text. In simpler terms, it is essential to determine the language of the political discourse of the thirteenth century.

Fortunately, al-Subki made our task much easier by meticulously preserving the conventions of the period. The biography's careful description, in painstaking detail, of Ibn ʿAbd al-Salam's political and *madhhab* activism has both elucidated 'the cultural context' of the thirteenth century and the language and vocabulary 'with and within which' Ibn ʿAbd al-Salam operated.[42] Al-Subki demonstrated a superb capacity to recreate an immaculate historical context and reconstructed meticulously Ibn ʿAbd al-Salam's thirteenth-century political and intellectual conventions, as one would expect from this Shafiʿi–Ashʿari *lieu de mémoire.* As such, the biography was laden with extensive coverage of political and theological confrontations that included major disagreements with Ayyubid sultans over their political choices or dynastic disputes. Furthermore, the biography covered the clashes with the traditionalist Hanbalis of Damascus, the fierce argument about theology, and Ibn ʿAbd al-Salam's *fatwa* against *tajsim*, *tashbih* and *hashawiyya* (derogatory terms used by rationalists when accusing traditionalists of anthropomorphism) that also dealt with the nature of the Qurʾan and endorsed the use of reason.[43]

While the specifics of this major thirteenth-century intellectual discourse between rationalists and traditionalists are not of primary relevance to this monograph, they nevertheless emphasise the role of inter- and intra-*madhhab* competition in the production of political thought and in shaping of the language and conventions of political discourse. Accordingly, and in order to extract these prevailing conventions, one must first engage with long passages of the biography dedicated to Ibn ʿAbd al-Salam's struggle against perceived innovations, his involvement in theological disputes, and the

[42] Pocock, 'Languages and Their Implications', 25. Skinner notes in *Visions of Politics: Regarding Method*, 1:125: 'More generally, the aim is to return the specific texts we study to the precise cultural contexts in which they were originally formed.'

[43] Al-Subki, *Tabaqat*, 4:360–8; supported by Ibn Wasil, *Mufarrij*, 5:141–2. Makdisi explains, 'Some of the Salaf exaggerated their affirmation of the divine attributes and thus fell into anthropomorphism, i.e., *tashbīh*, and were called the *mushabbiha*, partisans of *tashbīh* (the ascription of human characteristics to God)'; in 'Ashʿarī and the Ashʿarites', 51.

tensions with sultan al-Ashraf and the Shafiʿi and Hanbali traditionalists of Damascus.[44] For instance, al-Subki informed us that Ibn ʿAbd al-Salam 'stopped many innovations that were common among sermon-givers, like knocking the sword on the pulpit and other innovations, he invalidated the *ragha'ib* and the mid-Shaʿban prayers'.[45] When the Shafiʿi traditionalist–traditionist Ibn al-Salah al-Shahrazuri (577/1181–643/1245) defended upholding the *ragha'ib* prayer, Ibn ʿAbd al-Salam responded by rebuking him for relying on a 'fabricated *hadith* and for giving legal weight to popular practice'.[46] Additionally, the author related that when some 'deviant Hanbalis succeeded in dragging Ibn ʿAbd al-Salam into an argument about *kalam*', the *shaykh* willingly joined in and issued a legal opinion that al-Subki decided to reproduce so that it was 'benefited from and remembered'.[47] As discussed above, this *fatwa* attacked *tajsim*, *tashbih* and *hashawiyya*, or the perceived anthropomorphism of the Hanbali traditionalists. This legal opinion, most importantly for our purposes, made plenty of references to the ideal role of the *ʿulama'* in complementing the rulers' duties and moderating the exercise of power.[48] The whole affair escalated when Ayyubid sultan al-Ashraf joined in the debate and sent a letter to Ibn ʿAbd al-Salam accusing him of claiming to be an independent authority in reasoning and law (*mujtahid*) and inviting him, cynically, to proclaim a fifth *madhhab*.[49] Ibn ʿAbd al-Salam was then ordered to remain at home and refrain from meeting people, and was no longer allowed to issue legal opinions.[50] At this point, the leading scholars of Damascus sided with him. Al-Subki related that the *shaykh* of the Hanafi school rode to the Citadel on his donkey to meet the sultan. The Hanafi scholar asked al-Ashraf:

[44] Al-Subki, *Tabaqat*, 4:359–77.

[45] Ibid., 355. For more on the prayer of *ragha'ib* refer to Talmon-Heller and Ukeles, 'The Lure of a Controversial Prayer', 141–66; Hirschler, 'Pre-Eighteenth-Century Traditions of Revivalism', 201, 202, 213.

[46] Talmon-Heller and Ukeles, 'The Lure of a Controversial Prayer', 147. For more on the rivalry between Ibn al-Salah and Ibn ʿAbd al-Salam, refer to Sheibani, 'Islamic Law in an Age of Crisis', 134–48.

[47] Al-Subki, *Tabaqat*, 4:360.

[48] Ibid., 360–8.

[49] Ibid., 369.

[50] Ibid., 372.

> What is the issue between you and Ibn ʿAbd al-Salam? If a man of this prominence was in India or the far side of the world, then the sultan should have strived to bring him to his land, to add bliss to it and so the sultan can be prouder than other rulers![51]

The powerful brother of al-Ashraf, sultan al-Kamil (573/1177 or 576/1180–635/1238), 'who followed the true creed' of the Ashʿaris, as carefully noted by al-Subki, happened to be visiting Damascus from Egypt; he sided with the Shafiʿis and al-Ashraf was compelled to quell his dispute with Ibn ʿAbd al-Salam.[52] Al-Kamil was annoyed when he was informed that al-Ashraf had ordered both parties – rationalists and traditionalists – not to engage in this matter; he complained to his brother:

> By God this is unheard of! What sort of politics (*siyasa*) and rule (*saltana*) is this? You treat the righteous and the wicked equally! You forbid and silence those who seek to enjoin the good and forbid evil! You should have allowed the people of the *sunna* to express their arguments eloquently, so that they can uphold the true religion. You should have hanged twenty of those innovators to deter the rest. You should have helped the monotheists [the righteous group] to lead the Muslims on the right path.[53]

This account thus linked successful and righteous politics (*siyasa*) and rule (*saltana*) to the intellectual and theological discourses of the period and vice versa.

The contemporary sources confirm al-Subki's general story, although with stark variations.[54] According to Ibn Wasil's version, the sultan 'disliked sedition and intolerance amongst the *madhhabs*' and Ibn ʿAbd al-Salam was clearly 'biased' towards the Ashʿari creed.[55] He also related that al-Ashraf wrote to Ibn ʿAbd al-Salam quoting a known Prophetic tradition, 'Dissent lies dormant, may God curse him who stirs it up', and included offensive

---

[51] Ibid.; this account is confirmed in Ibn Fadl Allah al-ʿUmari, *Masalik al-absar fi mamalik al-amsar*, ed. Kamil Salman Juburi, 27 vols in 15 vols (Beirut: Dar al-Kutub al-ʿIlmiyya, 2010), 6:214.

[52] Al-Subki, *Tabaqat*, 4:374.

[53] Ibid.

[54] Ibn Wasil, *Mufarrij*, 5:141; this story is related under the obituary of al-Malik al-Ashraf, in the events of the year 635. This suggests that Ibn Wasil was reflecting the ruler's view, i.e., that of al-Ashraf.

[55] Ibid., 5:141.

verses of poetry.[56] According to Ibn Wasil, as soon as this warning letter reached Ibn ʿAbd al-Salam 'and the other pious-minded ones', they refrained from stirring up trouble and dissension subsided.[57] This account confirmed the historicity of the dispute, the theological leaning of Ibn ʿAbd al-Salam, and the customary involvement of the Ayyubid sultans in such theological quarrels.[58]

In this context where intra- and inter-*madhhab* rivalries played important roles in the political sphere, al-Subki sketched the ideal political role of the scholars in guiding the ruler. He narrated the role of Ibn ʿAbd al-Salam in moderating the Ayyubid rulers' dynastic feuds and their exercise of power in matters of taxation and justice. He related that Ibn ʿAbd al-Salam, at a later date, advised al-Ashraf not to escalate hostilities with his brother al-Kamil.[59] Furthermore, al-Subki claimed that al-Ashraf, now on his deathbed, asked for further guidance from Ibn ʿAbd al-Salam, who replied:

> While the sultan is in such a state of poor health and his life is in danger his regents indulge in fornication, drinking, committing sins, and imposing all kinds of unlawful taxes on Muslims; it is best that you, before meeting God, end all this foulness, stop all unlawful taxes, and rectify every injustice. So he [al-Ashraf], may God have mercy on his soul, did all that in time.[60]

The above anecdotes illustrate the preservation of the prevalent conventions of the political discourse of the late Ayyubid and Mamluk period in this Shafiʿi *lieu de mémoire*. Ibn ʿAbd al-Salam's political and theological activism, as related in al-Subki's biography, reflects how inter- and intra-*madhhab* competition plays a role in the political sphere, impacts the language of political discourse, and helps to articulate the Shafiʿi constitutional concerns

---

[56] Ibid., 5:142. Ibn Wasil mentions that he personally inspected this letter and the handwriting of al-Malik al-Ashraf.

[57] Ibid..

[58] The difference between the accounts of al-Subki and Ibn Wasil are not unexpected: one narrative was that of Ibn ʿAbd al-Salam's son as recounted by an ardent Shafiʿi–Ashʿari scholar, while the other was that of a court historian reflecting the ruler's outlook. On the other hand, al-ʿUmari (d. 749/1349) attributed the clash between Ibn ʿAbd al-Salam and al-Ashraf to the manoeuvering of the Shafiʿi traditionalist Ibn al-Salah who enlisted help 'from outside the *madhhab*' in his conspiracies, probably referring to the Hanbalis of Damascus; in *Masalik*, 5:330.

[59] Al-Subki, *Tabaqat*, 4:376.

[60] Ibid., 4:376.

of the period. We witness sultans al-Kamil and al-Ashraf conducting Ayyubid politics using the proprietary language and vocabulary of Hanbalis, Shafiʿis and Ashʿaris while, on the other hand, the *madhhab*s seem to be engaging in the political sphere using a distinctive political language that focuses on relevant public issues like taxation, justice, appeasing intra-dynastic tensions and protecting the populace. In this text, successful and righteous politics (*siyasa*) and rule (*saltana*) are now interlocked with the intellectual and theological discourses of the period. These disputes and intra- and inter-*madhhab* competitions between the traditionalists amongst the Hanbalis and Shafiʿis, on the one hand, and the Shafiʿi–Ashʿaris, on the other, offer a great insight into the Ayyubid dynasty's power dynamics and the leanings of various sultans. Furthermore, they highlight the tension between the scholars and rulers and its roots. Most importantly, the above passages show the scholars' use of legal opinions as weapons in the political sphere. Moreover, the accounts confirm the close involvement of Ayyubid sultans in religious and doctrinal affairs. They emphasise the competition between various *madhhab*s and intellectual groups in winning over the support of rulers in theological and other sorts of dispute amongst the scholars. As such, al-Subki preserved the conventions 'with and within which' members of the political and religious elites conducted their debates: he captured a period of Islamic history where politics and rule (*siyasa* and *saltana*) were conducted using the conventions of the *madhhab*s and vice versa.

The Contours of Shafiʿi Political Thought

With the prevalent conventions deciphered, the biography can now be read as a form of political thought. Ibn ʿAbd al-Salam's acts, as remembered and preserved by al-Subki, exemplified the contours of Shafiʿi political thought during the late Ayyubid and Mamluk period according to three main themes linked to the role of the *madhhab* in the political sphere and threats to the primacy of Shafiʿism in politics. Accordingly, the political role of the Shafiʿi *madhhab* was based on the prerogative to provide political legitimation to rulers and ruling elites (theme 1), and the prerogative to moderate the exercise of power by the rulers and ruling elites and defend the populace (theme 2). The threats to this role, according to the author, came from the rising influence of other *madhhab*s in politics (theme 3). As such, it appears that the remembrance of Ibn ʿAbd al-Salam as a Shafiʿi *lieu de memoire* and his biography as a political text provide a repertoire of political acts that could resurrect the primacy of the Shafiʿi *madhhab*'s indispensable role in politics, uphold the concern for the rule of law, and deal with the various challenges that the *madhhab* faced. Below I will trace these three themes in five anecdotes selected from the biography while keeping a close eye on the historicity of al-Subki's accounts by contrasting them to the contemporary chronicles, although – as mentioned above – the exemplary significance of these accounts is of relevance here rather than their veracity. The selected anecdotes are spread over different reigns of the late Ayyubid and early Mamluk period.

1. De-legitimation of Sultan al-Salih Ismaʿil

The first selected anecdote highlights the Shafiʿi *madhhab*'s prerogative of legitimating and de-legitimating rulers (theme 1). Ibn ʿAbd al-Salam was hailed for rejecting sultan al-Salih Ismaʿil's above-mentioned alliance with the Franks.[61] Ibn Wasil related the ceding of al-Shaqif (Beaufort) and Safad to the Franks by al-Salih Ismaʿil of Damascus during his struggle with his nephew, sultan al-Salih Ayyub of Egypt; the surrender of the two forts led to widespread indignation among Muslims.[62] Ibn Wasil who, as discussed above, had harshly criticised Ibn ʿAbd al-Salam for taking sides in theological disputes in Damascus, now switched to praising him, rather hagiographically:

> *Shaykh* ʿAbd al-ʿAziz Ibn ʿAbd al-Salam – may God have mercy on his soul – was one of the leading *imams* of the Shafiʿi [*madhhab*] and its exegesis, and he was unrivalled in our time. He was pious and ascetic; he would fear no man's reprimand if it pleased God; he was then the preacher of the [Grand Umayyad] Mosque of Damascus.[63]

[61] In late 1240, al-Salih Ismaʿil proposed ceding castles in Lebanon and Galilee, including Beaufort, Safad, Tyron, Chastel-Neuf and Toron, to Theobold of Champagne (1201–1253), in exchange for forging an alliance against Egypt; refer to Jonathan Riley-Smith, *The Crusades: A History* (London: Continuum, 2009), 188–9.

[62] Ibn Wasil, *Mufarrij*, 5:301–3; narrated during the events of year 639. For a more detailed discussion of this affair, refer to El-Merheb, 'Political Censure', 358–61.

[63] Ibn Wasil, *Mufarrij*, 5:302. See El-Merheb, 'Political Censure', 360.

Ibn Wasil related that Ibn ʿAbd al-Salam, aided by the Maliki jurist Ibn al-Hajib, had rejected the arrangement with the Franks, maligned it and was outspoken in his criticism of it; both jurists had to leave Damascus, as they had enraged al-Salih Ismaʿil, and ended up in Egypt.[64]

Although al-Subki related the same general story, he emphasised and celebrated the de-legitimation of the sultan. The biography stressed the constitutional prerogative of Ibn ʿAbd al-Salam to publicly strip al-Salih Ismaʿil's reign of its legitimacy. He narrated:

> *Shaykh* ʿIzz al-Din remained in Damascus until the rule of al-Salih Ismaʿil, known [derogatorily] as *Abu al-khaysh. Abu al-khaysh* entered an alliance with the Franks and granted them Sidon and the Beaufort castle; as such, *shaykh* ʿIzz al-Din renounced him and removed his name from the Friday sermon aided by the Maliki *shaykh* Abu ʿAmr Ibn al-Hajib. They both left Egypt around the year 639 as they infuriated the sultan.[65]

According to al-Subki, the arms merchants of Damascus asked Ibn ʿAbd al-Salam for his legal opinion before making sales to the Franks. His answer was that such a transaction was unlawful since it was inevitable that these arms would be used to kill Muslims.[66] Al-Subki related that Ibn ʿAbd al-Salam took this matter to the blessing at the end of the Friday sermon (*duʿaʾ*) at the Grand Mosque of Damascus where he prayed, 'May God assign to this community a judicious leadership that will be obedient to you and will forbid what is evil, so that your follower is valued and your enemy is disrespected' and 'people would respond *amen*'.[67]

That was al-Subki's first demonstration of Shafiʿi political thought in action during the late Ayyubid period. This narrative is unmistakably devoted to portraying political legitimation as a Shafiʿi prerogative. This anecdote can be considered similar to classical cases of scholar–ruler disagreement that end with the former removing the ruler's name from the Friday sermon.[68] In

64 Ibn Wasil, *Mufarrij*, 5:302–3.

65 Al-Subki, *Tabaqat*, 4:355; also see 377. Al-Subki named Sidon as opposed to Safad in Ibn Wasil's narrative. See El-Merheb, 'Political Censure', 360.

66 Al-Subki, *Tabaqat*, 4:378.

67 Ibid., 4:378. See El-Merheb, 'Political Censure', 360.

68 Mentioning the name of the ruler in the Friday sermon (like minting coins) is a convention reflecting obedience and legitimacy. For more on this check Crone, *Medieval Islamic*

a medieval Islamic political context, this translates as the scholar (i.e., the Shafiʿi authority) exercising his prerogative to withdraw legitimacy from any ruler, that is, conditional obedience or 'obedience in return for justice' as treated in Chapter 2.[69] Moreover, the Shafiʿi authority outlined what was and was not permissible in the context of Muslim political competition in dynastical feuds between Ayyubid sultans. Additionally, the Shafiʿi jurist was the ultimate authority to the people and it was to him that they turned to validate any sultanic order. As such, the prayer at the end of the Friday sermon became a fearsome political weapon that was used to delegitimise the ruler.

2. Moderating Rulers: the Reign of al-Salih Ayyub

Al-Subki used anecdotes that covered the relation between Ibn ʿAbd al-Salam and al-Salih Ayyub, the last effective Ayyubid sultan of Egypt, in order to highlight the Shafiʿi *madhhab*'s role in moderating rulers (theme 2). While contemporary sources did report several accounts confirming that Ibn ʿAbd al-Salam's uncompromising attitude towards the excesses of those in power persisted during his time in Egypt, al-Subki portrayed this personal quality within embellished anecdotes in order to emphasise the self-proclaimed Shafiʿi role of moderating the exercise of power.

Following his escape from Damascus, Ibn ʿAbd al-Salam quickly established himself as the ultimate Shafiʿi authority in Cairo. That he was prominent in Egypt was a matter of consensus among the contemporary sources and al-Subki. Abu Shama related that when Ibn ʿAbd al-Salam reached Egypt, he was well received by al-Salih Ayyub and was appointed the *khutba* and judgeship.[70] By contrast, Ibn Wasil attributed this warm welcome to the earlier maligning of al-Salih Ismaʿil, thus providing another indication of the intermingling of late Ayyubid politics with the *madhhabs*.[71] Al-Subki related, 'When the sultan built al-Salihiyya school, known in Cairo as *bayna*

Political Thought, 289–90; especially Norman Calder, 'Friday Prayer and the Juristic Theory of Government: Sarakhsī, Shīrāzī, Māwardī', *BSOAS* 49(1) (1986): 35–47; Jackson, *Islamic Law and the State*, 9. Refer to El-Merheb, 'Political Censure', for a study on the use of Friday sermons to censure rulers.

[69] Chapter 2, 60, 62.

[70] Abu Shama, *al-Dhayl ʿala al-rawdatayn*, 171.

[71] Ibn Wasil, *Mufarrij*, 5:303.

al-qasrayn, he commissioned the teaching seat of the Shafiʿi *madhhab* to *shaykh* ʿIzz al-Din.'[72] Al-Subki reported that a renowned Egyptian Shafiʿi scholar declared, 'We used to issue legal opinions before *shaykh* ʿIzz al-Din's coming, but now that he is here the *fatwa* seat is firmly taken.'[73] Al-Subki's confirmation that Ibn ʿAbd al-Salam became the prime authority of the Shafiʿi *madhhab* in Egypt was essential to what will follow in the narrative.[74]

In al-Subki's narrative, a showdown with the political authority was inevitable. While Ibn ʿAbd al-Salam had no reason to question the legitimacy of al-Salih Ayyub, he nonetheless strived to exercise his prerogative, as the Shafiʿi authority, to moderate the sultan's rule and his exercise of power (theme 2). As such, it was vital to illustrate that Ibn ʿAbd al-Salam continually commanded the upper hand in relation to sultan al-Salih Ayyub. Al-Subki related:

> *Shaykh* ʿIzz al-Din went to meet the sultan in the Citadel on a day of ʿId.[75] As per the custom of Egyptian sultans, ʿId was a ceremonial day where the sultan would show his splendour to his people, and so the soldiers were lined up along with the council of the sultanate while the *amirs* went on kissing the ground before the sultan. The *shaykh* called the sultan, 'Ayyub! How shall you answer God when he asks you: Did I grant you the rule of Egypt so you sanction the sale of liquor?' The sultan asked, 'Is that the case?' The *shaykh* responded, 'So-and-so tavern sells liquor and other evils; you thus renounce the blessing of ruling this kingdom!' So he shouted at him, in a loud voice, in front of the soldiers! To this, the sultan said, 'Master, I am not responsible for this, as this is from my father's reign.' He [Ibn ʿAbd al-Salam] replied, 'Are you one of those who say [quoting the Qurʾan], "We found our fathers following a way [and are following their example]."' The sultan immediately instructed the closure of the tavern.[76]

According to al-Subki's narrative, Ibn ʿAbd al-Salam stated, 'When I saw him [the sultan] in this splendidness, I intended to insult him for his own good, so

[72] Al-Subki, *Tabaqat*, 4:356.
[73] Ibid.
[74] Check Jackson, *Islamic Law and the State*, 10, on Ibn ʿAbd al-Salam being '*the* legitimizing authority' of Cairo.
[75] Muslim festive day.
[76] Al-Subki, *Tabaqat*, 4:356.

he does not become too proud.' When asked, 'Were you not afraid, master?' Ibn ʿAbd al-Salam replied: 'I evoked the greatness of God and so the sultan turned into a cat before my eyes.'[77]

Al-Subki carefully stages this 'performance' of political thought by the Shafiʿi authority in his account. It is not a simple piece of *adab* or hagiography employed to enrich a jurist's biography, but a political text loaded with references to power symbolism and ceremonialism. Ibn ʿAbd al-Salam's evocation of the greatness of God in this confrontation is al-Subki's way of attributing Shafiʿi constitutional prerogatives to the divine. Furthermore, Ibn ʿAbd al-Salam, as per the self-proclaimed Shafiʿi privilege, reminded the sultan to enforce doing what was good and forbidding what was evil, which was resonant with his previously mentioned prayer at the Friday sermon in Damascus. Unlike his injudicious Damascene uncle, the Egyptian sultan followed the advice of Ibn ʿAbd al-Salam and closed down the taverns. Moreover, the confrontation with the fearsome sultan al-Salih Ayyub takes place in a very evocative ceremonial setting. Al-Subki carefully selected this setting to announce the Shafiʿi prerogative of moderating the ruler's exercise of power: it is in front of soldiers and on the festive day of ʿId – at the Citadel, the symbolic heart of Ayyubid and Mamluk political power – that Ibn ʿAbd al-Salam chooses to caution the sultan, thus highlighting the official and public nature of this confrontation.[78] Given the ruthlessness of al-Salih Ayyub, it is extremely implausible that Ibn ʿAbd al-Salam addressed him in this manner in public.[79] However, historicity was not al-Subki's main concern, which was rather the exemplary value of Ibn ʿAbd al-Salam's act; what counted most to him was to underline the Shafiʿi prerogative to solemnly caution the ruler and moderate his exercise of power.

Yet there are credible indications to suggest that Ibn ʿAbd al-Salam's role as moderator of political power was indeed respected, to an extent, by

---

77 Ibid.

78 The Citadel became 'both the focus and the symbol of Ayyubid and Mamluk power' in Carole Hillenbrand, *The Crusades: Islamic Perspectives* (Edinburgh: Edinburgh University Press, 1999), 479; for a full study refer to Nasser O. Rabbat, *The Citadel of Cairo: A New Interpretation of Royal Mamluk Architecture* (Leiden: Brill, 1995).

79 'Ibn Wāṣil [*q.v.*] gives a penetrating pen-portrait, stressing Ayyūb's mixture of forbidding authority and diffident and introspective solitariness', in D. S. Richards, 'Al-Malik Al-Ṣāliḥ Ayyūb', *EI*[2].

the military and political elites. Al-Yunini narrated on the authority of the powerful *amir* Husam al-Din Ibn Abi ʿAli al-Hadhabani (d. 658/1260) that Ibn ʿAbd al-Salam refused to accept his testimony in a legal case that involved his patron the sultan. Al-Yunini related:

> *Amir* Husam al-Din Ibn Abi ʿAli, God have mercy on his soul, related, 'I was called as a witness [in court] in favour of al-malik al-Salih Najm al-Din [Ayyub]. The sultan instructed me to go to pronounce my testimony to *shaykh* ʿIzz al-Din who was at the time the judge in Egypt. I said [to the sultan]: my lord, he [Ibn ʿAbd al-Salam] will not accept me as a witness. The sultan insisted, so I told him: my lord, get me the *shaykh*'s consent. He [the sultan] sent a request to *shaykh* ʿIzz al-Din who replied, 'I do not accept his testimony' and the case was kept on hold until the judgeship came to judge Badr al-Din al-Sinjari, who welcomed me at the door and accepted my testimony. When it came to upholding justice, *shaykh* ʿIzz al-Din, God have mercy on his soul, did not favour anyone'.[80]

Al-Yunini's account showed how Ibn ʿAbd al-Salam succeeded in securing a reasonable extent of immunity for the judiciary from the interventions of the ruling military elites. As for the less plausible anecdote of the public scorning of sultan al-Salih Ayyub, it reflects al-Subki's yearning for a golden age when the role of the Shafiʿi political thought was publicly recognised.

3. Caliph, Sultan, Amirs *and* ʿulamaʾ

The following selected account treats both the legitimation and moderation of the ruling elites (themes 1 and 2). Related by contemporary sources and embellished in a retelling by al-Subki, the anecdote reflected the self-proclaimed constitutional duties of Shafiʿi thought in a novel and complex political scene: a caliph devoid of any real power; the recurrent rise of new members of the military elites; and a sultan who among his *amir*s was sometimes merely *primus inter pares*.[81] As such, the 'affair of the *tablakhana*' (the

---

[80] Al-Yunini, *Dhayl mirʾat al-zaman*, 17:235.

[81] Robert Irwin considers that Baybars had such status, while Qalawun's rule was 'more absolute', in *The Middle East in the Middle Ages*, 71. For more on this refer to Amalia Levanoni, 'The Mamluk Conception of the Sultanate', *International Journal of Middle East Studies* 26 (1994): 374; P. M. Holt, 'The Position and Power of the Mamlūk Sultan', *BSOAS* 38 (1975): 242.

military music band of an *amir*) was an example of the *ʿulamaʾ* trying to moderate and restrain the power of the *amirs* and a form of political thought, like others discussed in this book, which was interested in the question of politics and rule under a sultan and in the absence of an effective caliph.[82] This incident was first reported as a matter of straightforward spitefulness between two rival *amirs* in the entourage of sultan al-Salih Ayyub: both previously mentioned, Fakhr al-Din Ibn Shaykh al-Shuyukh Ibn Hamawiyya (d. 647/1250) and Husam al-Din Ibn Abi ʿAli al-Hadhabani.[83] Ibn Wasil, a close friend of the latter, related:

> Some of the servants of al-sahib Muʿin al-Din Ibn Shaykh al-Shuyukh [brother of Fakhr al-Din] – the vizier of al-malik al-Salih Ayyub – built on the roof of a mosque in Cairo a building to house Muʿin al-Din's *tablakhana*. When news of this reached *shaykh* ʿIzz al-Din, he rejected it and went in person with his sons to demolish the construction on the roof of the mosque. *Shaykh* ʿIzz al-Din knew very well that this would provoke al-malik al-Salih Ayyub and al-sahib Muʿin al-Din, so he proclaimed in the presence of witnesses that he no longer recognised the authority of Muʿin al-Din and removed himself from the judgeship of Cairo and its environs.[84]

Sultan al-Salih Ayyub was advised by Muʿin al-Din to remove Ibn ʿAbd al-Salam from the *khutba* so the latter could not attack him, as he had attacked al-Salih Ismaʿil over his alliance with the Franks in Damascus; the sultan took the advice and dismissed Ibn ʿAbd al-Salam.[85]

As a matter of course, al-Subki reported this matter in an embellished fashion.[86] The author dragged the caliph of Baghdad into the affair to assert, first, that the caliph's constitutional authority was transferred to Shafiʿi scholars and, secondly, that Shafiʿi legitimating power was independent of holding an official office. Al-Subki related:

---

82 Refer to Irwin, *The Middle East in the Middle Ages*, 40; R. Stephen Humphreys, 'The Emergence of the Mamluk Army', *Studia Islamica* 46 (1977): 167–73.

83 For more on Ibn Wasil and al-Hadhabani refer to Hirschler, *Medieval Arabic Historiography*, 23.

84 Ibn Wasil, 5:303–4.

85 Ibid., 5:304. Likewise, al-Yunini, confirms the anecdote of the *tablakhana* in *Dhayl mirʾat al-zaman*, 17:234–5.

86 Al-Subki, *Tabaqat*, 4:355.

> The sultan's *ustadar* Fakhr al-Din ʿUthman Ibn Shaykh al-Shuyukh [sic., should be Muʿin al-Din], who was in charge of the affairs of the sultanate, allowed a *tablakhana* to be housed and to operate on top of a mosque. Upon discovering it, *shaykh* ʿIzz al-Din ruled that the building should be demolished and that Fakhr al-Din Ibn al-Shaykh's tenure in office was no longer legitimate. Moreover, he removed himself from the judgeship. Although the sultan did not re-appoint him as a judge, his standing was not affected by this ruling. As for Fakhr al-Din, he assumed that this ruling would not affect his own status outside Egypt; soon this proved to be incorrect when the sultan decided to send an envoy to caliph al-Mustaʿsim (r. 640/1247–656/1258) in Baghdad. When the envoy reached the *diwan* and addressed the message to the caliph, the latter asked him, 'Did you hear this message from the sultan?' The envoy replied, 'No, I have been instructed to deliver it by the sultan's *ustadar* Fakhr al-Din Ibn Shaykh al-Shuyukh.' To this, the caliph responded, 'We take no message from the said person as he has been removed by Ibn ʿAbd al-Salam.' The envoy returned to the sultan, who this time instructed him personally to deliver the message to the caliph, and so he did.[87]

Al-Subki's account treated the prerogatives of legitimation and moderation of ruling elites (themes 1 and 2). It reflected how Shafiʿi thought granted itself caliphal constitutional authority to delegitimise senior office holders and curb powerful *amirs*. Primarily, the caliph of Baghdad was brought into the affair in order to suggest that his legitimating authority was transmitted to the Shafiʿi scholars personified by Ibn ʿAbd al-Salam. As such, the caliph would not deal with any official who had been removed by the Shafiʿi authority of Cairo. Strikingly, the version of contemporary historian Ibn Wasil framed the involvement of the caliph in the entirely opposite fashion: a caliphal envoy had in fact proposed to the sultan a new suitable candidate to replace Ibn ʿAbd al-Salam.[88] Additionally, what emerges from al-Subki's account is that Shafiʿi political thought envisaged a notion of legitimacy of the *amirs*

[87] Although al-Subki confused Fakhr al-Din for his brother Muʿin al-Din, this was not of major consequence to the narrative or to this interpretation of the affair.

[88] Contrary to al-Subki's account, the envoy of caliph al-Mustaʿsim visited al-Salih Ayyub along with the judge Afdal al-Din al-Khawanji and praised him, and based on this recommendation the latter was appointed to replace Ibn ʿAbd al-Salam; in Ibn Wasil, *Die Chronik*, 23.

independently from that of the sultan himself. The legitimacy of the *amirs* was to be decided, likewise, by the Shafiʿi *ʿulamaʾ*. Lastly, removing Ibn ʿAbd al-Salam from the judgeship did not reduce his status as the legitimating authority; this idea will recur below in the discussion of the investiture of the ʿAbbasid caliph of Cairo. As such, the political role of scholars rested outside official appointments and, hence, outside the power of the sultan or outside executive power altogether.

4. Defending the Populace

This anecdote primarily treats the intransigence of Shafiʿi thought towards unlawful taxation and thus addresses the moderation of the exercise of power and defending the populace (theme 2). During the preparations for war against the Mongol invasion, Ibn ʿAbd al-Salam aimed to defend Egypt from invaders while, simultaneously, protecting its populace against unjust taxation.[89] This was arguably one of the most celebrated deeds of Ibn ʿAbd al-Salam by contemporary and later sources. Ibn Wasil related that Qutuz, who was not yet officially sultan in Cairo, received an envoy from the Ayyubid sultan of Aleppo al-Malik al-Nasir (r. 634/1237–658/1260) asking for assistance against the Mongol threat.[90] Qutuz invited the jurists, judges and Cairene notables to the Citadel to deliberate and propose levying new taxes in order to finance the imminent war against the Mongols.[91] Ibn Wasil, who was present at this meeting, related that Ibn ʿAbd al-Salam did not attend in an official capacity.[92] Ibn Wasil provided a thorough account of the deliberations and noted, 'It was a consensus among all those present at the meeting to follow the opinion of *shaykh* ʿIzz al-Din Ibn ʿAbd al-Salam', which was:

> If the enemy threatened the lands of Islam, it is a duty for all to fight back. Levying taxes from the people to fund the preparation for war is authorised on one condition: that nothing shall remain in the treasury (*bayt al-mal*),

[89] This same case was selected to illustrate the use of *fatwas* as a tool for political censure in premodern Islamic societies in, El-Merheb, 'Political Censure', 364–67.

[90] Ibn Wasil, *Die Chronik*, 189.

[91] The meeting took place in the presence of the nominal child-sultan al-Mansur, son of al-Muʿizz Aybak, the slain master of Qutuz; ibid., 190

[92] Ibid.; Qutuz and the emerging Mamluks, 'felt it necessary to seek Ibn ʿAbd al-Salam's approval, despite the fact that the latter was at the time retired from public office and serving in no official capacity', in Jackson, *Islamic Law and the State*, 10.

> and that you [Mamluk *amirs*] shall sell all your golden and precious possessions, and that every soldier shall be solely equipped for his ride and his weapon, so they [the Mamluks] are treated similarly to the public. As for levying money from the populace while soldiers [Mamluks *amirs*] preserve their money and precious holdings, the answer is no![93]

While al-Subki's account of Ibn ʿAbd al-Salam's famous legal opinion is in complete agreement with the contemporary sources, his interpretation endows the account with a deeper political significance.[94] For the author, the moderation of the ruling elites, the protection of the populace and victory over the invading enemy were successfully achieved only because the ruling elites followed the Shafiʿi authority's directives. Al-Subki concluded, 'He [Ibn ʿAbd al-Salam] was so great and prestigious among them [the Mamluks] that they could not contradict him and they always recognised his directives; so they won the battle.'[95] This was a case of successful praxis of Shafiʿi political thought leading to victory.

This well-corroborated account was a founding political model. It revealed the stance of Shafiʿi political thought on the duty of *jihad* and unjust taxation, and proved the partaking of the civilian elite in the political sphere led by the Shafiʿi authority. Ibn Wasil's account showed that the civilian elite was composed of jurists, judges and notables, and that the sultan and his *amirs* consulted with it in a forum before taking major decisions. Furthermore, Ibn ʿAbd al-Salam's role as the leader of the civilian elite, as a mediator between the civilian and military elites, as a defender of the populace, and as a leading and indispensable counsellor for rulers was evident. As such, Ibn ʿAbd al-Salam ensured that the primacy of the duty of defending the lands of Islam against invaders was not to be taken as permission to unjustly tax the populace.

Subsequent scholars attempted to resuscitate and emulate Ibn ʿAbd al-Salam's legal opinion.[96] Forty years later, almost identical conditions occurred during the second reign of al-Nasir Muhammad Ibn Qalawun.

---

93 Ibn Wasil, *Die Chronik*, 190; al-ʿAyni mentions al-malik al-Mansur the son of Aybak but not Qutuz, in *ʿIqd al-juman*, 1:218–19. See El-Merheb, 'Political Censure', 365.

94 El-Merheb, 'Political Censure', 366.

95 Al-Subki, *Tabaqat*, 4:358.

96 The same case is discussed – with fewer details – in El-Merheb, 'Political Censure', 367.

Al-ʿAyni related that following the defeat of Wadi al-Khaznadar against the Mongol Ilkhanate in 699/1299, the Mamluk *amirs* convened in the presence of the sultan and intended to impose a new tax on the merchants of Cairo to re-equip the army.[97] The *amirs* instructed the market inspector (*naʾib al-hisba* or *muhtasib*) to secure a *fatwa* from the judges sanctioning this taxation; the market inspector claimed to possess the original copy of Ibn ʿAbd al-Salam's above-mentioned legal opinion.[98] *Amir* Sayf al-Din Salar, one of two main contenders for the sultanate during the second reign of al-Nasir Muhammad, requested this *fatwa* be taken immediately for ratification by the Shafiʿi chief judge Taqi al-Din Ibn Daqiq al-ʿId (625/1228–702/1302), a renowned pupil of Ibn ʿAbd al-Salam.[99] When the judge saw the legal opinion he recognised it and threw it to one side saying, 'You do not need my *fatwa*. If those in charge wish for something, the people will acquiesce.'[100] The *amirs*, evidently not satisfied with this reply, requested a meeting with Ibn Daqiq al-ʿId in order to 'get his blessing'. When the judge arrived for the meeting, Salar took his right arm and Baybars al-Jashankir, the second contender for the sultanate, took the left. They asked him to sit between the two of them as a sign of honour.[101] Eventually, Salar made clear their request, 'Master, we wish to acquire this *fatwa* so we do not commit any sin in our decisions.' Ibn Daqiq al-ʿId refused once again and said, 'This *fatwa* is conditional on every *amir* coming before me and swearing to God that he owns no silver or gold, and that his wife and children own no jewellery and things of the sort.'[102] Al-ʿAyni claims that Ibn Daqiq al-ʿId only ratified Ibn ʿAbd al-Salam's *fatwa* after every *amir* had brought his possessions before him.[103]

---

97 Al-ʿAyni, *ʿIqd al-juman*, 4:72. Al-ʿAyni relates on the authority of al-Yusufi (d.1358), a well-positioned witness to the reign of al-Nasir Muhammad and author of *Nuzhat al-nazir*. The same account is in al-Maqrizi, *Suluk*, 2:327.

98 Al-ʿAyni, *ʿIqd al-juman*, 4:72–3.

99 For more on the competition between the two commanders, refer to Irwin, *The Middle East in the Middle Ages*, 85–6. Ibn Daqiq al-ʿId was a student of Ibn ʿAbd al-Salam and the first to style his professor *sultan al-ʿulamaʾ*. He was appointed to the judgeship in 675/1295. Ibn Daqiq al-ʿId was also a poet and an alchemist who attempted to 'transmute quicksilver and sulphur into gold, and quicksilver and arsenic into silver'; refer to Ebied and Young, 'Ibn Daḳīḳ al-ʿĪd', *EI*[2].

100 Al-ʿAyni, *ʿIqd al-juman*, 4:73; El-Merheb, 'Political Censure', 367.

101 Al-ʿAyni, *ʿIqd al-juman*, 4:74.

102 Ibid.; El-Merheb, 'Political Censure', 367.

103 Ibid.

Ibn Daqiq al-ʿId was in many aspects the heir to what Ibn ʿAbd al-Salam signified to the Shafiʿi *madhhab*'s collective memory. Like his teacher before him, Ibn Daqiq al-ʿId represented the endurance of the Shafiʿi prerogative of conferring legitimacy to the competing military elites, moderating the exercise of power, and protecting the populace and, as such, upholding the cherished Shafiʿi ideal of the rule of law.

Salar and Baybars al-Jashankir were in a comparable position to sultans Qutuz and Baybars I. While they both held the keys to political power, they nevertheless desperately needed the endorsement of the legitimating Shafiʿi authority to maintain their grip on power. When sultan al-Mansur Lajin (r. 696/1297–698/1299) was killed, al-Nasir Muhammad, now fourteen years of age, was called up from Karak for his second reign. The two real holders of power were, however, his father's mamluks, Salar and Baybars al-Jashankir. These influential *amir*s were rivals waiting for the right moment to seize power, yet they managed to coexist and ruled jointly for ten years. Throughout their rule, they both cooperated with Shafiʿi jurists like Ibn Daqiq al-ʿId and Ibn Jamaʿa to legitimate and stabilise their ever-precarious positions. Nevertheless, both Salar and Baybars al-Jashankir – like Baybars I before them – dreaded the dominance of the Shafiʿi jurists and their political thought, and solicited different conceptions of political thought from Sufis, in the case of Baybars al-Jashankir, and Ibn Taymiyya, in the case of Salar.

The Mamluk defeat at the battle of Wadi al-Khaznadar complicated the joint position of Salar and Baybars al-Jashankir even further. There was a pressing need to regain control of the realm and the trust of the populace by quickly re-organising and equipping the army. People lost confidence in the rulers and mocked the soldiers and their two *amir*s Salar and Baybars al-Jashankir, and at every opportunity they would say, according to al-ʿAyni, 'by God, they are but a joke!'[104] The sultan increased military spending from the treasury, but the cost of the mission was exorbitant and there was soon a need to raise more taxes.[105] Consequently, Salar and Baybars al-Jashankir found themselves in the same position that Qutuz had found himself in: their political legitimacy was dependent on the military elite carrying out its

[104] Al-ʿAyni, *ʿIqd al-juman*, 4:68–70. This account is supported by al-Yusufi's contemporary and well-informed chronicle.

[105] Ibid., 4:70–2; see also al-Maqrizi, *Suluk*, 2:327.

duty to defend Islamic lands which, in turn, demanded levying more taxes in order to recruit and equip soldiers. The case of Salar and Baybars al-Jashankir was even shakier after the humiliating defeat at Wadi al-Khaznadar. Once again, the Shafi'i scholars were in a position to exercise their prerogative of bestowing political legitimacy on the military ruling elite and protecting the populace from unlawful and excessive taxation.

5. Baybars: Legitimation and Tension

Al-Subki's treatment of the relation between Baybars and Ibn 'Abd al-Salam reflects the Shafi'i prerogative of legitimating rulers, including sultan Baybars and the 'Abbasid caliph of Cairo (theme 1), and the threat of the rising influence of other *madhhab*s (theme 3). He recounted, 'Further proof of his great prominence among them [the Mamluks] is that al-malik al-Zahir Baybars was sure to follow *shaykh* 'Izz al-Din before swearing allegiance to both caliph al-Musta'sim and caliph al-Hakim. The *shaykh* would swear allegiance first, followed by the sultan, and then the judges.'[106] Al-Subki greatly exaggerated this legitimating role as he claimed that when Ibn 'Abd al-Salam's impressive funeral procession passed under the Citadel, Baybars confided to his close advisers, 'Only now is my reign secure. If this *shaykh* had wished to incite the people against my rule, I would have lost it!'[107] Although this sounds too dramatic to have been uttered by Baybars, there are indications that the sultan recognised Ibn 'Abd al-Salam's stature during his reign.

Most accounts of the ceremony of the oath of allegiance (*bay'a*) of the first 'Abbasid caliph in Egypt confirm that sultan Baybars respected Ibn 'Abd al-Salam's legitimating authority. The contemporaneous sources corroborate that the prerogative of Shafi'i political thought to legitimate the ruler was somehow put into practice during the reign of Baybars. Several accounts reveal a specific hierarchy during the political legitimation ceremony of

[106] Al-Subki, *Tabaqat*, 4:358; Ibn 'Abd al-Zahir mentions that Ibn 'Abd al-Salam was only present at the *bay'a* of the first caliph, in *al-Rawd*, 100; similarly in al-Qalqashandi, *Subh al-a'sha*, 3:264–5; Baybars al-Mansuri makes no mention of this participation, in *Zubdat al-fikra fi tarikh al-hijra*, ed. Donald Sidney (Beirut and Berlin: al-Ma'had al-Almani li-al-Abhath al-Sharqiyya and al-Kitab al-'Arabi, 1998), 60–1; al-Suyuti relates a different order of performing the *bay'a*, in *Tarikh al-khulafa'*, ed. Ibrahim Salih (Beirut: Dar Sadir, 1997), 562–3.

[107] Al-Subki, *Tabaqat*, 4:358; Ibn al-'Imad, *Shadharat al-dhahab fi akhbar man dhahab*, ed. Mahmud al-Arna'ut and 'Abd al-Qadir al-Arna'ut, 10 vols (Beirut: Dar Ibn Kathir, 1986), 7:524.

the ʿAbbasid caliph. Ibn Wasil narrated that Ibn ʿAbd al-Salam attended the *bayʿa* of the caliph in the Citadel of Cairo with the chief judge Ibn Bint al-Aʿazz.[108] First, the chief judge attested to the candidate's genealogy. Subsequently, Ibn ʿAbd al-Salam was the first to perform the *bayʿa*, followed by the chief judge, sultan Baybars and then everyone else. Likewise, Ibn ʿAbd al-Zahir's account, being the close secretary of Baybars, was very telling. He related that, 'The sultan summoned the jurists, leading *imams*, *amirs*, Sufis, merchants, and many people to the hall of ʿAmd; *shaykh* ʿIzz al-Din ʿAbd al-Salam joined, so did the caliph – God be pleased with him – and the sultan.'[109] It is noteworthy that Ibn ʿAbd al-Salam, once again attending in no official capacity, is mentioned ahead of the sultan at the ceremony.

Conversely, there are indications of an uneasy relation between Baybars and Ibn ʿAbd al-Salam. Unlike other contemporaneous sources, Ibn ʿAbd al-Zahir was generally silent on Ibn ʿAbd al-Salam, which is very suggestive.[110] Considered the 'official' biographer of Baybars, Ibn ʿAbd al-Zahir's main aim was to embellish and legitimate Baybars' rule and, as such, his silence could have reflected discomfort with the influential role of Ibn ʿAbd al-Salam as the legitimating authority. This is supported by indications that Baybars continuously tried to appease and win over Ibn ʿAbd al-Salam. For instance, al-Yunini narrated that Ibn Hanna, Baybars' vizier, proposed to Ibn ʿAbd al-Salam that his son take over his post after his (Ibn ʿAbd al-Salam's) death, but the offer was swiftly declined by Ibn ʿAbd al-Salam.[111] Some later sources were more explicit in covering the issue of legitimation by pointing out Baybars' background as a slave. Al-Kutubi (d. 686/1287–764/1363) relayed that Ibn ʿAbd al-Salam shouted out during the *bayʿa* of Baybars, 'Rukn al-Din, I know you are the *mamluk* of al-Bunduqdar!'[112] Ibn ʿAbd al-Salam purportedly refused to swear the oath of allegiance until it was attested

[108] Ibn Wasil, *Die Chronik*, 231.

[109] Ibn ʿAbd al-Zahir, *al-Rawd*, 100. Also refer to Shafiʿ Ibn ʿAli, *Husn al-manaqib al-sirriyya al-muntazaʿa min al-sira al-Zahiriyya*, ed. ʿAbd al-ʿAziz al-Khuwaytir (al-Riyad: Matbaʿat Safir, 1989), 79–80.

[110] Ibn ʿAbd al-Zahir's work 'was known to have been commissioned by Baybars', in Little, 'Historiography of the Ayyūbid and Mamlūk Epochs', 421.

[111] Al-Yunini, *Dhayl mirʾat al-zaman*, 17:242–3; al-ʿUmari, *Masalik*, 6:216.

[112] Al-Kutubi, *Fawat al-wafayat*, 2:352.

that Baybars was indeed sold to al-Salih Ayyub, who later manumitted him.[113] Such an anecdote would surely not be found in Ibn ʿAbd al-Zahir's biography of Baybars.

Despite such accounts, Shafiʿi political thought seems to have been functioning well and in relative agreement under the joint watch of Ibn ʿAbd al-Salam and Baybars. Although the Shafiʿi self-proclaimed prerogative of legitimating rulers led to some tensions between them, contemporaneous sources corroborate the existence of a certain political arrangement between the sultan, the Shafiʿi authority and the civilian elite. Likewise, they confirm the legitimating authority of Ibn ʿAbd al-Salam and his role as leader of Cairo's civilian elite during the *bayʿa* of the caliph.

Yet six months after the death of Ibn ʿAbd al-Salam, Baybars attempted to tamper with this arrangement by instituting his legal reforms.[114] This attempt only exacerbated the Shafiʿi collective memory's 'will to remember' and preserve this arrangement that had secured the *madhhab*'s dominance. It is against this background that al-Subki raised his warning against the rising influence of other *madhhab*s in the political sphere (theme 3) and claimed that Baybars was reprimanded in a dream by Imam al-Shafiʿi for instituting the legal reform of the four chief judges.[115] Al-Shafiʿi scorned Baybars, 'How dare you insult my *madhhab*? Are these lands mine or yours? I shall depose you and your progeny till Judgement Day!"[116] According to al-Subki, Baybars soon died, his son never succeeded in establishing his rule, and Baybars' descendants ended up living in abject poverty. Once again, the *Tabaqat* linked *madhhab* to politics by reiterating that any deviation from Shafiʿi dominance leads to unsuccessful politics, loss of rule and other dire consequences.

Shafiʿi Political Thought in a Later Subki Work

The political themes detected in Ibn ʿAbd al-Salam's biography in the *Tabaqat* re-emerge in a later work composed by al-Subki. Although seldom viewed in this fashion, *Muʿid al-niʿam wa-mubid al-niqam* (*The Restorer of Favours and*

---

113 Ibid.

114 Jackson, *Islamic Law and the State*, 10–11.

115 Nielsen, 'Sultan Al-Ẓāhir Baybars', 173–4; al-Subki, *Tabaqat*, 4:425.

116 Al-Subki, *Tabaqat*, 4:425.

the Restrainer of Chastisements) is a source of political thought that clearly upholds Shafiʿi constitutional concerns for the rule of law and limited government.[117] This work treats the conduct and duties of the holders of 113 public posts and professions of the Mamluk period. Most importantly, it is a political text that asserts Shafiʿi conceptions of political authority and Shafiʿi constitutional concerns. The *Muʿid* promotes upholding them through the moderation of the exercise of power and the division of political, judicial and administrative labour. Throughout this treatise, al-Subki's doctrinal affiliations and loyalties were asserted over and over again, as is evident in his praise of prominent Shafiʿi–Ashʿari figures like al-Juwayni, al-Ghazali and al-Razi, and his sympathy towards Sufism.[118] Moreover, the treatment of political themes in the *Muʿid* is evident throughout the discussions of the conduct of the caliph, sultan, vice-regents and judges using a stylistic blend that draws from administrative and statecraft manuals, and Shafiʿi juridical writings.[119]

A brief examination of the *Muʿid* supports the methodology of this chapter. Some anecdotes in this treatise reflect the same interpretation of Shafiʿi political thought that was identified in the biography of Ibn ʿAbd al-Salam in the *Tabaqat*. For instance, the *Muʿid*'s treatment of the function of the *amirs* and the recollection of Ibn ʿAbd al-Salam's legal opinion on taxation reassert the contours of Shafiʿi political thought of the period by reproducing the same above-mentioned political themes.[120] First, al-Subki cited the prerogative of the *ʿulamaʾ* to legitimate the ruling elites (theme 1). He related the story of a sinful jurist who was flogged by an *amir* for his drunkenness; the jurist, now sober, went to the judge and demanded that he be flogged one more time as he considered the ruling of the *amir* unlawful.[121] The allegory here fits (theme 1) as even a sinful jurist is capable of de-legitimating the judicial decision (*hukm*) of an *amir* and the dispensation of justice is the

---

117 Refer to 'al-Subkī', *EI*². The title translation is from an earlier edition by D. W. Myhrman (London, 1908), otherwise this edition is not used in this book.

118 Al-Subki, *Muʿid al-niʿam*, 78–80, 119.

119 Ibid., 13–15. For more on this stylistic blend, refer to Chapters 1 and 4, above; El-Merheb, 'Islamic Political Thought and Professional Mobility'.

120 Ibid., 46–7. The deep influence of some familiar premises of Ibn Jamaʿa's *Tahrir* on the *Muʿid al-niʿam* is evident in the discussion, for instance, on the duty of the *amirs* to train with soldiers and keep them in form.

121 Al-Subki, *Muʿid al-niʿam*, 48–9. Al-Subki, however, was careful to exonerate the vice-regent of Syria from the accusations he levels against other *amirs*, see 50–1.

prerogative of Shafiʿi judges. Furthermore, the author recounted Ibn ʿAbd al-Salam's famous *fatwa* to Qutuz on the eve of the Mongol invasion in a version rich with detail that went unmentioned in the *Tabaqat*.[122] In the version in the *Muʿid*, which reproduced a more detailed report of Ibn ʿAbd al-Salam's speech, Baybars and Qalawun were also present when Ibn ʿAbd al-Salam pronounced his legal opinion to Qutuz. This anecdote fits with the proclaimed prerogative of moderating the exercise of power and defending the populace (theme 2). Additionally, al-Subki's discussion of the office of the vice-regent (*naʾib al-saltana*) in the *Muʿid* reflects the recurring Shafiʿi concern with avoiding unbalanced and harsh punishments while upholding justice.[123] Again, this fits well with the moderation of the ruling elites and accordingly with (theme 2) of Shafiʿi political thought.

Yet unlike the *Tabaqat*, the *Muʿid* treats Shafiʿi political thought head-on. The palpable influence of Shafiʿi political treatises like Ibn Jamaʿa's *Tahrir* is difficult to miss in the *Muʿid*. For instance, al-Subki's discussion of the office of sultan reveals how entrenched Shafiʿi political thought of the period was within his work. The author started by noting that many jurists had previously written on the subjects of the *imama* and sultanic ordinances. In complete agreement with Ibn Jamaʿa's *Tahrir*, al-Subki then explained that by sultan he meant the greater *imam* (*al-imam al-aʿzam*).[124] Such an interpretation of sultan encapsulated, in striking simplicity, one of Ibn Jamaʿa's main contributions to political thought and his tripartite conception of the highest political authority of Islam, which was covered in Chapter 2. Al-Subki listed the duties of the sultan as: raising armies; upholding the duty of *jihad* and protecting the abode of Islam; proper handling of land grants; attending to the *ʿulamaʾ* and the needy by respecting the charitable endowments that support them; preserving the treasury; and upholding ritual prayer duties and religion. Much of this discussion echoed the writings of Ibn Jamaʿa and other earlier Shafiʿi political thinkers, but also reflected concerns and priorities of al-Subki's time.[125]

---

122 Ibid., 51.
123 Ibid., 21–3.
124 Ibid., 16. Refer to the detailed discussion in Chapter 2, 84.
125 Al-Subki, *Muʿid al-niʿam*, 16–21.

Conclusion

The selected anecdotes of Ibn ʿAbd al-Salam's biography in the *Tabaqat* highlight the contours of the Shafiʿi *madhhab*'s political thought. Al-Subki's narrative featured three major themes: the two self-proclaimed prerogatives of political legitimation and delegitimation of rulers (theme 1); moderating the exercise of power and defending the populace (theme 2); and warning against the rising influence of other *madhhab*s in the political sphere (theme 3). In sum, the first two themes relate to the Shafiʿi constitutional concerns for upholding the rule of law and limited government, as advocated in the political treatises of Ibn Jamaʿa, while the third theme points to the role of *madhhab* competition in the production of political thought. As such, reading Mamluk historiography as a form of political thought proved to be very beneficial.

This chapter recovered the prevailing conventions in the treatment of political themes of the period by following the guidelines of Skinner and Pocock. That was possible owing to al-Subki's scrupulous preservation of the intellectual context and political language of the late Ayyubid and Mamluk period 'with and within which' Ibn ʿAbd al-Salam operated.[126] This exercise uncovered an entire repertoire of political ideas disguised in the language of theological and juristic disputes between the Ashʿari–Shafiʿis and traditionalist Hanbalis. These disputes were often conducted with the tacit or explicit involvement of Ayyubid and Mamluk rulers and members of the military elites. Furthermore, this chapter emphasised the interrelatedness between *madhhab* and politics, especially as per the vision of al-Subki who presented Shafiʿism as the official or preferred *madhhab* of the state and linked adherence to it to successful politics and prolonged rule.

Three important conclusions can be drawn here. First, the remembrance of Ibn ʿAbd al-Salam's life and career epitomised a model relation between rulers, civilian elite and populace that secured the rule of law to a certain extent during the late Ayyubid and early Mamluk period. As such, al-Subki portrayed a Shafiʿi *madhhab* political thought that was already in praxis and well in place by the time of Ibn Jamaʿa. Secondly, the evoking of the

[126] Pocock, 'Languages and Their Implications', 25.

prerogatives of legitimating and moderating rulers and protecting the populace was effectively a call by al-Subki for the revival of this rule of law in the fourteenth century. It was a yearning for a golden age when the dominance of Shafiʿism as the preferred *madhhab* secured the rule of law. Thirdly, the 'will to remember' Ibn ʿAbd al-Salam and to preserve Shafiʿi political thought was intended to defend the Shafiʿi *madhhab* from threats arising from competition in a period of political uncertainty. As such, the competition amongst the *madhhab*s in this period spread into the domain of constitutional and public law, thus stimulating the production of political thought.

Bibliography

Primary Sources

Abū Shāma. *Tarājim rijāl al-qarnayn al-sādis wa-al-sābiʿ al-maʿrūf bi al-dhayl ʿalā-al-rawḍatayn*, ed. ʿIzzat al-ʿAṭṭār al-Ḥusaynī. Beirut: Dār al-Jīl, 1974.

Al-ʿAbbāsī (al-Ṣafadī). *Āthār al-uwal fī tartīb al-duwal*. Cairo: al-Maṭbaʿa al-Maymaniyya, 1878.

Al-ʿAbbāsī (al-Ṣafadī). *Nuzhat al-mālik wa-al-mamlūk fī mukhtaṣar sīrat man waliya Miṣr min-al-mulūk*, ed. ʿUmar ʿAbd al-Salām Tadmurī. Ṣaydā and Beirut: al-Maktaba al-ʿAṣriyya, 2003.

Al-ʿAynī. *ʿIqd al-jumān fī taʾrīkh ahl-al-zamān*, ed. Muḥammad Muḥammad Amīn. 5 vols. Cairo: Dār al-Kutub wa-al-Wathāʾiq al-Qawmiyya, 2009.

Al-Birzālī. *Mashyakhat qāḍī al-quḍāt shaykh al-Islām Badr al-Dīn Ibn Jamāʿa*, ed. Muwaffaq Bin ʿAbd al-Qādir, 2 vols. Beirut: Dār al-Gharb al-Islāmī, 1988.

Al-Dhahabī. *Siyar aʿlām al-nubalāʾ*, ed. Shuʿayb al-Arnaʾūṭ, 25 vols. Beirut: Muʾassasat al-Risāla, 1991, vol. 23.

Al-Ghazālī. *Al-Mustaẓhirī (Faḍāʾiḥ al-bāṭiniyya)*, ed. ʿAbd al-Raḥmān Badawī. Kuwait: Dār al-Kutub al-Thaqāfiyya,1964.

Al-Ghazālī (Pseudo-Ghazālī). *Counsel for Kings (Naṣīḥat al-Mulūk)*, trans. F. R. C. Bagley. London: Oxford University Press, 1964.

Al-Juwaynī. *Al-Ghiyāthī: Ghiyāth al-umam fī-iltiyāth al-ẓulam*, ed. ʿAbd al-ʿAẓīm al-Dīb. Cairo: Maṭbaʿat Nahḍat Miṣr, 1981 or 1982.

Al-Kutubī. *Fawāt al-wafayāt*, ed. Iḥsān ʿAbbās, 5 vols. Beirut: Dār Ṣādir, 1973.

Al-Manṣūrī, Baybars. *Zubdat al-fikra fī tārīkh al-hijra*, ed. Donald Sidney Richards. Beirut and Berlin: al-Maʿhad al-Almānī li-al-Abḥāth al-Sharqiyya and al-Kitāb al-ʿArabī, 1998.

Al-Maqrīzī. *Al-Sulūk li-maʿrifat duwal al-mulūk*, ed. Muḥammad ʿAbd al-Qādir ʿAṭā, 8 vols. Beirut: Dār al-Kutub al-ʿIlmiyya, 1997.

Al-Māwardī. *Qawānin al-wizāra wa-siyāsat al-mulk*, ed. Raḍwān al-Sayyid. Beirut: Dār al-Ṭalīʿa, 1979.

Al-Māwardī. *Tashīl al-naẓar wa taʿjīl al-ẓafar fī akhlāq al-malik wa-siyāsat al-mulk*, ed. Ḥasan al-Saʿātī and Muḥyī Hilāl al-Sarḥān. Beirut: Dār al-Nahḍa, 1981.

Al-Māwardī. *Adab al-dunyā wa-al-dīn*, ed. Muḥammad Karīm Rājiḥ. Beirut: Dār Iqraʾ, 1985.

Al-Māwardī. *Kitāb al-aḥkām al-sulṭāniyya wa-al-wilāyāt al-dīniyya*, ed. Aḥmad Mubārak al-Baghdādī, 2 vols. Kuwait: Dār Ibn Qutayba, 1989.

Al-Qalqashandī. *Ṣubḥ al-aʿshā fī ṣināʿat al-inshāʾ*, 14 vols. Cairo: al-Maṭbaʿa al-Amīriyya, 1913.

Al-Qalqashandī. *Maʾāthir al-ināfa fī maʿālim al-khilāfa*, ed. ʿAbd al-Sattār Aḥmad Farrāj. Beirut: ʿĀlam al-Kutub, 2006.

Al-Qarāfī, and Mohammad H. Fadel. *The Criterion for Distinguishing Legal Opinions from Judicial Rulings and the Administrative Acts of Judges and Rulers*, World Thought in Translation. New Haven, CT: Yale University Press, 2017.

Al-Qarāfī. *Al-Iḥkām fī tamyīz al-fatāwā ʿan al-aḥkām wa taṣarrufāt al-qāḍī wa-al-imām*, ed. Abū Ghudda. Aleppo and Beirut: Maktab al-Maṭbūʿāt al-Islāmiyya and Dār al-Bashāʾir al-Islāmiyya, 1995.

Al-Qarāfī. *Al-Furūq*, ed. ʿUmar Ḥasan al-Qayyām, 4 vols. Beirut: Muʾassasat al-Risāla, 2003.

Al-Rāzī (Najm al-Dīn). *The Path of God's Bondsmen from Origin to Return (Merṣād al-ʿibād min al-mabdāʾ ilā-al-maʿād): A Sufi Compendium*, trans. Hamid Algar. Delmar, NY: Caravan Books, 1982.

Al-Rāzī (Najm al-Dīn). *Manārāt al-sāʾirīn wa maqāmāt al-ṭāʾirīn*, ed. Saʿīd ʿAbd al-Fattāḥ. Kuwait: Dār Suʿād al-Ṣubāḥ, 1993.

Al-Rāzī (Najm al-Dīn). *Falsafat al-taṣawwuf wa-al-daʿwa ilā-Allāh fī kitāb Mirṣād al-ʿibād min-al-mabdāʾ ilā-al-maʿād*, trans. ʿAlī Ismāʿīl. Cairo: Etrac Publishing, 2002.

Al-Ṣafadī. *Al-Wāfī bi-al-wafayāt*, 29 vols. Beirut: Dār Iḥyāʾ al-Turāth al-ʿArabī, 2000.

Al-Shayzarī. *Al-Nahj al-maslūk fī siyāsat al-mulūk*, ed. Muḥammad Ismāʿīl and Aḥmad al-Mazīdī. Beirut: Dār al-Kutub al-ʿIlmiyya, 2003.

Al-Subkī, Tāj al-Dīn. *The Restorer of Favours and the Restrainer of Chastisements*, ed. D. W. Myhrman. London, 1908.

Al-Subkī, Tāj al-Dīn. *Ṭabaqāt al-Shāfiʿīya al-Kubrā*, ed. Maḥmūd Muḥammad al-Ṭanāḥī and ʿAbd al-Fattāḥ Muḥammad al-Ḥulū, 10 vols. Cairo: Maṭbaʿat ʿĪsā al-Bābī al-Ḥalabī wa-Shurakāh, 1964, vol. 1.

Al-Subkī, Tāj al-Dīn. *Muʿīd al-niʿam wa-mubīd al-niqam*, ed. Muḥammad ʿAlī al-Najjār, Abū Zayd Shalabī and Muḥammad Abū al-ʿUyūn. Cairo: Maktabat al-Khānjī, 1993.

Al-Subkī, Tāj al-Dīn. *Ṭabaqāt al-Shāfiʿiyya al-kubrā*, ed. Muṣṭafā ʿAbd al-Qādir Aḥmad ʿAṭā, 6 vols. Beirut: Dār al-Kutub al-ʿIlmiyya, 1999.

Al-Suyūṭī. *Ḥusn al-muḥāḍara fī akhbār miṣr wa-al-Qāhira*, ed. Muḥammad Abū Faḍl Ibrāhīm, 2 vols. Cairo: Dār Iḥyāʾ al-Kutub al-ʿArabiyya, 1968.

Al-Suyūṭī. *Tārīkh al-khulafāʾ*, ed. Ibrāhīm Ṣāliḥ. Beirut: Dār Ṣādir, 1997.

Al-Ṭurṭūshī, *Sirāj al-mulūk*, ed. Muḥammad Abū Bakr. Cairo: al-Dār al-Miṣriyyah al-Lubnāniyya, 1994.

Al-Ṭarsūsī. *Tuḥfat al-Turk fī-mā yajib an yuʿmal fī al-mulk*, 2nd edn, ed. Riḍwān al-Sayyid. Beirut: Ibn al-Azraq Center for Political Heritage Studies, 2012.

Al-Yāfiʿī. *Mirʾāt al-jinān wa-ʿibrat al-yaqẓān fī maʿrifat mā yuʿtabar min ḥawādith al-zamān*, 4 vols. Beirut: Dār al-Kutub al-ʿIlmiyya, 1997.

Al-Yūnīnī. *Dhayl mirʾāt al-zamān*, ed. Ḥamza Aḥmad ʿAbbās, 3 vols. Abū Dhabī: Hayʾat Abū Dhabī li-al-Thaqāfa wa-al-Turāth, al-Majmaʿ al-Thaqāfī, 2007.

Al-Yūsufī. *Nuzhat al-nāẓir fī sīrat al-Malik al-Nāṣir*, ed. Aḥmad Ḥuṭayṭ. Beirut: ʿĀlam al-Kutub, 1986.

Al-ʿUlaymī. *Kitāb al-uns al-jalīl bi-tārīkh al-Quds wa-al-Khalīl*, ed. ʿAdnān Yūnus ʿAbd al-Majīd Abū Tabbāna, 2 vols ʿAmmān: Al-Khalīl, 1999.

Ibn ʿAbd al-Ẓāhir. *Al-Rawḍ al-zāhir fī sirāt al-Malik al-Ẓāhir*, ed. ʿAbd al-ʿAzīz al-Khuwayṭir. al-Riyāḍ, 1976.

Ibn al-Dawādārī. *Kanz al-durar wa-jāmiʿ al-ghurar*, 9 vols. Deutsches Archäologisches Institut, 1960.

Ibn al-Jawzī, Sibṭ. *Mirʾāt al-zamān fī tārīkh al-aʿyān*, ed. Salmān Al-Jubūrī. Beirut: Dār al-Kutub al-ʿIlmiyya, 2013.

Ibn Faḍl Allāh al-ʿUmarī. *Masālik al-abṣār fī mamālik al-amṣār*, ed. Kāmil Salmān Jubūrī, 27 vols, in 15 vols. Beirut: Dār al-Kutub al-ʿIlmiyya, 2010.

Ibn Fātik, Mubashshir. *Mukhtār al-ḥikam wa-maḥāsin al-kalim*, ed. ʿAbd al-Rahṃān Badawī. Beirut: al-Mu'assasa al-ʿArabiyya li-al-Dirāsāt wa-al-Nashr, 1980.

Ibn al-Ḥaddād. *Al-Jawhar al-nafīs fī siyāsat al-raʾīs (649/1251–2)*, ed. Riḍwān al-Sayyid. Beirut: Dār al-Ṭalīʿa, 1983.

Ibn Ḥajar al-ʿAsqalānī. *Al-Durar al-kāmina fī aʿyān al-miʾa al-thāmina*, 4 vols. Beirut: Dār al-Jīl, 1993.

Ibn Ḥamawiyya (Tāj al-Dīn). 'Kitāb al-siyāsa al-mulūkiyya', MS Topkapi, Istanbul. TSMK A. 1116.

Ibn al-ʿImād. *Shadharāt al-dhahab fī akhbār man dhahab*, ed. Maḥmūd al-Arnāʾūṭ and ʿAbd al-Qādir al-Arnāʾūṭ, 10 vols. Beirut: Dār Ibn Kathīr, 1986.

Ibn Jamāʿa. *Taḥrīr al-aḥkām fī tadbīr ahl al-Islām*, ed. Fuʾād ʿAbd al-Munʿim Aḥmad. Qatar: Riʾāsat al-Maḥākim al-Sharʿiyya wa-al-Shuʾūn al-Dīniyya, 1985.

Ibn Jamāʿa. *Tadhkirat al-sāmiʿ wa-al-mutakallim fī adab al-ʿālim wa-al-mutaʿallim*, ed. Muḥammad Ibn Mahdī al-ʿAjamī. Beirut: Dār al-Bashāʾir al-Islāmiyya li-al-Ṭibāʿa wa-al-Nashr wa-al-Tawzīʿ, 2008.

Ibn Jamāʿa. *Mustanad al-ajnād fī ālāt al-jihād wa-mukhtaṣar fī faḍl al-jihād wa-Faḍāʾil al-rāmī fī sabīl Allāh*, ed. Usāma Nāṣir al-Naqshbandī. Damascus: Dār al-Wathāʾiq li-al-Dirāsāt wa-al-Ṭabʿ wa-al-Nashr wa-al-Tawzīʿ, 2008.

Ibn Kathīr. *Al-Bidāya wa-al-nihāya*, ed. Muḥyī al-Dīn Dīb Mistū, 20 vols in 11 vols. Damascus-Beirut: Dār Ibn Kathīr li-al-Ṭibāʿa wa-al-Nashr wa-al-Tawzīʿ, 2010.

Ibn Nubāta. *Al-Mukhtār min kitāb tadbīr al-duwal*, ed. Salwā Qindīl. Beirut: al-Abḥāth li-al-Tarjama wa-al-Nashr wa-al-Tawzīʿ, 2006.

Ibn Taghrībirdī. *Al-Nujūm al-zāhira fī mulūk Miṣr wa-al-Qāhira*, ed. Muḥammad Ḥusayn Shams al-Dīn, 17 vols. Beirut: Dār al-Kutub al-ʿIlmiyya, 1992.

Ibn Ṭalḥa. *Al-ʿIqd al-farīd li-al-malik al-Saʿīd*, ed. Yūsuf bin ʿUthmān al-Ḥazīm. Riyadh: Ibn al-Azraq Center for Political Studies, 2013.

Ibn al-Waḥīd. 'Al-Urjūza al-maʿrūfa bi-niṣf al-ʿaysh fī tadbīr hādhihi al-ḥayāt', MS University Library of Leipzig, 1297, Vollers 0553.

Ibn al-Waḥīd. *Niṣf al-ʿAysh*, ed. ʿĀdil al-Bakrī. Al-Mawṣil: Maṭbaʿat al-Jumhūriyya, 1969.

Ibn Wāṣil. *Mufarrij al-kurūb fī akhbār banī Ayyūb*, ed. Ḥasanayn Muḥammad Rabīʿ and Saʿīd ʿAbd al-Fattāḥ ʿĀshūr, 5 vols. Cairo: Maṭbaʿat Dār al-Kutub, 1972.

Ibn Wāṣil. *Die Chronik des ibn Wasil: Ǧamāl ad-Dīn Muḥammad ibn Wāṣil, Mufarriǧ al-Kurūb fī Aḫbār Banī Ayyūb: kritische Edition des letzten Teils (646/1248–659/1261) mit Kommentar: Untergang der Ayyubiden und Beginn der Mamlukenherrschaft*, ed. Mohamed Rahim, Arabische Studien, Bd. 6. Wiesbaden: Harrassowitz, 2010.

Marsilius and Annabel S. Brett. *The Defender of the Peace*, Cambridge Texts in the History of Political Thought. Cambridge: Cambridge University Press, 2005.

Meisami, Julie Scott (ed.), *The Sea of Precious Virtues: A Medieval Islamic Mirror for Princes (Baḥr al-favāʾid)*. Salt Lake City: University of Utah Press, 1991.

'Qadaḥ al-dirāsa fī manāhij al-siyāsa'. MS British Library, London. Or.1534.

Shāfiʿ Ibn ʿAlī. 'Tārīkh al-salāṭīn wa-al-ʿasākir', MS Bibliothèque nationale de France, Paris. Arabe 1705.

Shāfiʿ Ibn ʿAlī. *Ḥusn al-manāqib al-sirriyya al-muntazaʿa min-al-sīra al-Ẓāhiriyya*, ed. ʿAbd al-ʿAzīz al-Khuwayṭir. al-Riyāḍ: Maṭbaʿat Safīr, 1989.

Unknown. 'Miṣbāḥ al-hidāya fī ṭarīq al-imāma', MS Bodleian Library, Oxford. OR 579.

Secondary Sources

Abou El Fadl, Khaled. *Rebellion and Violence in Islamic Law*. Cambridge: Cambridge University Press, 2001.

Alam, Muzaffar. *The Languages of Political Islam: India 1200–1800*. Chicago, IL: University of Chicago Press, 2004.

Anjum, Ovamir. *Politics, Law and Community in Islamic Thought: The Taymiyyan Moment*, Cambridge Studies in Islamic Civilization. Cambridge: Cambridge University Press, 2012.

Anjum, Ovamir. 'Political Metaphors and Concepts in the Writings of an Eleventh-Century Sunni Scholar, Abū Al-Maʿālī Al-Juwaynī (419–478/1028–1085)', *Journal of the Royal Asiatic Society* 26(1/2) (2016): 7–18.

Ayalon, D. 'Studies on the Structure of the Mamluk army [III]', in Gerald R. Hawting (ed.), *Muslims, Mongols and Crusaders: An Anthology of Articles Published in The Bulletin of the School of Oriental an African Studies*. London: Routledge, 2007, 97–130.

Banister, Mustafa. *The Abbasid Caliphate of Cairo, 1261–1517: Out of the Shadows*, Edinburgh Studies in Classical Islamic History and Culture. Edinburgh: Edinburgh University Press, 2021.

Bauer, Thomas. 'Mamluk Literature: Misunderstandings and New Approaches', *Mamlūk Studies Review* 9(2) (2005): 105–32.

Berkey, Jonathan Porter. *The Transmission of Knowledge in Medieval Cairo: A Social History of Islamic Education*, Princeton Studies on the Near East. Princeton, NJ: Princeton University Press, 1992.

Black, Antony. *The West and Islam: Religion and Political Thought in World History*. New York: Oxford University Press, 2008.

Black, Antony. *The History of Islamic Political Thought: From the Prophet to the Present*, 2nd edn. Edinburgh: Edinburgh University Press, 2011.

Bori, Caterina. 'The Collection and Edition of Ibn Taymīyah's Works: Concerns of a Disciple', *Mamlūk Studies Review* 13(2) (2009): 47–67.

Bori, Caterina. 'Ibn Taymiyya Wa-Jamāʿatuhu: Authority, Conflict and Consensus in Ibn Taymiyya's Circle', in Yossef Rapoport and Shahab Ahmed (eds), *Ibn Taymiyya and His Times*, Studies in Islamic Philosophy 4. Karachi: Oxford University Press, 2010, 23–52.

Bori, Caterina. 'Theology, Politics, Society: The Missing Link. Studying Religion in the Mamluk Period', in Stephan Conermann (ed.), *Ubi Sumus? Quo Vademus?: Mamluk Studies – State of the Art*. Goettingen: V & R Unipress and Bonn University Press, 2013, 56–94.

Bori, Caterina. 'Ibn Taymiyya (14th to 17th Century): Transregional Spaces of Reading and Reception', *The Muslim World* 108(1) (2018): 87–123.

Bosworth, Clifford Edmund. *The New Islamic Dynasties: A Chronological and Genealogical Manual.* Edinburgh: Edinburgh University Press, 1996.

Böwering, Gerhard, Patricia Crone and Mahan Mirza (eds), *The Princeton Encyclopedia of Islamic Political Thought*, Princeton Reference. Princeton, NJ: Princeton University Press, 2013.

Broadbridge, Anne F. *Kingship and Ideology in the Islamic and Mongol Worlds*, Cambridge Studies in Islamic Civilization. Cambridge: Cambridge University Press, 2008.

Calder, Norman. 'Friday Prayer and the Juristic Theory of Government: Sarakhsī, Shīrāzī, Māwardī', *Bulletin of the School of Oriental and African Studies* 49(1) (1986): 35–47.

Canning, Joseph. *Ideas of Power in the Late Middle Ages, 1296–1417.* Cambridge: Cambridge University Press, 2011.

Chamberlain, Michael. *Knowledge and Social Practice in Medieval Damascus, 1190 –1350*, Cambridge Studies in Islamic Civilization. Cambridge: Cambridge University Press, 1995.

Cobb, Paul M. 'Usāma Ibn Munqidh's Lubāb al-Ādāb (The Kernels of Refinement): Autobiographical and Historical Excerpts', *Al-Masāq* 18(1) (2006): 67–8.

Crone, Patricia. 'Did Al-Ghazālī Write a Mirror for Princes? On the Authorship of Naṣiḥat Al-Mulūk', *Jerusalem Studies in Arabic and Islam* 10 (1987): 167–91.

Crone, Patricia. *Medieval Islamic Political Thought*, The New Edinburgh Islamic Surveys. Edinburgh: Edinburgh University Press, 2005.

Crone, Patricia and Martin Hinds. *God's Caliph: Religious Authority in the First Centuries of Islam.* Cambridge: Cambridge University Press, 2003.

El-Hibri, Tayeb. *Reinterpreting Islamic Historiography: Hārūn Al-Rashīd and the Narrative of the 'Abbasid Caliphate*, Cambridge Studies in Islamic Civilization. New York: Cambridge University Press, 1999.

El-Merheb, Mohamad. 'Louis IX in Medieval Arabic Sources: The Saint, the King, and the Sicilian Connection', *Al-Masāq* 28(3) (2016): 282–301.

El-Merheb, Mohamad. '"There Is No Just Ruler at This Time!" Political Censure in Pre-Modern Islamic Juristic Discourses', in Karina Kellermann, Alheydis Plassmann and Christian Schwermann (eds), *Criticising the Ruler in Pre-Modern Societies: Possibilities, Chances, and Methods: Kritik Am Herrscher in Vormodernen Gesellschaften:Möglichkeiten, Chancen, Methoden*, Macht Und Herrschaft, Band 6. Göttingen: V&R Unipress and Bonn University Press, 2019, 349–75.

El-Merheb, Mohamad. Review. 'Sohaira Z. M. Siddiqui: Law and Politics under the Abbasids: An Intellectual Portrait of al-Juwayni, Cambridge: Cambridge University Press, 2019', *Bulletin of the School of Oriental and African Studies* 82(3) (2019): 533–5.

El-Merheb, Mohamad. 'Islamic Political Thought and Professional Mobility: The Intellectual and Empirical Worlds of Ibn Ṭalḥa and Ibn Jamāʿa', in Mohamad El-Merheb and Mehdi Berriah (eds), *Professional Mobility in Islamic Societies (700–1750): New Concepts and Approaches*, Handbook of Oriental Studies. Section One, the Near and Middle East. Leiden: Brill, 2021, 207–30.

Emon, Anver M. *Religious Pluralism and Islamic Law: 'Dhimmīs' and Others in the Empire of Law*, 1st edn, Oxford Islamic Legal Studies. Oxford: Oxford University Press, 2012.

Emon, Anver M. 'Shariʿa and the Rule of Law', in Robin Griffith-Jones and Mark Hill (eds), *Magna Carta, Religion and the Rule of Law*. Cambridge: Cambridge University Press, 2015, 196–215.

Encyclopaedia of Islam, 2nd edn. Leiden: E. J. Brill (*EI²*).

Encyclopaedia of Islam, 3rd edn. Leiden: E. J. Brill (*EI³*).

Escovitz, Joseph H. 'Patterns of Appointment to the Chief Judgeships of Cairo during the Baḥrī Mamlūk Period', *Arabica* 30(2) (1983): 147–68.

Eychenne, Mathieu. *Liens Personnels, Clientélisme et Réseaux de Pouvoir dans le Sultanat Mamelouk (Milieu XIIIe–Fin XIVe Siècle)*. Beirut: Presses de l'Ifpo, 2013.

Fadel, Mohammad. 'State and Sharia', in Rudolph Peters and P. J. Bearman (eds), *The Ashgate Research Companion to Islamic Law*, Ashgate Research Companion. Farnham: Ashgate, 2014, 93–107.

Gardiner, Noah. 'The Occultist Encyclopedism of ʿAbd Al-Raḥmān al-Bisṭāmī', *Mamlūk Studies Review* 20 (2017): 3–38.

Garnett, George. *Marsilius of Padua and 'the Truth of History'*. Oxford: Oxford University Press, 2006.

Gibb, Hamilton A. R. 'Constitutional Organization', in Majid Khadduri and Herbert J. Liebesny (eds), *Law in the Middle East*. Washington, DC: The Middle East Institute, 1955, 3–27.

Gibb, Hamilton A. R. 'The Heritage of Islam in the Modern World (I)', *International Journal of Middle East Studies* 1(1) (1970): 3–17.

Gibb, Hamilton A. R. and Stanford J. Shaw. 'Al-Mawardi's Theory of the Caliphate', in *Studies on the Civilization of Islam*. Princeton, NJ: Princeton University Press, 1982, 151–65.

Gilbert, Joan E. 'Institutionalization of Muslim Scholarship and Professionalization of the ʿUlamaʾ in Medieval Damascus', *Studia Islamica* 52 (1980): 105–34.

Godthardt, Frank. 'The Life of Marsilius of Padua', in Gerson Moreno-Riaño and Cary J. Nederman (eds), *A Companion to Marsilius of Padua*, Brill's Companions to the Christian Tradition, vol. 31. Leiden: Brill, 2012, 13–55.

Gutas, Dimitri. *Greek Wisdom Literature in Arabic Translation: A Study of the Graeco-Arabic Gnomologia*. New Haven, CT: American Oriental Society, 1975.

Gutas, Dimitri. 'The Study of Arabic Philosophy in the Twentieth Century: An Essay on the Historiography of Arabic Philosophy', *British Journal of Middle Eastern Studies* 29(1) (2002): 5–25.

Haghighat, Seyed Sadegh. 'Persian Mirrors for Princes: Pre-Islamic and Islamic Mirrors Compared', in Regula Forster and Neguin Yavari (eds), *Global Medieval: Mirrors for Princes Reconsidered*, Ilex Foundation Series 15. Cambridge, MA and Washington, DC: Center for Hellenic Studies, Trustees for Harvard University and Ilex Foundation, distributed by Harvard University Press, 2015, 83–93.

Hallaq, Wael B. 'Caliphs, Jurists and the Saljūqs in the Political Thought of Juwaynī', *The Muslim World* 74(1) (1984): 26–41.

Hassan, Mona. *Longing for the Lost Caliphate: A Transregional History*. Princeton, NJ: Princeton University Press, 2017.

Hillenbrand, Carole. 'Islamic Orthodoxy or Realpolitik? Al-Ghazālī's Views on Government', *Iran* 26 (1988): 81–94.

Hillenbrand, Carole. *The Crusades: Islamic Perspectives*. Edinburgh: Edinburgh University Press, 1999.

Hillenbrand, Carole. 'A Little-Known Mirror for Princes of Al-Ghazālī', in Rüdiger Arnzen, Jörn Thielmann and Gerhard Endreß (eds), *Words, Texts and Concepts Cruising the Mediterranean Sea: Studies on the Sources, Contents and Influences of Islamic Civilization and Arabic Philosophy and Science; Dedicated to Gerhard Endress on His Sixty-Fifth Birthday*, Orientalia Lovaniensia Analecta 139. Leuven: Peeters, 2004, 593–601.

Hirschler, Konrad. 'Pre-Eighteenth-Century Traditions of Revivalism: Damascus in the Thirteenth Century', *Bulletin of the School of Oriental and African Studies* 68(2) (2005): 195–214.

Hirschler, Konrad. *Medieval Arabic Historiography: Authors as Actors*. London: Routledge, 2006.

Hirschler, Konrad. *The Written Word in the Medieval Arabic Lands: A Social and Cultural History of Reading Practices*. Edinburgh: Edinburgh University Press, 2012.

Hirschler, Konrad. *Medieval Damascus: Plurality and Diversity in an Arabic Library: The Ashrafiya Library Catalogue*, Edinburgh Studies in Classical Islamic History and Culture. Edinburgh: Edinburgh University Press, 2016.

Hodgson, Marshall G. S. and Edmund Burke. *Rethinking World History: Essays on Europe, Islam, and World History*, Studies in Comparative World History. Cambridge: Cambridge University Press, 1993.

Hofer, Nathan. 'The Origins and Development of the Office of the "Chief Sufi" in Egypt, 1173–1325', *Journal of Sufi Studies* 3(1) (2014): 1–37.

Hofer, Nathan. *The Popularisation of Sufism in Ayyubid and Mamluk Egypt, 1173–1325*, Edinburgh Studies in Classical Islamic History and Culture. Edinburgh: Edinburgh University Press, 2015.

Holt, P. M. 'The Position and Power of the Mamlūk Sultan', *Bulletin of the School of Oriental and African Studies* 38(2) (1975): 237–49.

Holt, P. M. 'An Early Source on Shaykh Khaḍir Al-Mihrānī', *Bulletin of the School of Oriental and African Studies* 46(1) (1983): 33–9.

Hoover, Jon. 'Early Mamluk Ash'arism against Ibn Taymiyya on the Nonliteral Reinterpretation (Ta'wīl) of God's Attributes', in Ayman Shihadeh and Jan Thiele (eds), *Philosophical Theology in Islam: Later Ash'arism East and West*, Islamicate Intellectual History, vol. 5. Leiden: Brill, 2020, 195–230.

Humphreys, R. Stephen. *From Saladin to the Mongols: The Ayyubids of Damascus, 1193–1260*. Albany, NY: State University of New York Press, 1977.

Humphreys, R. Stephen. 'The Emergence of the Mamluk Army', *Studia Islamica* 46 (1977): 148–82.

Hurvitz, Nimrod. *Competing Texts: The Relationship between Al-Mawardi's and Abu Ya'la's Al-Ahkam Al-Sultaniyya*, Occasional Publications 8. Cambridge, MA: ILSP, Harvard Law School, 2007.

Irwin, Robert. *The Middle East in the Middle Ages: The Early Mamluk Sultanate 1250–1382*. London and Carbondale: Croom Helm and Southern Illinois University Press, 1986.

Jackson, Sherman A. 'From Prophetic Actions to Constitutional Theory: A Novel Chapter in Medieval Muslim Jurisprudence', *International Journal of Middle East Studies* 25(1) (1993): 71–90.

Jackson, Sherman A. *Islamic Law and the State: The Constitutional Jurisprudence of Shihāb Al-Dīn Al-Qarāfī*, Studies in Islamic Law and Society, vol. 1. New York: E. J. Brill, 1996.

Johansen, Baber. 'A Perfect Law in an Imperfect Society. Ibn Taymiyya's Concept of "Governance in the Name of the Sacred Law"', in Peri J. Bearman, Wolfhart Heinrichs, Bernard G. Weiss and Frank E. Vogel (eds), *The Law Applied: Contextualizing the Islamic Shari'a; a Volume in Honour of Frank E. Vogel*. London: I. B. Tauris, 2008, 259–94.

Kerr, Malcolm. *Islamic Reform: The Political and Legal Theories of Muḥammad 'Abduh and Rashīd Riḍā*. Berkeley: University of California Press, 1966.

Khalaf, ʿAbd al-Jawād. *al-Qāḍī Badr al-Dīn Ibn Jamāʿ: Ḥayātuh wa-āthāruh*. Karachi: Jāmiʿat al-Dirāsāt al-Islāmiyya, 1988.

Khismatulin, Alexey. 'The Art of Medieval Counterfeiting: The Siyar al-Mulūk (The Siyāsat-Nāma) by Niẓām al-Mulk and the "Full" Version of the Naṣīḥat al-Mulūk by al-Ghazālī', *Manuscripta Orientalia* 14(1) (2008): 3–31.

Khismatulin, Alexey. 'Two Mirrors for Princes Fabricated at the Seljuq Court: Nizām al-Mulk's Siyar al-Mulūk and al-Ghazālī's Nasīhat al-Mulūk', in Edmund Herzig and Sarah Stewart (eds), *The Age of the Seljuqs: The Idea of Iran*, vol. 6. London: I. B. Tauris, 2015, 94–130.

Krawietz, Birgit. 'Ibn Qayyim Al-Jawzīyah: His Life and Works', *Mamlūk Studies Review* 10(2) (2006): 19–64.

Kuhn, Thomas S. *The Structure of Scientific Revolutions*. Chicago, IL: University of Chicago Press, 1962.

Lambton, A. K. S. 'Justice in the Medieval Persian Theory of Kingship', *Studia Islamica* 17 (1962): 91–119.

Lambton, A. K. S. 'Islamic Mirrors for Princes'. in *La Persia Nel Medioevo*. Rome: Accademia Nazionale dei Lincei, 1971, 419–42.

Lambton, A. K. S. *State and Government in Medieval Islam: An Introduction to the Study of Islamic Political Theory; the Jurists*, reprinted, London Oriental Series 36. Oxford: Oxford University Press, 1981.

Leder, Stefan. 'Sultanic Rule in the Mirror of Medieval Political Literature', in Neguin Yavari and Regula Forster (eds), *Global Medieval: Mirrors for Princes Revisited*. Cambridge, MA: Harvard University Press, 2015, 93–111.

Levanoni, Amalia. 'The Mamluk Conception of the Sultanate', *International Journal of Middle East Studies* 26 (1994): 373–92.

Lewis, Bernard. *The Political Language of Islam*. Chicago, IL: University of Chicago Press, 1988.

Little, Donald P. 'Historiography of the Ayyūbid and Mamlūk Epochs', in Carl F. Petry (ed.), *The Cambridge History of Egypt, vol. 1: Islamic Egypt, 640–1517*. Cambridge: Cambridge University Press, 1998, 412–44.

Madelung, Wilferd. 'A Treatise on the Imamate Dedicated to Sultan Baybars I', in *Proceedings of the 14th Congress of the Union Européenne Des Arabisants et Islamisants, Pt. 1*, Budapest, 1995, 91–102.

Madelung, Wilferd. 'The Spread of Māturīdism and the Turks', in *Religious Schools and Sects in Medieval Islam*, Variorum Collected Studies Series CS213. Aldershot: Ashgate/Variorum, 1999, 109–69.

Makdisi, George. 'Ashʿarī and the Ashʿarites in Islamic Religious History I', *Studia Islamica* 17 (1962): 37–80.

Makdisi, George. '"Ṭabaqāt" – Biography: Law and Orthodoxy in Classical Islam', *Islamic Studies* 32(4) (1993): 371–96.

Marlow, Louise. 'Kings, Prophets and the 'Ulamā' in Mediaeval Islamic Advice Literature', *Studia Islamica* 81 (1995): 101–20.

Marlow, Louise. *Hierarchy and Egalitarianism in Islamic Thought*. Cambridge: Cambridge University Press, 1997.

Marlow, Louise. 'The Way of Viziers and Lamp of Commanders (Minhāj Al-Wuzarā' Wa Sirāj Al-Umarā') of Aḥmad Al-Iṣfahbādhī and the Literary and Political Culture of Early Fourteen-Century Iran', in Beatrice Gruendler and Louise Marlow (eds), *Writers and Rulers: Perspectives on Their Relationship from Abbasid to Safavid Times*, Literaturen Im Kontext 16. Wiesbaden: Reichert, 2004, 169–93.

Marlow, Louise. 'Advice and Advice Literature', *EI*[3], 2007.

Marlow, Louise. *Counsel for Kings: Wisdom and Politics in Tenth-Century Iran: The Naṣīḥat Al-Mulūk of pseudo-Māwardī: Contexts and Themes*, 2 vols. Edinburgh: Edinburgh University Press, 2016.

McGregor, Richard. *Sanctity and Mysticism in Medieval Egypt: The Wafā' Sufi Order and the Legacy of Ibn 'Arabī*. Albany, NY: State University of New York Press, 2004.

McGregor, Richard. 'The Problem of Sufism', *Mamlūk Studies Review* 13(2) (2009): 69–84.

Mubārak, Zakī. *Al-Akhlāq 'ind-al-Ghazālī*. Cairo: Dār al-Sha'b, 1924.

Murphey, Rhoads. *Exploring Ottoman Sovereignty: Tradition, Image and Practice in the Ottoman Imperial Household, 1400–1800*. London: Continuum, 2008.

Natij, Salah. 'Murū'a: Soucis et Interrogations éthiques dans la culture Arabe classique (1ere Partie)', *Studia Islamica* 112 (2017): 206–63.

Natij, Salah. 'Murū'a: Soucis et Interrogations éthiques dans la culture Arabe classique (2e Partie)', *Studia Islamica* 113 (2018): 1–55.

Nielsen, Jorgen S. 'Sultan Al-Ẓāhir Baybars and the Appointment of Four Chief Qāḍīs, 663/1265', *Studia Islamica* 60 (1984): 167–76.

Nora, Pierre. 'Between Memory and History: Les Lieux de Mémoire', *Representations* 26 (1989): 7–24.

Nora, Pierre and Lawrence D. Kritzman (eds), *Realms of Memory: Rethinking the French Past*, European Perspectives. New York: Columbia University Press, 1996.

Ohlander, Erik S. *Sufism in an Age of Transition: 'Umar al-Suhrawardī and the Rise of the Islamic Mystical Brotherhoods*, Islamic History and Civilization: Studies and Texts, vol. 71. Leiden: Brill, 2008.

Peacock, A. C. S. 'Advice for the Sultans of Rum: The "Mirrors for Princes" of Early Thirteenth-Century Anatolia', in Bill Hickman, Gary Leiser and Robert Dankoff (eds), *Turkish Language, Literature, and History: Travellers' Tales, Sultans, and Scholars since the Eighth Century*, Routledge Studies in the History of Iran and Turkey. London: Routledge, 2016, 276–307.

Peacock, A. C. S. 'Politics, Religion and the Occult in the Works of Kamal al-Din Ibn Talha, a Vizier, 'Alim and Author in Thirteenth-Century Syria', in Carole Hillenbrand (ed.), *Syria in Crusader Times: Conflict and Coexistence*. Edinburgh: Edinburgh University Press, 2020, 34–60.

Petry, Carl F. *Civilian Elite of Cairo in the Later Middle Ages*. Princeton, NJ: Princeton University Press, 1981.

Pocock, J. G. A. 'Burke and the Ancient Constitution – A Problem in the History of Ideas', *The Historical Journal* 3(2) (1960): 125–43.

Pocock, J. G. A.. 'The Reconstruction of Discourse: Towards the Historiography of Political Thought', *MLN* 96(5) (1981): 959–80.

Pocock, J. G. A. 'Languages and Their Implications: The Transformation of the Study of Political Thought', in *Politics, Language, and Time: Essays on Political Thought and History*. Chicago, IL: University of Chicago Press, 1989.

Pocock, J. G. A. 'The Politics of Historiography', *Historical Research* 78(199) (2005): 1–14.

Pocock, J. G. A. 'The Historian as Political Actor in Polity, Society and Academy', in *Political Thought and History: Essays on Theory and Method*. Cambridge: Cambridge University Press, 2009, 217–38.

Pocock, J. G. A. 'Historiography as a Form of Political Thought', *History of European Ideas* 37(1) (2011): 1–6.

Pomerantz, Maurice A. 'A Maqāma Collection by a Mamlūk Historian: Al-Maqāmāt Al-Ğalāliyya by Al-Ḥasan B. Abī Muḥammad Al-Ṣafadī (fl. First Quarter of the 8th/14th C.)', *Arabica* 61(6) (2014): 631–63.

Pomerantz, Maurice A. 'The Play of Genre: A Maqāma of "Ease after Hardship" from the Eighth/Fourteenth Century and Its Literary Context', in Maurice A. Pomerantz and Aram A. Shahin (eds), *The Heritage of Arabo-Islamic Learning*. Leiden: Brill, 2015, 461–82.

Pouzet, Louis. *Damas au VIIe–XIIIe siècle: vie et structures religieuses d'une métropole islamique*, 2nd edn, Recherches Nouvelle série A, Langue arabe et pensée islamique 15. Beirut: Dār el-Machreq, 1991.

Rabbat, Nasser O. *The Citadel of Cairo: A New Interpretation of Royal Mamluk Architecture*, Islamic History and Civilization: Studies and Texts, vol. 14. Leiden: E. J. Brill, 1995.

Rapoport, Yossef. 'Ibn Taymiyya's Radical Legal Thought', in Yossef Rapoport and

Shahab Ahmed (eds), *Ibn Taymiyya and His Times*, Studies in Islamic Philosophy 4. Karachi: Oxford University Press, 2010, 191–226.

Rapoport, Yossef. 'Royal Justice and Religious Law: Siyāsah and Shariʿah under the Mamluks', *Mamlūk Studies Review* 16 (2012): 71–102.

Riley-Smith, Jonathan Simon Christopher. *The Crusades: A History*, 2nd edn, repr. London: Continuum, 2009.

Rosenthal, Erwin I. J. *Political Thought in Medieval Islam: An Introductory Outline*. Cambridge: Cambridge University Press, 1958.

Rubin, Uri. 'Prophets and Caliphs: The Biblical Foundations of the Umayyad Authority', in Herbert Berg (ed.), *Method and Theory in the Study of Islamic Origins*, Islamic History and Civilization 49. Leiden: Brill, 2003, 73–99.

Savage-Smith, Emilie, Simon Swain, G. J. H. van Gelder and Ignacio Javier Sánchez Rojo (eds), *A Literary History of Medicine: The 'Uyūn al-Anbā' Fī Ṭabaqāt al-Aṭibbā', of Ibn Abīuṣaybi'ah*, Handbook of Oriental Studies, Section One, Near and Middle East, 5 vols. Leiden: Brill, 2020.

Al-Ṣarrāf, Shihāb. 'Mamluk Furūsīyah Literature and Its Antecedents', *Mamlūk Studies Review* 8(1) (2004): 141–200.

Sheibani, Mariam. 'Islamic Law in an Age of Crisis and Consolidation: ʿIzz al-Dīn Ibn ʿAbd al-Salām (577–660/1187–1262) and the Ethical Turn in Medieval Islamic Law', PhD thesis, University of Chicago, 2018. ProQuest (10841014).

Sheibani, Mariam. 'Innovation, Influence, and Borrowing in Mamluk-Era Legal Maxim Collections: The Case of Ibn ʿAbd al-Salām and al-Qarāfī', *Journal of the American Oriental Society* 140(4) (2020): 927–54.

Siddiqui, Sohaira Zahid. *Law and Politics under the Abbasids: An Intellectual Portrait of al-Juwayni*, Cambridge Studies in Islamic Civilization. Cambridge: Cambridge University Press, 2019.

Skinner, Quentin. 'Meaning and Understanding in the History of Ideas', *History and Theory* 8(1) (1969): 3–53.

Skinner, Quentin. 'Motives, Intentions and the Interpretation of Texts', *New Literary History* 3(2) (1972): 393–408.

Skinner, Quentin. *The Foundations of Modern Political Thought*. Cambridge: Cambridge University Press, 1978.

Skinner, Quentin. *Visions of Politics*, 3 vols. Cambridge: Cambridge University Press, 2002.

Snouck Hurgronje, Christiaan. *Selected Works of C. Snouck Hurgronje*, ed. Georges-Henri Bousquet and Joseph Schacht. Leiden: E. J. Brill, 1957.

Steenbergen, Jo van. 'Appearances of Dawla and Political Order in Late Medieval Syro-Egypt: The State, Social Theory, and the Political History of the Cairo Sultanate (Thirteenth–Sixteenth Centuries)', in Stephan Conermann (ed.),

History and Society during the Mamluk Period (1250–1517), Studies of the Annemarie Schimmel Institute for Advanced Study I. Göttingen, V&R Unipress, 2016, 51–85.

Sweeney, Michael J. 'The Spirituality of the Church: Scripture, Salvation, and Sacraments', in Gerson Moreno-Riaño and Cary J. Nederman (eds), *A Companion to Marsilius of Padua*, Brill's Companions to the Christian Tradition, vol. 31. Leiden: Brill, 2011, 181–227.

Talmon-Heller, Daniella. 'Muslim Martyrdom and Quest for Martyrdom in the Crusading Period', *Al-Masāq* 14(2) (2002): 131–9.

Talmon-Heller, Daniella and Raquel Ukeles. 'The Lure of a Controversial Prayer: Ṣalāt Al-Raghā'ib (the Prayer of Great Rewards) in Medieval Arabic Texts and from a Socio-Legal Perspective', *Der Islam* 89(1/2) (2012): 141–66.

Thorau, Peter. *The Lion of Egypt: Sultan Baybars I and the Near East in the Thirteenth Century*. London: Longman, 1995.

Van Den Bossche, Gowaart. 'Literarisierung Reconsidered in the Context of Sultanic Biography: The Case of Shāfiʿ b. ʿAlī's Sīrat al-Nāṣir Muḥammad (BnF MS Arabe 1705)', in Jo van Steenbergen and Maya Termonia (eds), *New Readings in Arabic Historiography from Late Medieval Egypt and Syria*. Leiden: Brill, 2021, 466–89.

Van Gelder, Geert Jan. 'Mirror for Princes or Vizor for Viziers: The Twelfth-Century Arabic Popular Encyclopedia "Mufīd al-ʿulūm" and Its Relationship with the Anonymous Persian "Baḥr al-Fawā'id"', *Bulletin of the School of Oriental and African Studies, University of London* 64(3) (2001): 313–38.

Yavari, Neguin. *Advice for the Sultan: Prophetic Voices and Secular Politics in Medieval Islam*. New York: Oxford University Press, 2014.

Yilmaz, Huseyin. *Caliphate Redefined: The Mystical Turn in Ottoman Political Thought*. Princeton, NJ: Princeton University Press, 2018.

Zakeri, Mohsen. 'From Futuwwa to Mystic Political Thought – The Caliph al-Nāṣir Li-Dīn Allāh and Abū Ḥafṣ Suhrawardī's Theory of Government', in Shahrokh Raei (ed.), *Islamic Alternatives: Non-Mainstream Religion in Persianate Societies*, Göttinger Orientforschungen. III, Reihe, Iranica 16. Wiesbaden: Harrassowitz, 2017, 29–55.

Index

al-ʿAbbasi
Athar al-uwal fi tartib al-duwal (*Foregoing Examples of Statecraft*), 129
ʿAbbasids, 3, 16, 21, 22, 28, 104, 148
and caliphate in Cairo, 70, 82, 151–2, 159, 182, 186, 187
and Ibn Jamaʿa, 77
and Ibn Talha, 140
and military manuals, 59–60
and Sufism, 87, 92, 93–5
ʿAbd al-Latif, Sharaf al-Din (son of Ibn ʿAbd al-Salam), 164
Abu Bakr, 20, 35
Abu Shama, 162–3, 167, 176
Abu Yaʿla, 35, 63, 70
Abu Yusuf, 63
accountability, 5, 113, 142
and *muʾakhadha*, 116, 140
adab, 16, 29, 41, 59, 60, 178
and Ibn Talha, 132, 133, 141–2, 143
ʿadl (justice), 3, 4, 8, 24–5, 26, 36, 189, 190
and Ashrafiyya Library, 36
and Ibn Jamaʿa, 55, 59, 60, 61, 62, 81, 83
and Ibn Talha, 45, 133, 134, 137, 138, 140, 142, 144
and Lambton, 24–5
and al-Subki, 172, 173, 176, 179
and Sufism, 94, 100, 104, 106, 107, 109, 110, 111, 104, 107, 113, 114
administration, 8, 24, 49, 71–4
and Ibn Talha, 139–42, 143
and al-Qarafi, 153, 154
administrative manuals, 8, 24, 35, 36, 86, 132, 139, 140
and Ibn Jamaʿa, 71, 73
and Ibn Talha, 132, 139, 140
advice literature, 25, 28, 89, 91, 156
and Ibn Talha, 125, 127–8, 129, 131, 132, 133, 142, 143
advisers, 25, 107, 114, 137, 186
ʿahd (oath), 45–6, 79
ahistoricism, 30–1
ahkam al-qital (rules of combat), 60–1
Aḥmad b. Tulun, 35
ʿajab (pride), 136
Alexander, 91
ʿAli, 35, 105
ʿAlids, 104, 105
ʿalim (knowledgeable), 104, 116–17
Almohads, 90
aman (safe conduct), 75
al-Amidi, Sayf al-Din, 158
amirate (*imara*), 8, 17, 25, 70, 87, 153, 179–82, 189–90
al-Amuli, Karim al-Din, 97, 98
anachronism, 6, 30–1
Anatolia, 93
Anjum, Ovamir, 39
'Political Metaphors and Concepts', 43
Politics, Law and Community in Islamic Thought: the Taymiyyan Moment, 31–2
anthropomorphism, 40, 134, 143, 161, 169, 170
ʿaqaʾid (creeds), 132
ʿaqil (judicious), 104
Ardashir, 35
Aristotle, 35, 91
Politics, 167
Arjuwash, 52
army, the, 55, 139, 153, 184, 185

Artuqids, 124, 126, 128, 129, 139
asceticism, 89, 90, 127, 174
Ashʿari tradition, 5, 26, 39, 46
  and Ibn Jamaʿa, 58–9
  and Ibn Talha, 133–4, 143
  and *Misbah al-hidaya fi tariq al-imama*, 120
  and al-Subki, 161
  and Sufism, 88, 92–3, 102
al-Ashraf Khalil Ibn Qalawun, Sultan, 48, 49, 51, 130
  and Mukhtasar fi fadl al-jihad, 61, 71
al-Ashraf Musa, Sultan al-Malik, 34, 159, 170–3
Ashrafiyya Library (Damascus), 26, 34–6
astrolabe, 56
astrology, 127
Awlad al-Shaykh see Fakhr al-Din Ibn Shaykh al-Shuyukh Ibn Hamawiyya; Hamawiyya (*banu*) family
al-ʿAyni, 184, 185
Ayyubid period, 1, 3, 6–7, 23, 24, 159, 160
  and Ibn Talha, 125, 126, 128, 129, 132, 134, 137–9
  and Mamluk transition, 124
  and al-Qarafi, 146
  and al-Subki, 167, 168, 169, 170–3, 174–6, 178, 191
  and Sufism, 40, 88–90, 93, 99

al-Badawi, Ahmad, 86
Badr al-Din Luʾluʾ, Sultan, 129
Baghdad, 14, 21, 22–3, 31, 122, 125
  and Ibn Jamaʿa, 48
  and al-Subki, 180, 181
  and Sufism, 94, 104, 105
Bahr al-fawaʾid (*Sea of Precious Virtues*) (anon), 25–6, 130
baligh (mature), 104
batin (hidden and esoteric knowledge), 117
Bauer, Thomas, 41
bayʿa (oath of allegiance), 65, 67, 186–8
Baybars I, Sultan, 4, 86, 95–6, 123, 130, 147, 151–2, 159, 185–9
  and *Misbah al-hidaya fi tariq al-imama*, 100–1, 115, 117, 118
  and al-Subki, 161, 167
Baybars II al-Jashankir, Sultan, 53, 54, 76, 77, 78, 82, 95, 97–8
  and al-ʿAbbasi, 129
  and legitimation, 186–8
  and Salar, 184, 185–6
Berkey, Jonathan P., 41
al-Birzali, 161
Black, Antony, 2, 13, 14, 15–16, 30
Bori, Caterina, 39
Böwering, Gerhard
  The Princeton Encyclopedia of Islamic Political Thought, 23
Brett, Annabel, 12

Cairo, 3, 7, 10, 11, 39, 124, 128, 159
  and ʿAbbasid caliphate, 70, 82, 115, 151–2, 159, 180–2, 186, 187
  and Ibn ʿAbd al-Salam, 176–7, 188
  and Ibn Jamaʿa, 36, 50–1, 53–4, 56
  and Khidr, 96
  and merchants, 184
  and *Nasihat al-muluk*, 26–7
  and al-Nasir Muhammad, 78
  and al-Qarafi, 38, 147, 149
  and scholars, 41
  and Sufism, 40, 88–9, 95, 97–8
  and Taj al-Din, 161
caliphate, 2, 8, 17–22, 113
  and Baghdad, 22–3
  and Cairo, 70, 82, 115, 151–2, 159, 180–2, 186, 187
  and Ibn Jamaʿa, 13, 48, 57, 83
  and Ottoman Empire, 109
  and al-Qarafi, 147–8, 150–2, 153, 154
  and al-Subki, 179–82
  and Sufism, 94–5
  and *Tahrir al-ahkam fi tadbir ahl al-Islam*, 64–71, 79–82, 122–3
'Cambridge School,' 6, 30
Canning, Joseph, 12–13
Chamberlain, Michael, 41
checks and balances, 8, 49, 57
Christians, 32, 96, 100; *see also* non-Muslims
citadel, 34, 51, 124
  and Cairo, 54, 97, 98, 182, 186–7
  and Damascus, 52, 170, 177, 178
coercive authority, 103–7, 115, 119, 134–9
community *see umma*
companions of the Prophet, 26, 36, 116–17
conquest (*futuh*), 60
constitution, 17–19, 33, 38–40, 45–6, 168, 172–3, 191–2
  and Ibn Jamaʿa, 49, 68–70, 72, 77–8, 80–3
  and Ibn Talha, 129, 132, 134, 144
  and proto-, 8, 9, 83–4, 122
  and al-Qarafi, 145–6, 147–55
  and al-Subki, 175, 178, 179–81, 189

and *Tahrir al-ahkam fi tadbir ahl al-Islam*, 57, 58
contextualism, 1, 6–7, 11, 29–34, 168
Coulson, Noel, 18
court etiquette, 25, 36, 133
Crone, Patricia, 2, 18, 143
God's Caliph, 19–20
Medieval Islamic Political Thought, 14–15, 23
Crusades, 16; *see also* Franks

Damascus, 3, 7, 124, 126–7, 159
and Ashrafiyya Library, 34–6
and Ibn Jamaʿa, 51, 52–3, 56
and Sufism, 88, 89–91
al-Dawadari, ʿAlam al-Din Sanjar, 50
dawla, 43, 97
de-legitimation, 174–6
delegation, 38, 45, 46, 126
and Ibn Jamaʿa, 48, 49, 52, 57, 58, 64, 65, 69–70, 71, 72, 77–8, 80, 81, 82, 83–4
and Ibn Talha, 134, 135, 136, 139–42
and legitimate, 1, 7–9, 123, 144–5, 155
and al-Qarafi, 146, 148, 150, 153–4
and Sufism, 114–16, 118–19, 120
al-Dhahabi, 161
dhimmis see non-Muslims
divorce, 154
diwan al-inshaʾ (chancery), 8, 36, 41, 131, 133, 139, 141–2
and Ibn Jamaʿa, 50, 55, 57, 78, 80, 82

Egypt, 23, 79, 80, 87, 93, 143
and al-Subki, 158, 159, 171, 175, 178–9
see also Cairo
elites
and military, 7, 10, 49, 59, 120, 159, 179, 185, 191
and political, 16, 32, 40, 94, 127, 159, 179, 183
see also amirate; caliphate; imamate; sultanate
emirate *see* amirate
Emon, Anver, 45
epistemology, 31, 32, 37, 38–9
ethics, 10, 24, 133–4, 135
and Sufism, 8, 107–11, 113–14, 118, 119–20

Fadel, Mohammad H., 18, 38, 148
Fakhr al-Din Ibn Shaykh al-Shuyukh Ibn Hamawiyya, 90, 180, 181; *see also* Hamawiyya (*banu*) family
al-Farabi, 35
fasiq, 66, 104
fatwa and legal opinion, 37, 150, 152, 154
and Ibn Jamaʿa, 59, 76, 78, 79, 82
and al-Subki, 169, 170, 173, 174, 177, 183, 184, 189, 190
fiqh (jurisprudence), 26, 57, 93, 109, 116–17, 148, 161, 166
and speculative, 38, 124–5, 146, 158
Franks, 124, 159, 174–5; *see also* Crusades
Frederick II Hohenstaufen, Emperor, 90
frontiers, 137
futuwwa, 60, 94–5

Galen, 91
Garnett, George, 12
genealogy, 141, 142–5
genre, 23–7, 129–32, 142–3
al-ghadab (anger), 113
ghanima (booty/spoils), 64, 74, 75, 154
al-Ghazali, 14, 17, 26–7, 35, 42
and caliphate, 68
Fadaʾih al-batiniyya wa-fadaʾil al-Mustazhiriyya (*The Scandals and Esoterics and the Virtues of the Party of [Caliph] al-Mustazhir*), 106–7, 119
and Ibn Jamaʿa, 84
and Ibn Talha, 143
and *Misbah al-hidaya fi tariq al-imama*, 113
and al-Subki, 162, 164, 165, 189
and Sufism, 87, 88, 93, 99, 104
and sultanate, 118
and *Tahrir al-ahkam fi tadbir ahl al-Islam*, 47
Ghazan, 52
ghurur (vanity), 136
Gibb, H. A. R., 2, 13, 17–18
Gilbert, Joan E., 41
gnomologia, 91–2
gnostics, 132
governance, 2, 4, 5, 18, 24, 28, 32, 36, 45, 56, 111; *see also* limited government
Guide for the Listener and the Speaker on the Etiquette of the Teacher and the Pupil, The (Ibn Jamaʿa), 56

hadith, 26, 59, 62, 90, 170
Hadrian, 35
Hallaq, Wael, 21

Hamawiyya (*banu*) family, 89–90, 92–3; *see also* Fakhr al-Din Ibn Shaykh al-Shuyukh Ibn Hamawiyya; Mu'in al-Din Ibn Shaykh al-Shuyukh
Hanafi school, 29, 39, 166–7, 170–1
Hanbali, 3, 39, 95, 157, 159, 161, 169, 170
haqa'iq (core duties), 151
haqiqa (mystical reality), 32
al-Harastani, 'Abd al-Samad, 158
hashawiyya see antropomorphism
Hassan, Mona
  Longing for the Lost Caliphate, 22
al-hawa' (passion), 113
heavenly mandate, 87
Hellenism, 91, 92
Hermes, 91
Hillenbrand, Carol, 106
Hinds, Martin
  God's Caliph, 19–20
Hirschler, Konrad, 35, 41
hisba (market inspection), 8, 140, 141, 153–4, 184
historicism *see* contextualism
Hobbes, Thomas, 34
Hofer, Nathan, 40, 87
  The Popularisation of Sufism in Ayyubid and Mamluk Egypt, 1173–1325, 88–9, 92, 97
hudud (prescribed punishment), 60, 110, 135, 137
Hulegu, 128
Huma'i, J., 26
hurr (free), 104
Husam al-Din Ibn Abi 'Ali al-Hadhabani, 179, 180

Ibn 'Abd al-Salam, 'Izz al-Din, 42, 55, 148, 156–60, 191; see also *Tabaqat al Shafi'iyya al-kubra*
Ibn 'Abd al-Zahir, 162–3, 167, 187
Ibn Abi Usaybi'a, 91
Ibn al-Athir, 'Ala' al-Din, 54
Ibn al-Azraq
  Bada'i al-sulk fi taba'i' al-mulk (*The Exquisite Path to the Modes of Kingship*), 146
Ibn al-Dawadari, 96
Ibn al-Haddad
  al-Jawhar al-nafis fi siyasat al-ra'is (*The Exquisite Kernel of the Ruler's Statecraft*), 129
Ibn al-Hajib, 166, 175
Ibn al-Muqaffa', 35
Ibn al-Salah al-Shahrazuri, 170
Ibn al-Sal'us, Shams al-Din, 50–1
Ibn al-Wahid
  al-Urjuza al-ma'rufa bi-Nisf al-'aysh fi tadbir hadhihi al-hayat (*The Metric Poem [Titled] Half of One's Life is Based on His Proper Administration*), 130
Ibn al-Waziri, 55
Ibn 'Arabi, 42, 53, 86, 109, 111, 118
  Fusus al-hikam (*The Bezels of Wisdom*), 97, 98
Ibn 'Asakir, Fakhr al-Din, 158
Ibn 'Ata' Allah al-Iskandari, 97, 98
Ibn Bint al-A'azz, Taj al-Din, 147, 187
Ibn Bint al-A'azz, Taqi al-Din, 51
Ibn Daqiq al-'Id, 159, 165–6, 184–5
Ibn Hajar, 161–2
Ibn Jama'a, 1, 9, 48–50, 105
  and biography, 47–8, 50–6
  and caliphate, 17–18, 22
  and Ibn Talha, 141
  and Ibn Taymiyya, 97–8
  and language, 45–6
  and al-Subki, 165
  and Sufism, 88
  and sultanate, 87
  see also *Mukhtasar fi fadl al-jihad* (*A Compendium of the Virtues of* jihad); *Mustanad al-ajnad fi alat al-jihad* (*The Soldiers' Guide to War Engines*); *Tahrir al-ahkam fi tadbir ahl al-Islam* (*Drafting Ordinances towards Running the Affairs of the People of Islam*)
Ibn Kathir, 53, 98, 161
Ibn Khaldun, 3–4, 15, 23, 30
Ibn Qutayba, 35
Ibn Rushd (Averroes), 14
Ibn Talha, 10, 47, 122, 126–8; see also *al-'Iqd al-farid li-al-malik al-Sa'id*
Ibn Taymiyya, 3, 17, 23, 31–2, 39
  and Ibn Jama'a, 52, 53
  and Salar, 185
  and al-Subki, 161
  and Sufism, 95, 96–8
Ibn Wasil, 162–3, 167, 171–2, 174–5, 180, 181
  and Ibn 'Abd al-Salam, 182–3, 187
  and al-Salih Ayyub, Sultan, 176
idioms, 44–5, 46
al-Ihkam fi tamyiz al-fatawa 'an al-ahkam wa tasarrufat al-quadi wa al-imam (*Book of Perfection in Distinguishing*

Legal Opinions from Judicial Rulings and Discretionary Actions of Judges and Rulers) (al-Qarafi), 5, 124–5, 145–8, 150–5
ijtihad (legal reasoning), 8, 37, 57, 83; see also *mujtahid*
Ilkhanids, 52
'ilm (religious knowledge), 106, 107, 117
'ilm al-awfaq (science of magic squares), 127
'ilm al-hurruf (science of numerical values of letters), 127, 128, 130, 142
imam *see* imamate
imam al-din (imam of religion), 110, 112
imamate, 17–18, 21, 39, 43, 174
  and Ibn Jama'a, 47, 49, 52, 60, 61–3, 64–72, 76, 80–2, 83
  and al-Qarafi, 145–6, 150, 151–2, 153, 154
  and al-Subki, 160, 187–8, 190
  and Sufism, 85, 87
  and ten duties, 136–8, 145
  see also *Misbah al-hidaya fi tariq al-imama* (*The Guiding Lamp to the Path of the Imamate*) (anon)
India, 35
intellectual context, 34–6
investigation (*istidlal*), 102, 103
al-'Iqd al-farid li-al-malik al-Sa'id (*The Unique Necklace for a Content King*) (Ibn Talha), 5, 44–5, 124–6, 127–8
  and administration, 139–42
  and coercive power, 134–9
  and ethics, 133–4
  and genealogy of political thought, 142–5
  and genres, 129–32
Iraq, 92, 93; *see also* Baghdad
Islamic political thought, 1–4, 6–7, 12–14
  and contextualisation, 29–34, 42–6
  and genealogy of, 141, 142–5
  and Ibn Talha, 125–6, 142–3
  and intellectual context, 34–5
  and long durée, 14–17
  and *Misbah al-hidaya fi tariq al-imama*, 98–102, 118–21
  and *Mu'id al-ni'am wa-mubid al-niqam*, 188–90
  and origins, 123–4
  and paradigms, 17–23
  and al-Qarafi, 145–55
  and sources, 4–5
  and Sufism, 85–93
  and Tahrir al-ahkam fi tadbir ahl al-Islam, 56–9, 64–71, 77–84, 122–3
  and text availability, 27–9
  see also genre; Ibn Jama'a

Jackson, Sherman, 38, 147, 148, 150, 152
al-Jahiz, 35
Jamal al-Din 'Abdallah, 54
al-Jashankir *see* Baybars II al-Jashankir, Sultan
Jews, 96, 100; *see also* non-Muslims
jihad, 26, 56, 58, 59, 61, 110, 183, 190
jizya (poll tax), 75
Johansen, Baber, 39
Judgement Day, 114, 116
judges (*al-hukkam*), 8, 79, 116, 148; see also *nuwwab*; *qadi*
judgeship (*qada'*), 50–4, 73, 116, 126, 140, 141, 149–50, 153, 176, 179, 180–2
judicial offices, 8, 49, 152–4, 155
jurisprudence see *fiqh*
jurists, 1, 4–5, 8–9, 15, 17–21, 24–7, 32, 44–6, 182–3, 185, 187
  and Ibn Jama'a, 48, 50, 53, 57–8, 64, 77, 78–9, 82, 83–4
  and Ibn Talha, 129, 132, 133–5, 137–8, 140, 143
  and al-Qarafi, 37–38, 125, 145, 147–8, 151
  and al-Subki, 156–7, 160, 164, 166, 175–6, 178, 189–90
  and Sufism, 40–1, 86, 87–90, 93, 97, 99–100, 103–5, 107–9, 119–20
justice see *'adl*
al-Juwayni, Abu 'Abd Allah Muhammad (Imam al-Haramaya), 17, 42, 93
  and epistemology, 32, 38–9
  Ghiyath al-umam fi-iltiyath al-zulam (*Aid to Nations Shrouded in Darkness*), 21, 105–6, 107, 119
  and Ibn Jama'a, 60, 65, 84
  and *imamate*, 68
  and *Misbah al-hidaya fi tariq al-imama*, 113
  and al-Subki, 162, 164, 166, 189
  and Sufism, 87, 93, 99, 104
  and sultanate, 118
  and *Tahrir al-ahkam fi tadbir ahl al-Islam*, 47
al-Juwayni, 'Imad al-Din Abu al-Fath 'Umar b. 'Ali Ibn Hamawiyya, 90, 93; *see also* Hamawiyya (*banu*) family

kadhib (deceit), 136
kafi (capable, competent to govern), 104, 106, 107
kalam', 170
al-Kamil, Sultan, 89, 90, 123, 171, 172–3
Kerr, Malcolm, 18, 30–1
Khalid Ibn al-Walid, 101
Khalifat Allah (deputy of God), 19–21
khalifat Rasul Allah (deputy of the Prophet), 19–21
khanqah, 53, 54, 88, 94
kharaj (land tax), 16, 36, 58, 75, 120, 184
  and Ibn ʿAbd al-Salam, 182–3
  and Ibn Talha, 137
  and imamate, 109, 110
Khidr al-Mihrani, 95–6, 98, 99–100
khilaf (disputation), 126
Khurasan, 90, 92, 93
Khusraw, 35
al-Khusrushahi, Shams al-Din, 149
Khwarazmians, 128
kibar (arrogance), 136, 144
kifaya (competence to govern), 104, 106, 107
kingship, 24–5, 112–14, 131
Kitab al-Ahkam al-sultaniyya wa-al-wilayat al-diniyya (*The Book of Ordinances of Government*) (al-Mawardi), 18, 72, 129, 139, 141, 167, 111, 119
  and Ibn Jamaʿa, 57, 64, 66
Kitab al-Siyasa al-mulukiyya (*The Book of Kingly Rulership*) (Taj al-Din Ibn Hamawiyya), 89, 91, 92–3, 99, 120
Kitab nasihat al-muluk (*Book of Counsel for Kings*) (anon), 26–7
Kitbugha, al-Malik al-ʿAdil, 51–2, 77
Kobra, Najm al-Din, 86

Lambton, Ann K. S., 2, 13, 14, 15, 48, 143
  and caliphate, 17–18, 19, 22
  and genre, 24, 25
  and *Tahrir al-ahkam fi tadbir ahl al-Islam*, 64, 67
language, 5, 10, 33–4, 87, 108
  and constitutional, 38
  and Ibn Talha, 133
  and political, 7, 19, 29–30, 42–6, 85, 103, 157
  and al-Subki, 162, 167–9, 172–3, 191
  and Sufism, 101, 109, 111, 112, 115, 118–20
legitimate authority, 13, 40, 49, 135

Lewis, Bernard
  The Political Language of Islam, 43
libraries, 26, 34–6
lieux de mémoire, 164–6, 169
limited government, 1, 7, 8, 126, 189, 191
  and Ibn Jamaʿa, 46, 49, 57, 58, 64, 82, 83
  and Ibn Talha, 142, 144, 145, 148, 150, 153, 154, 155, 157
literary theory, 24
literati, 24
Locke, John, 34
long durée, 14–17
Lubab al-Adab (*The Kernels of Refinement*) (Usama Ibn Munqidh), 91
Luqmān, 91

McGregor, Richard, 40
Machiavelli, Niccolò, 34
Madelung, Wilferd, 21, 99–101, 104–5, 112
madhhabs (legal schools), 10, 16, 37–8
  and Ibn ʿAbd al-Salam, 156–7
  and Ibn Jamaʿa, 59, 63
  and Ibn Talha, 144
  and politics, 166–8, 169, 170, 172–4
  and al-Qarafi, 146–7, 148, 149–50, 152, 154–5
  and al-Subki, 161, 162, 191–2
  and Sufism, 86, 87
madrasa, 34, 53, 56, 124, 141
Maghrib, 93
Mahmud b. Sebüktigin, Sultan, 166
al-Malik al-Zahir *see* Baybars I, Sultan
Mamluk period, 1, 3, 6–7, 10
  and Ayyubids, 124, 128
  and caliphate, 20, 22
  and genre, 24
  and libraries, 34–5
  and *shariʿa*, 19
  and Sufism, 40, 85–6, 88–9, 95–7
  see also Ibn Jamaʿa
al-Maʾmun, 35
al-Manbiji, Nasr, 53, 95, 97, 98
al-Mansur Lajin, Sultan, 52, 185
al-Maqrizi, 55
maʿrifat al-bari (awareness of God), 102, 103
Marlow, Louise, 28–9
marriage, 154
Marsilius of Padua, 34
  Defensor pacis (*Defender of Peace*), 11, 12–14

ma'sum (infallible), 104–6
al-Mawardi, 17, 30–1, 35, 42
Adab al-dunya wa-al-Din (*The Ethics of the World and of Religion*), 102, 108, 110–11, 119, 130
and caliphate, 68, 70
and Ibn Jama'a, 63, 84
and Ibn Talha, 134, 143, 144
Qawanin al-wizara, 139
and Sufism, 87
and sultanate, 118
and *Tahrir al-ahkam fi tadbir ahl al-Islam*, 47
Tashil al-nazar, 130, 136
and text availability, 27–9
see also *Kitab al-Ahkam al-sultaniyya wa-al-wilayat al-diniyya*
mazalim see non-*shari'a* courts; *siyasa*
military arts manuals (*furusiyya*), 58, 59, 60, 63; see also *Mustanad al-ajnad fi alat al-jihad*
military commanders (*umara'*), 72–3
mirrors for princes, 5, 24, 25–6, 35, 36
and Ibn Talha, 125, 129, 131–2, 133, 142–3
and Sufism, 86
Misbah al-hidaya fi tariq al-imama (*The Guiding Lamp to the Path of the Imamate*) (anon), 4, 5, 9–10, 21, 85–6, 87, 92, 118–21
and coercive authority, 103–7
and ethics, 107–11
and Ibn Talha, 129–30
and *On the Nature of the Imamate*, 107–8, 112, 119–20
and political thought, 98–102, 123
and ruler's power, 111–14
and Sufism, 117–18
and sultanate, 136
and *'ulama'*, 116–17
Miskawayh, 35
al-Mizzi, 161
Mongols, 22, 23, 122, 124, 128, 184
and Ibn 'Abd al-Salam, 159, 182, 183
Morocco, 90
Mubarak, Zaki, 26
muftiship (*fitya*), 140, 141, 148, 150; see also *fiqh*
Muhammad, Prophet, 19, 20, 53, 60, 62, 97, 147, 150, 154
and companions, 26, 36, 116–17
Mu'id al-ni'am wa-mubid al-niqam (*The Restorer of Favours and the Restrainer of Chastisements*) (al-Subki), 5, 129, 156, 157, 166, 188–90
Mu'in al-Din Ibn Shaykh al-Shuyukh, 180–1; *see also* Hamawiyya (*banu*) family
mujtahid (independent investigator), 104, 106, 107, 170; see also *ijtihad*
Mukhtar al-hikam wa-mahasin al-kalim (*A Collection of Wise Maxims and Beneficial Words*) (al-Mubashshir Ibn Fatik), 91–2
Mukhtasar fi fadl al-jihad (*A Compendium of the Virtues of* jihad) (Ibn Jama'a), 12, 56, 58, 60, 61–3, 65, 71, 81
al-Mustakfi bi-Allah (caliph), 78–9, 82
Mustanad al-ajnad fi alat al-jihad (*The Soldiers' Guide to War Engines*) (Ibn Jama'a), 12, 56, 58, 59–61, 62, 63
al-Mu'tadid III, 20
Mu'tazilism, 102
mysticism, 87, 88–9, 107–8; *see also* Sufism

Nafa'is al-'anasir li-majalis al-Malik al-Nasir see *al-'Iqd al-farid li-al-malik al-Sa'id* (*The Unique Necklace for a Content King*)
Nagel, Tilman, 21
najda (bravery), 106
Najm al-Din Abu al-Hasan 'Ali, 93; *see also* Hamawiyya (*banu*) family
al-Nasir li-Din Allah, Caliph, 87, 94
al-Nasir Muhammad Ibn Qalawun, Sultan, 48, 50, 51–2, 53–4, 57, 183–4, 185
and Sufism, 95, 97, 98
and Tahrir al-ahkam fi tadbir ahl al-Islam, 64, 77, 78–9, 82, 84
and vizierate, 71–2
al-Nasir Salah al-Din Yusuf, Sultan, 126–7, 128, 142
Nizam al-Mulk, 15–16, 162, 166
non-Muslims (*dhimmis*), 58, 74, 75, 77, 100
non-*shari'a* courts (*mazalim*), 44–5, 110, 137, 138, 153
Nora, Pierre
Les Lieux de Mémoire, 164
numerical values of letters see *'ilm al-hurruf*
Nur al-Din Zangi, Sultan, 90, 93, 166
Nusaybin (Syria), 126, 140
nuwwab (deputy judges), 54, 147, 149, 153

obedience, 59, 60, 62, 65–6, 69, 76, 135, 176
occultism, 127, 142, 143
Ottoman Empire, 15–16, 22, 87, 109

passion (*al-hawa'*), 113
peace, 12–13, 14
Peacock, Andrew, 128
Petry, Carl
  Civilian Elite of Cairo, 41
philosophers, 3, 4, 12, 14, 24, 25, 91–2
Plato, 35, 91
Pocock, J. G. A., 6, 30, 43–4, 191
  and contextualism, 33–4, 42, 168
political thought *see* Islamic political thought
populace, 7–8, 10, 55–6, 83, 88, 135, 158–9, 173, 182–6
Pouzet, Louis, 90
power, 1, 2, 3, 7–8, 13
  and delegation of, 69, 70–1
  and Ibn Jama'a, 49
  and Ibn Talha, 133–9
  and *imamate*, 66
  and military (*shawka*), 104
  and *Misbah al-hidaya fi tariq al-imamate*, 107–8, 111–14
  and al-Qarafi, 38
  and *Tahrir al-ahkam fi tadbir ahl al-Islam*, 57
practical philosophy, 109–11
praxis, 47–8, 50, 77–82
prayer, 62, 135, 159, 170, 176, 178, 190
Prophet *see* Muhammad, Prophet
prophethood (*nubuwwa*), 9, 113, 115, 119, 123, 135–6, 144
prophetic tradition see *hadith*
proto-constitutions, 8, 9, 83, 84, 122
Pythagoras, 91

Qadah al-dirasa fi manahij al-siyasa (*The Goblet of Instruction in the Ways of Government*) (anon), 130
qadi (chief judge), 52–3, 79–81, 159, 184, 187–8; *see also* Ibn Jama'a; Ibn Talha; al-Qarafi; al-Subki
Qalawun, Sultan, 130
al-Qalqashandi
  Ma'athir al-inafa fi ma'alim al-khilafa (*Foregoing Glories of the Caliphate Landmarks*), 20
al-Qarafi, 10, 38, 122
  al-Ikhkam fi tamyiz al-fatawa 'an al-ahkam wa-tasarrufat al-qadi wa-al-Imam (*The Book of Perfection in Distinguishing Legal Opinions from Judicial Rulings and the Discretionary Actions of Judges and Rulers*), 5, 124–5, 145–55
al-Qazwini, Imam al-Din, 52
Qur'an, 59, 62, 169
  and numerical values of letters, 127, 128
Quraysh (Qurashi), 21, 65, 67, 68, 104–7, 119
al-Qushayri, 134, 143
Qutuz, Sultan, 167, 182, 190

ragha'ib prayer, 159, 170
ra'iyya (subjects), 71
Rapoport, Yossef, 45
al-Rasa'il al-Subkiyya fi al-radd 'ala Ibn Taymiyya wa-tilmidhihi Ibn Qayyim al-Jawziyya (*al-Subki's Responses to Ibn Taymiyya and His Student Ibn Qayyim al-Jawziyya*) (al-Subki), 161
al-Razi, Fakhr al-Din, 149
al-Razi, Najm al-Din Daya, 17, 88, 119, 189
  Mirsad al-'ibad min al-mabda' ila-al-ma'ad (*The Path of God's Bondsmen from Origin to Return*), 108, 111–13, 118
reading, 6–7, 168
reason, 38, 45, 102, 103, 133, 134, 137, 169, 170
rebellion, 26, 58, 64, 74, 76, 77, 111, 120
restricted functions (*wilayat juz'iyya*), 154
ribat, 94; see also *khanqah*
Rida, Rashid, 31
right of necessity, 103–7
Roman Empire, 32
Rosenthal, Erwin E. J., 2, 13, 17–18, 64–5, 70
rule of law, 1, 7, 8, 10, 45–6, 159, 174, 185, 189, 191–2
  and Ibn Jama'a, 9, 49, 57–8, 60, 64, 74, 76–7, 2, 83
  and Ibn Talha, 140, 142, 144, 145
  and *Misbah al-hidaya fi tariq al-imama*, 107–14, 118–20, 126
  and al-Qarafi, 38, 148, 150–1, 152–5
  and al-Subki, 156–8
  and Sufism, 85, 86, 100
ruling duties (*'arif*), 104, 107
al-Rumi, Jalal al-Din, 86

Sadr al-Din Abu al-Hasan Muhammad, 90; *see also* Hamawiyya (*banu*) family
Sa'id al-Su'ada *khanqah*, 54, 88
al-Sa'id Najm al-Din Ghazi, Sultan, 128
Salah al-Din, Sultan of Aleppo, 126, 128
Salah al-Din (Saladin), Sultan, 129, 161, 162, 166

Salar, Sayf al-Din, 53, 95, 97, 184, 185–6
al-Salih Ayyub, Sultan, 159, 174, 176–9, 180
al-Salih Isma'il, Sultan, 159, 174–6
Sassanians, 24–5
al-Sayyid, Radwan, 28
Schacht, Joseph, 18
scholars (*'ulama'*), 26, 37, 41–2, 59, 73
  and Ottoman Empire, 109
  and al-Subki, 158–9, 170, 179–82, 189, 190
  and Sufism, 94, 114, 116–17
secretaries, 8, 36, 78, 79; see also *diwan al-insha'* (chancery),
Seljuqs, 16, 23
'Seth, 91
al-Shadhili, Abu al-Hasan, 86, 97
Shadhili brotherhood, 88–9
Shafi'i tradition, 5, 15–16, 26, 39
  and Ibn 'Abd al-Salam, 159
  and Ibn Jama'a, 58–9, 62–3, 83
  and Ibn Talha, 126, 133–4, 143–4
  and language, 46
  and *Misbah al-hidaya fi tariq al-imama*, 120
  and *Mu'id al-ni'am wa-mubid al-niqam*, 188–90
  and al-Qarafi, 147–9, 152
  and al-Subki, 160–1
  and Sufism, 87–8, 93
  and *Tahrir al-ahkam fi tadbir ahl al-Islam*, 47, 57, 77–80
  see also *Tabaqat al Shafi'iyya al-kubra*
Shafi' Ibn 'Ali
  Tarikh al-salatin wa-al-'asakir (*The History of Sultans and Military Commanders*), 77–82
shari'a, 2, 10, 17, 18, 110, 132, 150
  and caliphate, 19
  and Ibn Jama'a, 64, 68, 80
  and Ibn Talha, 135, 136, 137, 138–42, 144, 145
  and language, 43, 44–5, 46
  and *Misbah al-hidaya fi tariq al-imama*, 123
  and paradigms, 32
  and Sufism, 100
  and *Tahrir al-ahkam fi tadbir ahl al-Islam*, 73, 74, 75
shawka (military power), 66, 76, 104
shaykh al-shuyukh, 90, 92–3
Shaykh *see* 'Izz al-Din 'Abd al-'Aziz (Ibn 'Abd al-Salam)
al-Shayzari
  al-Nahj al-masluk fi siyasat al-muluk (*The Established Path to the Statecraft of Kings*), 129
Shi'a Islam, 104, 105
shihh (avarice), 136
shura, 43
Sibt Ibn al-Jawzi, 35
Siddiqui, Sohaira, 32, 38–9, 45
Siyar al-muluk (*Siyasat-nama*) (*Book of Government*), 15
siyasa (court), 4, 32, 35, 43, 44–5, 137, 173
Skinner, Quentin, 6, 12, 30, 191
  and contextualism, 33, 34, 42, 168
slavery, 104
Socrates, 35
sources, 4–5
spies, 138
spoils of war, 58; see also *ghanima*
al-Subki, Taj al-Din, 10, 22, 39, 158–60, 191–2
  Mu'id al-ni'am wa-mubid al-niqam, 5, 129, 156, 157, 166, 188–90
  see also *Tabaqat al Shafi'iyya al-kubra*
al-Subki, Taqi al-Din, 160–1, 164, 165
substantive law (*furu' al-fiqh*), 146
Sudan, 20
Sufism, 8, 9–10, 16, 40, 85–93
  and charity, 124
  and counsel, 116–18
  and delegation, 114–16
  and ethics, 107–11
  and genre, 26
  and Ibn Jama'a, 53, 54
  and Ibn Talha, 127, 132, 133–5
  and mystical reality (*haqiqa*), 32
  and politics, 93–8
  and al-Subki, 189
  see also *Misbah al-hidaya fi tariq al-imama* (*The Guiding Lamp to the Path of the imama*)
al-Suhrawardi, Shihab al-Din 'Umar, 86, 87, 88, 94–5, 118
sultanate, 17, 18, 24, 103
  and Ibn Jama'a, 58, 60, 61–3, 67–70, 83
  and Ibn Talha, 125–6, 134–9, 144–5
  and *Misbah al-hidaya fi tariq al-imama*, 113, 114, 115, 116, 123
  and al-Qarafi, 124–5, 145–55
  and rebellion, 76
  and *shari'a*, 44–5
  and al-Subki, 179–82, 190
sultanic courts *see* non-*shari'a* courts; *siyasa*

Sunni Islam, 15–16, 88, 94, 99
Syria, 25, 39, 41, 45, 158, 161
and Ibn Jamaʿa, 50, 72, 78–9, 80, 82
and Ibn Talha, 125, 130, 140, 143
and Sufism, 93, 97, 101
see also Damascus; Syro-Egyptian lands
Syro-Egyptian lands, 1, 5, 23, 89–90; *see also* Cairo; Damascus

Tabaqat al Shafiʿiyya al-kubra (*The Great Shafiʿi Biographical Dictionary*) (al-Subki), 15, 56, 157, 160–8, 173–4
and Baybars II al-Jashankir, Sultan, 186–8
and conventions, 168–73
and populace, 182–6
and ruling elites, 179–82
and al-Salih Ayyub, Sultan, 176–9
and al-Salih Ismaʿil, 174–6
tablakhana (military music band), 179–80, 181
tadbir (process of running the affairs of the people of Islam), 56–7, 65, 67, 69–71
tafwid see delegation
tahrir (process of drafting ordinances), 65, 67
Tahrir al-ahkam fi tadbir ahl al-Islam (*Drafting Ordinances towards Running the Affairs of the People of Islam*) (Ibn Jamaʿa), 4, 11–12, 13–14, 47, 83–4
and administration, 71–4
and caliphate, 20, 122–3
and Ibn Talha, 129
and political thought, 56–9, 64–71
and praxis, 77–82
and rules of war, 74–7
and al-Subki, 160
and synthesis, 63–4
Taj al-Din Abu Muhammad ʿAbdallah, 90–1, 92; *see also* Hamawiyya (*banu*) family
tajsim see anthropomorphism
Tamyiz see al-Qarafi
taqlid (legal conformity), 37–8, 45–6, 49, 79–82
al-Tarsusi, Najm al-Din, 105
tasfiya (refinement of the soul), 102
tashbih see anthropomorphism
taxation see *kharaj*; *zakat*
ten duties of the imam, 136–8, 145
terrorism, 15
al-Thaʿalibi, 35
theology, 38–40, 169–70
tolerance, 15
treasury, 139–40
truce, 74, 75
al-Turtushi, 35, 63
Siraj al-muluk (*The [Guiding] Lamp for Rulers*), 146

ʿulamaʾ see scholars
ʿUmar, 35
ʿUmar II b. ʿAbd al-ʿAziz, 35, 166
umaraʾ (military commanders), 72–3
umma (community), 31–2, 43, 71
Upper Egypt, 40, 89
usul al-fiqh (speculative jurisprudence), 38, 124–5, 146, 158
usurpation (*imarat al-istilaʾ*), 87
ʿUthman, 20
ʿUyun al-anbaʾ fi tabaqat al-atibbaʾ (*The Best Accounts of the Classes of Physicians*) (Ibn Abi Usaybiʿa), 91

vizierate (*wizara*), 8, 17, 114–15, 118–19
and conduct, 36
and Ibn Talha, 139
and al-Qarafi, 153
and *Tahrir al-ahkam fi tadbir ahl al-Islam*, 71–2
vocabulary *see* language

Wadi al-Khaznadar, battle of, 184, 185
Wafaʾiyya order, 40
wahdat al-wujud (unity of creation), 127
war, 49, 57–8, 74–7; *see also* military manuals; *Mukhtasar fi fadl al-jihad*
waraʿ (piety), 106, 107
wazir see vizierate
weapons of mass destruction (*ma yaʿimmu atharuh*), 77
Weber, Max, 18
wilayat (senior functions), 8, 45–6, 71–4, 80, 139, 153
wilayat al-awqaf (supervision of charitable endowments), 62, 140
wizarat al-tanfidh (vizierate of special delegation), 72, 139
women, 60, 75, 76, 104

Yilmaz, Huseyin, 87, 109
al-Yunini, 162–3, 167, 179, 187

zakat (alms tax), 62
zawiyas, 96; see also *khanqah*

EU representative:
Easy Access System Europe
Mustamäe tee 50, 10621 Tallinn, Estonia
Gpsr.requests@easproject.com

www.ingramcontent.com/pod-product-compliance
Lightning Source LLC
Chambersburg PA
CBHW052050220426
43663CB00012B/2508
9781474479653